# In a Nutshell

# In a Nutshell

*Cooking and Baking with Nuts and Seeds*

Cara Tannenbaum and Andrea Tutunjian

PHOTOGRAPHY BY GENTL & HYERS/EDGE

**W. W. Norton & Company**

*New York   London*

*Empty muffin liner from Upside-Down Cranberry-Pistachio Muffins (page 119)*

Page 354, Hazelnut and Vanilla Cream Macarons: Adapted from Kathyrn Gordon from *Les Petits Macarons: Colorful French Confections to Make at Home*. Co-written with Anne E. McBride. Copyright 2011. Reprinted with permission from Running Press, a member of the Perseus Books Group.

For information about permission to reproduce selections from this book, write to Permissions, W. W. Norton & Company, Inc., 500 Fifth Avenue, New York, NY 10110

For information about special discounts for bulk purchases, please contact W. W. Norton Special Sales at specialsales@wwnorton.com or 800-233-4830

Manufacturing by RR Donnelley, Shenzhen
Book design by Jan Derevjanik
Production manager: Anna Oler

Library of Congress Cataloging-in-Publication Data

Tannenbaum, Cara.
 In a nutshell : cooking and baking with nuts and seeds / Cara Tannenbaum and Andrea Tutunjian ; photography by Gentl & Hyers/Edge ; food styling by Michael Pederson. — First edition.
     pages cm
Includes bibliographical references and index.
ISBN 978-0-393-06558-9 (hardcover)
1.  Cooking (Nuts) 2.  Cooking (Seeds)  I. Tutunjian, Andrea. II. Title.
TX814.T36 2014
641.6′45—dc23

                    2014011418

W. W. Norton & Company, Inc.
500 Fifth Avenue, New York, N.Y. 10110
www.wwnorton.com

W. W. Norton & Company Ltd.
Castle House, 75/76 Wells Street, London W1T 3QT

1 2 3 4 5 6 7 8 9 0

*To our families:*
*Bruce, Leah, and Sophie Byland*
*and*
*Bill, Danielle, and Sean Heaney*

*Behind these recipes are the memories and moments*
*that provide the real sustenance in our lives.*

*Pistachio Biryani (page 285)*

# Contents

# Introduction

Nuts are like jewels: they are small, desirable, valuable gems. They have stories to tell, culled from their worldwide points of origin. They have both ancient histories and modern culinary flair. They have captured our imaginations with their charms, and after nibbling them endlessly, we felt it was time to stop just eating and start sharing.

Our fascination with nuts and seeds began years ago, as did our culinary collaboration. We met as chef-instructors at the Institute of Culinary Education when it was a small operation known as Peter Kump's New York Cooking School. We both loved to bake and taught in the professional pastry program. And boy, did we have nuts. And seeds. We had boxes and bags of all varieties stacked on the tall shelves of the back storeroom, waiting every day for students to pull them down, toast them, grind them, and fold them into beautiful baked goods.

Baking was not our only passion; we both also had a long, deep culinary history. After years as a restaurant chef and owner, Cara had settled into a busy catering business, also brimming with nuts and seeds. She not only baked with them at the school, she cooked with them too, creating a burgeoning folio of recipes that grew along with her business. Meanwhile, Andrea settled into her home at ICE writing curriculum, mastering recipes, developing formulas, and shaping the culinary path that thousands of students would travel.

We quickly found that we were a creative match, in the kitchen and behind the computer. When time came to test recipes or rewrite the school's curriculum, we worked together, laughing loudly while jotting down our thoughts. Nuts were included in nearly everything we did, serving as a common thread throughout our work. The time came to gather our thoughts and our recipes and pull together a thoughtful collection.

Our backgrounds made this easy to do. We were both born in Brooklyn and moved to Long Island at a young age. Our immigrant ancestors shared their love and their culinary roots with us. We sopped up our families' traditions, as disparate as they were. We use that perspective, a love of culinary history and regional specialties, to see nuts and seeds through a broad lens.

This is a natural view of nuts and seeds. Way before written and recorded history, nuts were a dietary mainstay, and as cultures evolved, people relied on what was at hand to sustain them. Rivers were tamed and fields were plowed as nuts and seeds were harvested from their natural settings. They took their place in agricultural fields, encouraging trade and commerce as they found their homes in the cuisines of the world.

We love the wide world of nuts and seeds. We hope our recipes reflect that love. We respect culinary tradition, but with a modern hand in the kitchen. We understand that nuts and seeds are nutritional powerhouses, filled with minerals and vitamins whose properties are just now being explored and appreciated. Crunchy, crusty, toasty, yummy—every bit is in this book. You will come to enjoy them as we do when you seek what is *In a Nutshell*.

In a Nutshell

# Welcome to Our World of Nuts and Seeds

# What Is a Nut?

Nuts and seeds are difficult morsels to define, as there are both culinary and botanical explanations for them. In the plant kingdom, the nuts and seeds we use to cook and bake with are actually seeds of fruits. True nuts are unusual, and there are only two featured here: hazelnut and chestnut. These two are defined as nuts because as they grow, they are a single seed housed in a thick, hard shell. The remainder of our nuts and seeds are botanically seeds, and can for the most part be categorized by the type of fruit or flower they grow in. The outlier is the peanut, a legume or bean with nut-like characteristics.

# Almonds

**ORIGINS:** First harvested and cultivated in the Middle East and southwest Asia thousands of years ago, almonds were introduced to the Americas in the mid-eighteenth century. After struggling for a foothold in the unsuitable climate of the Northeast, almond trees were planted by California pioneers, and a burgeoning industry was born during the Gold Rush of the 1850s. Now California is the world's largest source of cultivated almonds.

**FORMS AND USES:** Almonds are purchased whole with their skins on (natural) or skins off (blanched). Thinly sliced almonds are also available with skins on or off. Slivered almonds—wider wedges than sliced almonds—are cut from blanched almonds only. Almonds have a prominent place in many cuisines worldwide, from Europe through the Middle East and Asia to the Americas. Frequently used in both cooking and baking, almonds are used as sauce thickeners, fillings, coatings, and crunchy garnishes.

**TASTE, TEXTURE, AND APPEARANCE:** Almonds have a mild, distinct flavor that is floral and sweet. Roasting or toasting intensifies the flavor. Their texture is firm and dense. The inside of a fresh almond is creamy white, with a uniform, compact texture.

**CARE AND KEEPING:** Whole almonds with their skins on stay fresh longer than those without, and whole almonds have longer shelf lives than sliced or slivered almonds. Store almonds airtight in a cool, dark spot for up to 6 months. Freeze them for storage for up to a year.

**NUTRITION:** Almonds are a terrific source of vitamin E and magnesium. A handful of almonds—1 ounce, or about 23 pieces—provides the same amount of protein as 1 ounce of beef but is also packed with fiber, calcium, potassium, phosphorus, and iron. These properties promote heart health and may help insulin resistance and guard against cancer.

**NUT EXTRAS:** The nearly universal appeal of almonds has spurred the growth of products in addition to the nut itself. Almond milk, with its creamy, rich flavor, is a tasty substitute in many recipes for cow's milk. Almonds are ground into butter, have sugar added to create pastes for baking, and are pressed to create almond oil, which can be used in dressings and sauces. Finely ground almonds are used as a wheat flour alternative, adding nutty flavor to baked goods and thickening sauces without any gluten.

# Brazil Nuts

**ORIGINS:** Indigenous to the Amazon rainforest, Brazil nuts were completely unknown to Europeans until the sixteenth-century exploration of South America. They have never been cultivated, only harvested in a slow, difficult process of collection. The very large seeds of a very tall evergreen tree, Brazil nuts grow in heavy clusters of dozens surrounded by an outer shell that can weigh up to 4 pounds. Once collected from the forest floor, where workers risk head injuries caused by the falling nuts, the fibrous husks are removed. The nuts are then transported great distances from the rainforest in regions that have limited mechanized transportation.

**FORMS AND USES:** You don't often find Brazil nuts in their shells, because those dark brown, rock-hard shells are so difficult to crack. Most often purchased shelled whole or in pieces, Brazil nuts frequently have just a bit of their papery husk attached. Some nuts are ground into Brazil nut flour, but it is not commonly used. Some are ground for their oil, which has commercial but not culinary applications.

**TASTE, TEXTURE, AND APPEARANCE:** With its mild and mellow undertones, the flavor of the Brazil nut is often characterized as creamy. The nut's high fat content yields a rich, unctuous texture that can seem greasy if overprocessed. Its tropical roots reflect its ability to enhance other tropical flavors, such as banana, mango, pineapple, and coconut. When removed from their triple-sided shells, most Brazil nuts are the size of an adult's thumb or a bit smaller and have a pale yellow or slightly beige color.

**CARE AND KEEPING:** Their high fat content makes Brazil nuts extremely perishable. Wrapping them airtight will help avert spoilage, and refrigeration helps even more. Keep them well wrapped in the refrigerator for 3 months. Storage in the freezer will prolong their shelf life to 6 months.

**NUTRITION:** Brazil nuts are packed with nutrients, which puts them in the pantheon of healthy snacks. While their fat content is high, making them calorically dense, their fat is monounsaturated, the kind of fat that is believed to help lower LDL cholesterol. They are a great source of vitamin E, an antioxidant. Selenium, a mineral believed to inhibit or prevent cancer growth, is abundant, and only two of these giant nuts a day contain the daily recommended requirement. Other minerals, such as copper, magnesium, and manganese, and the vitamin thiamin are packed into Brazil nuts as well.

**NUT EXTRAS:** Old-fashioned clock gears are lubricated with Brazil nut oil, and certain cosmetics are made with it, but it is rare to find the oil used for anything edible. The nuts are infrequently used when compared to almonds and walnuts,

but we hope that their solid texture and buttery flavor will someday propel them into the culinary forefront. Their Amazonian harvest is seasonally balanced with rubber extraction, helping to keep the local workforce employed and aiding in environmental balance.

# Cashews

ORIGINS: A member of the same botanical family as poison ivy, the cashew tree is indigenous to Brazil and needs an extremely hot climate to thrive. In the late sixteenth century, Portuguese explorers transported the nuts to Goa, the Portuguese region of India, and to the African countries of Mozambique and Tanzania. Comfortable in the extreme heat, cashews thrived in their new habitats and spread through Asia. Now India and Mozambique are the world's largest producers. The cashew's earliest intrepid consumers had to find a way through the chemically irritating shell to find the luscious nut within. All cashews require roasting to render them edible; the blistering chemical urushiol can be extracted from them only in a hot oil bath.

FORMS AND USES: Because of the nut's caustic properties, consumers never find cashews available for purchase in the shell. The nut grows hanging from the base of the cashew apple, an edible but rarely eaten fruit. Shelling is done in a hands-free mechanized process. The shelled cashew is always roasted in oil, so

even when a cashew is labeled unroasted, it has had a short bath in hot oil to remove all traces of CNSL, or cashew nut shell liquid. Some cashews are ground into butter, but the majority of the heart-shaped nuts are sold roasted and whole. Very few commercial products are made with cashews, and most are eaten whole or in pieces, not used in baked goods, confections, or savory foods.

TASTE, TEXTURE, AND APPEARANCE: Cashews have a slightly sweet and corn-like taste and a buttery texture that is a bit mealy. The amount of roasting determines the color, which ranges from light beige for those called raw (remember, they are never totally raw because of CNSL) to a warm golden brown. Their curved silhouettes seem kidney-shaped, but their Latin name, *Anacardium*, likens them to the shape of a heart.

CARE AND KEEPING: All cashews have had plenty of processing and handling before they land in our kitchens, and the quality of that handling will affect their shelf life. Six months in a refrigerator or a year airtight in a freezer will keep cashews fresh. Whole nuts stay fresh longer than pieces, so shop for them whole.

NUTRITION: Cashews are filled with B vitamins and have plenty of iron, zinc, magnesium, and phosphorus.

NUT EXTRA: The huge percentage of starch in cashews makes them great sauce thickeners. They are often found in Indian curries.

# Chestnuts

**ORIGINS:** Different species of chestnut evolved in Europe, Asia, and North America. The American chestnut, once a staple for both food and strong timber, was nearly destroyed by a blight at the turn of the twentieth century. Now, over one hundred years later, botanists are slowly reviving stands of the American original. In the meantime, European, Chinese, and Japanese chestnuts have been imported to our shores, mostly for culinary purposes.

**FORMS AND USES:** The glossy brown chestnuts that we see in markets and for sale roasted on the streetcorners of New York City begin their lives in a porcupine-like burr that must be removed before use. Chestnuts can be found in their shells, ready for roasting. They can also be found shelled, roasted, and vacuum-packed. They are jarred whole and often packed in syrup. They are ground into flour and made into purees that are available both sweetened and unsweetened, in cans. They are also candied and rolled in sugar for a very sweet treat. Harvested in the cooler months, chestnuts are often associated with the winter holidays and are used in savory stuffings and sweet baked goods, as flour, and in pureed form. In Europe chestnut flour was used like polenta, cooked into a tasty porridge, before corn was introduced.

**TASTE, TEXTURE, AND APPEARANCE:** Chestnuts have a mild and mellow flavor. Roasting gives them a distinctive toasty quality. High in starch and low in fat, they have a mealy, floury texture.

**CARE AND KEEPING:** Before roasting, raw chestnuts must be kept like vegetables, wrapped in plastic and stored in a cold spot in the refrigerator. They will last 2 to 3 weeks like this. Vacuum-packed and jarred chestnuts, generally roasted, are good for a year if their containers remain sealed. Once they are opened, they should be refrigerated in an airtight container and used within 2 to 3 weeks. Sweetened products generally last a bit longer, but again, once opened, should be used within 1 month. Freezing can prolong shelf life up to a year.

**NUTRITION:** The starchiest of all nuts, chestnuts are low in fat and contain no gluten. They have lots of dietary fiber and a high proportion of vitamin C. Folates are found in large quantities, as are calcium, magnesium, manganese, phosphorus, and potassium.

**NUT EXTRAS:** Chestnut trees may bear life-sustaining nuts, but the strong wood has been influential in the growth of this country. One of the hardest and longest of woods, chestnut has been used for everything from ship masts to telephone poles and railroad ties. These three items alone affected many areas of the economy, and when they were needed and used the economy grew. The chestnut blight put an end to that. Now botanists try to combine various species genetically, intending to bring back a tree that once meant so much to the American economy.

# Coconuts

**ORIGINS:** Believed by botanists to be natives of the Philippines, coconuts drifted their way across the ocean to many other parts of Asia. Coconut palms grow in India and South America as well. They have been productive for thousands of years.

**FORMS AND USES:** Coconuts grow in clusters where the fronds sprout on the tree, and each mature tree can produce up to 60 nuts a year. Fresh nuts are difficult to crack, and may yield nothing if mold or rot has arrived first. Commercially, the flesh is often shredded or flaked, and then sweetened, or not. Shredded coconut is made from the coconut as it dries. Chipped coconut, grated coconut, coconut oil, coconut milk, and coconut water can all come from the same nut. Worldwide, coconut is a ubiquitous ingredient in soups, stews, curries, and countless baked goods. It easily crosses the line between sweet and savory dishes. Coconut water has health-food status and is used by many as an electrolyte replacement beverage, like a reduced-sugar Gatorade. Coconut oil, a favorite of vegans as a butter substitute, is available in jars that can be stored at room temperature.

**TASTE, TEXTURE, AND APPEARANCE:** Coconut has a distinctive flavor that is sunny and tropical. Fresh coconut meat is fibrous and pleasantly chewy. Either fresh or dried, the color remains creamy white.

**CARE AND KEEPING:** Choose whole coconuts for their intact shells, firmness, and water content (if you shake the nut, you can hear the water within and make an educated guess as to how full of water it is). Keep them in a cool place, intact, for 3 or 4 months. Shredded or flaked coconut is available sweetened or unsweetened. Generally found in airtight bags, it will stay fresh if unopened for 3 months. Once opened, wrap the bag airtight and use within a month. Coconut milk or coconut cream, both products created by cooking coconut flesh with water and straining the mix, keeps for years in the can, like evaporated milk.

**NUTRITION:** Coconuts are about 65 percent fat, and some of the fat is saturated. There is also a large proportion of dietary fiber in fresh coconut. If the oil is naturally extracted, it is believed to be heart-healthy. Significant quantities of potassium are available from coconut (and from the water within). Phosphorus, calcium, magnesium, manganese, copper, and iron all contribute to the coconut's nutritional profile.

**NUT EXTRA:** Even the fibrous, hairy husks of the coconut have useful applications: they can be decorative, used as vessels, or burned and used as a source of fuel.

# Hazelnuts

**ORIGINS:** The hazelnut, aka the filbert, is a small nut with a point at one end. Wild hazelnuts first sprouted in what are now Italy and Greece and the nut has been cultivated in Europe since the first century AD. Hazelnut fossils have been discovered in archeological excavations in Pompeii,

Italy, and other locations. Though today hazelnuts are grown in the United States—especially in Oregon and Washington—the trees planted there are the European hazelnut variety, not the wild American hazelnut, which is not considered to be of very high quality. The European hazelnuts grown in the United States tend to be larger in size than those grown in Europe.

**FORMS AND USES:** Hazelnuts are sold either shelled or unshelled but are always roasted. They are available whole or in pieces. They are ground into flour and pressed for their oil. The papery skin surrounding hazelnuts can be removed by the user, but we are finding that more and more they are skinned before sale. Hazelnuts are commercially ground with sugar to form praline paste. Chefs, bakers, and confectioners all use hazelnuts.

**TASTE, TEXTURE, AND APPEARANCE:** Hazelnuts are among the crunchiest nuts, with a mellow, smooth flavor. Their bitter skins can be difficult to remove, however. The best way is to roast them in the oven (a toaster oven works well) for about 5 minutes, then gather the nuts in a clean dishtowel and rub them vigorously. The dry skins just flake off, though a few scraps will always stick to the nuts.

**CARE AND KEEPING:** Shelled hazelnuts should be kept carefully sealed airtight in a cool, dry spot, where they will keep for a few weeks. In the refrigerator they will remain fresh for 3 months, and in the freezer they will remain fresh for 6 months. Praline paste must be stored in the refrigerator. Hazelnut oil belongs in the refrigerator as well and should

be purchased in small quantities. When vacuum-packed, the flour will remain fresh. Once the vacuum seal has been opened, use the flour quickly or freeze it to maintain quality.

**NUTRITION:** Hazelnuts provide substantial amounts of vitamin E, folate, and B vitamins and are believed to improve heart health. One ounce of hazelnuts contains 32 milligrams of calcium, 2.7 grams of fiber, 1.33 milligrams of iron, and a host of other excellent properties. Hazelnuts are made up of monounsaturated fat, which is thought to lower LDL cholesterol, in the amount of 78 percent.

**NUT EXTRA:** The unique flavor of hazelnuts, which matches particularly well with chocolate and coffee, derives from a chemical compound called filbertone contained in the raw nuts.

# Macadamia Nuts

**ORIGINS:** Although macadamia nuts are strongly associated with Hawaii, they are native to Australia. The trees were spread from Australia to Hawaii by a number of travelers. The first known exchange occurred in 1882, when William Herbert Purvis planted several macadamia trees in Hawaii, one of which is still living. In 1892 a sailor named Robert A. Jordan was given a bag of macadamia nuts when his ship docked in Brisbane, and in an early example of regifting, he passed them on to his brother, E. W. Jordan, who lived on the island of Oahu and planted the nuts in his backyard. A few small macadamia nut plantations were planted, and then, in 1926, the Territory of Hawaii exempted all lands used exclusively to grow macadamia nuts from taxes and macadamia production shot up. The state is home to many extensive plantations. Today Hawaii and Australia vie for the position of the world's largest producer of this nut. They are followed by South Africa.

**FORMS AND USES:** Macadamia nuts are usually sold in jars or vacuum packaging, either roasted or raw but almost always shelled, because their shells are extremely hard and difficult to remove at home. Bakers and chefs use them whole and in pieces. The oil is occasionally used in dressings and sauces.

**TASTE, TEXTURE, AND APPEARANCE:** Macadamia nuts are slightly mealy in texture and taste rich and buttery. They have a yellow-beige color and greatly resemble chickpeas. They marry beautifully with other tropical flavors, such as coconut and banana, and they have a special affinity with honey as well.

**CARE AND KEEPING:** Macadamia nuts have a high oil content—about 74 percent—which gives them their rich taste but can also cause them to go rancid very quickly. While we tend to keep more common nuts, such as almonds and walnuts, on hand at all times, we purchase macadamia nuts only when we intend to use them for a specific purpose, because of their high price and their tendency to spoil. Before the vacuum pack or jar is opened, macadamia nuts will remain in good condition for up to 2 years, but after opening the nuts should be stored in the refrigerator or freezer and used within a couple weeks' time.

**NUTRITION:** Since a good 74 percent of macadamia nuts is made up of beneficial oil, almost all of it monounsaturated fat, they are an extremely healthful food. They are also more than 9 percent protein and more than 6 percent fiber. These nuts offer high levels of potassium, phosphorus, magnesium, and calcium as well.

**NUT EXTRA:** Macadamia nuts grow on trees that can reach 60 feet in height and have shiny green leaves. The nuts are harvested after they fall from the trees, either by hand or mechanically.

# Peanuts

**ORIGINS:** Peanuts date back to pre-Columbian times, when they grew on and around the Andes. In the sixteenth century, the peanut began to spread as Portuguese explorers took it to Africa and India and the Spanish took it to the Philippines. In 1920, when boll weevils invaded cotton fields in the United States and growing cotton stopped being profitable, George Washington Carver, a botanist, came up with more than three hundred ways to use peanuts (though contrary to popular belief, he did not invent peanut butter). Today China is by far the world's largest producer of peanuts. India, in the number-two slot, grows less than half the number of peanuts produced in China. Nigeria is the world's third largest producer, with the United States in fourth place.

**FORMS AND USES:** There are four commonly grown varieties of peanuts in the United States: the Virginia, a large variety eaten out of hand; the Runner, the most common form, with the highest yield; the Spanish, which is smaller and reddish brown; and the Valencia, which is a little redder and sweeter. Peanuts can be purchased in or out of the shell, be raw or roasted. And they are ground into flour or into butter, the all-American sandwich favorite. Often salted out of the shell for eating, they are also available unsalted for cooking and baking. Peanut butter is available raw or roasted and salted or unsalted as well.

**TASTE, TEXTURE, AND APPEARANCE:** Peanuts, which are legumes, do have a faintly beanlike flavor, but mostly they taste nutty and sweet. Raw peanuts have a mealy texture, but most peanuts, whether shelled or not, are roasted before they are sold, and therefore they taste toasty and sweet and have a crisp snap to them. They are pale before roasting and skinless and golden after they are shelled and roasted.

**CARE AND KEEPING:** Peanuts should be stored in a cool, dry place. Shelled peanuts will last about 3 months if kept airtight in the refrigerator, while nuts in the shell will last longer. Both can be frozen for longer-term storage.

**NUTRITION:** About 26 percent of a peanut (depending on the variety) is protein. This percentage is higher than the amount of protein found in milk and eggs and even in some types of meat. Peanuts are also a rich source of antioxidants. They contain large amounts of phosphorus, magnesium, niacin, and thiamin. Peanuts do, however, trigger allergic reactions in a large number of people—estimated as high as 11 million in the United States alone—and those reactions can be so intense that they lead to anaphylactic shock.

**NUT EXTRAS:** Peanut butter, which is usually classified as crunchy or smooth, is available in two forms, commercial and natural. Peanut butter is such a staple in the United States that 75 percent of American homes have a jar of it on hand at any given time. It was introduced at the 1893 Chicago Exhibition by an anonymous doctor, who considered it a medicinal source of protein. By 1903 another medical professional, Dr. Ambrose Straub, patented a machine that could grind peanuts into butter, and an industry was born.

# Pecans

**ORIGINS:** The name *pecan* derives from the Algonquin Indian word *paccan,* which meant any nut with a shell hard enough for someone to need a rock to crack it. The pecan's Latin name, *Carya illinoinensis,* also derives from its native American roots: in the mid-1700s, fur traders exported pecans from the area inhabited by the Illinois Indians to the East Coast. The nuts' popularity grew after the Civil War, when soldiers returning north from the South brought pecans with them. While pecan trees grow throughout the Midwest and the South, they are perhaps most closely associated with Texas, and

Georgia, the two states with more pecan trees than any others.

**FORMS AND USES:** Pecans are graded by size and are available in or out of the shell. The halves may be intact or in pieces. Flour and butter are never made from pecans, as they are from other nuts. Used in savory and sweet recipes, pecans' shining role may be in pecan pie, an American dessert favorite. No commercial oil is processed from pecans.

**TASTE AND TEXTURE:** Pecans have a buttery, sweet flavor and an extremely appealing medium-crunchy texture with just the right amount of snap. The shelled nuts are long, not very thick ovals with two parallel grooves down the center. Pecans are firm but are not as hard and crunchy as almonds, or even walnuts. Pecan shells are smooth medium-brown ovals, often with darker streaks down the sides.

**CARE AND KEEPING:** Pecan pieces are generally less expensive than intact halves. If you buy pecans in the shells, keep in mind that 2½ pounds of pecans in the shell will yield about 1 pound, or 4 cups, of shelled nuts. Look for intact nuts without any discoloration and a faintly sweet, nutty smell. Store pecans airtight in the refrigerator for up to 9 months or in the freezer for up to 2 years.

**NUTRITION:** Pecans contain large amounts of unsaturated fat and protein as well as fiber. A study published in the *Journal of Nutrition* in 2001 suggested that eating a handful of pecans daily was as effective at lowering cholesterol as taking cholesterol-lowering drugs, probably owing to their high vitamin E content. Pecans are a good source of omega-3 fatty acids and of magnesium, potassium, phosphorous, zinc, and sulfur. A trace chemical in pecans is believed to delay age-related muscle and nerve degeneration, leading us to believe that they help slow the aging process.

**NUT EXTRAS:** Pecans are an American success story. Members of the hickory tree family, they grow in a wide swath of North America that stretches from Illinois through Kentucky, Missouri, and Texas and down into the Oaxaca region of Mexico. While other nuts are grown in North America, they are generally cultivated in much smaller areas than pecans are. Pecans grow in the Southeast (Georgia, Florida, Alabama, Mississippi, Louisiana), the Southwest (Texas, New Mexico, Arizona, Oklahoma), and the Midwest (Kansas, Illinois, Missouri, Iowa, Kentucky, Tennessee, Indiana). Pecans have even made it into space: NASA packaged Texas pecans as snacks for *Apollo* flight crews.

# Pine Nuts

**ORIGINS:** Humans have eaten pine nuts since the Stone Age: there is archeological evidence that pine nuts were eaten 6,000 years ago in what is now Nevada and 3,000 years ago in what is now Utah. Early Spanish explorers noted that the natives ground the nuts and used them as meal. Use of pine nuts in Europe at the same time has been noted, though the nuts were culled from a different species of evergreen tree. Pine nuts were also harvested and utilized in Korea and China.

**FORMS AND USES:** Pine nuts are always sold removed from the cone. The different varieties that come from around the world are different in their taste and texture and have different associated costs. They are sold whole. A derived oil is not commercially available, and pine nuts may be processed and ground by their user but are not sold in that way. European pine nuts are known for their large size and good quality. Chinese pine nuts are less expensive and smaller. Although there are many pine trees in the Americas, not enough of them can be harvested to yield a native commercial crop.

**TASTE, TEXTURE, AND APPEARANCE:** Fortunately, pine nuts compensate for their cost with a fairly intense flavor, so that a mere handful of pine nuts, especially when toasted, can lend a great deal of character to a dish. A pine nut is small, about the size of a newly sharpened pencil tip, and sweet. The texture of pine nuts is slightly mealy, though it firms up when they are toasted.

**CARE AND KEEPING:** Pine nuts are harvested from pine cones, and the process for extracting them is labor-intensive, accounting for their high price. Unlike most nuts, pine nuts should *not* be tightly sealed. They tend to get moldy and need to breathe. The best way to store pine nuts is in a paper bag in a cool, dry place. You can freeze pine nuts, but be sure to thaw only the amount you need (they thaw quite quickly because of their small size.)

Pine nuts that have been frozen and then thawed will begin to grow mold after 4 or 5 days. Freezing will extend the shelf life of all pine nuts for 3 to 6 months.

**NUTRITION:** Because pine nuts are small and generally are not eaten in large amounts, their excellent nutritional profile is somewhat muted. They're just as good for you as other nuts are, but you're unlikely to eat enough of them to get any significant benefit. The protein content of pine nuts ranges from 10 percent to 34 percent.

**NUT EXTRAS:** The pine tree was a symbol of the god Neptune in Greek mythology, and its nuts played a part in Pueblo Indian mythology as well: one legend had it that a woman ate a pine nut and became pregnant with a baby who grew up to become the Aztec emperor Montezuma. Navajo Indians rubbed pine pitch on corpses before they were buried, and the Hopi marked the foreheads of the living with that same pitch for protection.

# Pistachios

**ORIGINS:** Pistachios made their way to Italy from Syria when Tiberius was emperor, and they were a favorite of the Queen of Sheba. A man named William E. Whitehouse brought pistachios to the United States, in 1930. He entered Iran through Russia, collected 20 pounds of pistachios, smuggled them into the country, and then planted them in Chico, California. Today pistachios grow not only in California but throughout the

Mediterranean and as far east as Pakistan and India. Wild pistachios grow in the hills of northern Iran and Afghanistan, but they are slightly different from the variety found elsewhere—smaller, and with a definite turpentinelike flavor.

**FORMS AND USES:** Pistachios are available for purchase shelled or unshelled, roasted or raw, and salted or unsalted. In spite of its expense, pistachio oil is sometimes used as a commercial product. Pistachio flour and pistachio paste are also available and are used in baked goods.

**TASTE, TEXTURE, AND APPEARANCE:** Pistachios have a somewhat mealy texture, similar to that of cashews, which are in the same family. Different varieties of pistachios have different appearances, but the nuts are various shades of green, though their tints may range from a yellow-green to a dark color that almost looks purple. The nuts are small and sweet, with a faintly bitter aftertaste in some varieties. Pistachios are used widely in Middle Eastern cooking and desserts. They are the basis for the traditional filling in flaky baklava. Pistachio is a popular flavor for ice cream as well; pistachio ice cream is a characteristic pale green color.

**CARE AND KEEPING:** Pistachios are best purchased in the shell and stored in a cool area, but this is practical only for snacking, not for cooking and baking. Shelled pistachios should be used within 2 months of purchase. Pistachios in the shell can be placed in plastic bags (be extra-sure to expel any air from the bag before sealing) and refrigerated for up to 6 months or frozen for up to 1 year.

**NUTRITION:** Pistachios are nutritious, with the added benefit that they often replace less healthful snacks such as potato chips. They offer large amounts of thiamin, vitamin $B_6$, copper, and manganese. About 90 percent of the fat in pistachios is unsaturated. Pistachios also contain a large amount of the antioxidant lutein—more than any other nut—which is thought to reduce the risk of macular degeneration.

**NUT EXTRAS:** Behavioral eating expert James Painter coined the phrase "the pistachio principle" to describe the positive effect of eating pistachios straight from their shells. Apparently snackers feel satisfied with fewer pistachios than other nuts, because cracking the shells to get at the nuts forces them to eat more slowly. Because of their semisplit shells, pistachios can be roasted and salted while still in the shell.

# Poppy Seeds

**ORIGINS:** The poppy plant, *Papaver somniferum,* is one of the oldest cultivates in human history. Poppy flowers have long had both medicinal and culinary uses. The ancient Sumerians called the poppy plant *hul gil*, meaning "flower of joy." The plant's origins may lie in the western Mediterranean, southern Europe, or western Asia. The ripe seeds have had a place in the cuisines of central and eastern Europe, India, and the Middle East for centuries.

**FORMS AND USES:** Poppy seeds have a lovely taste and crunchy texture.

Slate-blue poppy seeds are used in breads, cakes, salad dressings, and pastries in Western cuisines, while the white variety is more often ground and used to thicken sauces for curries from northern India. Poppy seeds can simply be sprinkled on top of baked goods such as bread, but often they are soaked and ground into a paste.

**TASTE, TEXTURE, AND APPEARANCE:** Poppy seeds are used in both sweet and savory foods; they are among those chameleonlike seeds that seem to reflect the taste of the ingredients surrounding them. Their slightly sweet flavor is most often described as faintly nutty, but it is a little hard to define. The elusive taste can be augmented by toasting.

**CARE AND KEEPING:** Like any high-fat nut or seed, poppy seeds are prone to rancidity. Their high oil content means that they must be refrigerated or frozen. While some purveyors suggest keeping them for only 6 months, others feel poppy seeds can maintain freshness, moisture, and flavor for up to 3 years if sealed in an airtight container and stored in a cool, dry, dark place. We mark the date of purchase on packages of poppy seeds and try to store them in the freezer and use them within 1 year. When purchasing poppy seeds, look for uniform color. (White seeds can be found in some South Asian specialty stores but may be hard to track down.) If at all possible, taste the seeds before buying them. Old seeds will have a noticeably rancid flavor.

**NUTRITION:** Poppy seeds have a high percentage of edible oils, from 44 percent to 50 percent. The seeds are also a good source of calcium, although you would have to eat an awful lot of them to achieve the recommended daily amount.

**NUT EXTRAS:** Poppy seeds are harvested from the ripened base of the poppy flower. The milk harvested from the unripe pod, with its sleep-inducing properties, gives the poppy its species name, *somniferum*. The juice of that unripe poppy seed pod can be transformed into opium, morphine, and ultimately heroin. The plant has been used to make these drugs for just as long as the seeds have been used in cooking. This is why consuming a large number of poppy seeds could cause someone to test positive for drug use.

# Pumpkin Seeds

**ORIGINS:** Archeologists have found traces of pumpkin seeds dating back nearly 9,000 years in Mexico. From there the seeds spread through the New World and were eaten by nearly all the native populations. Native peoples not only consumed the seeds for food but utilized them for medicinal purposes and for their oil. European settlers in the Americas quickly adopted the pumpkin and used the flesh as well as the seeds. Pumpkin seeds and the methods for their cultivation traveled back to Europe from the colonies, and from there spread throughout the world.

**FORMS AND USES:** Pumpkin seeds are sold in and out of the shell, roasted or unroasted, salted or unsalted. Commercial uses require them to be shelled, but snacking is another matter, and folks like to crack the shell and pull out the nutmeat. There is no commercially available pumpkin seed butter or flour, but oil is extracted from the seeds and is used frequently in eastern Europe. The seeds are used in both baking and cooking.

**TASTE, TEXTURE, AND APPEARANCE:** The shells of pumpkin seeds are usually white or beige, and the seeds themselves are dark green. They are small, thin, and pleasantly crunchy. Pumpkin seeds do taste slightly of squash and complement many vegetable flavors. A handful of toasted pumpkin seeds scattered over almost any winter vegetable dish makes a lovely finishing touch, and they complement the taste of their vegetable of origin in baked goods as well.

**CARE AND KEEPING:** When buying pumpkin seeds in the shell, look for uniform color and avoid shells with any black spots. Shelled pumpkin seeds should be green, and if you are buying from a bin, look for most of the seeds to be intact—broken seeds indicate rough handling. Be sure they don't smell musty or moldy at all. Pumpkin seeds can be stored in the refrigerator in an airtight container for 2 months, though the shelled seeds do tend to fade a little in terms of flavor with the passage of time. We prefer to purchase them in small amounts and use them as soon as possible. When roasting pumpkin seeds, use low temperatures to keep from destroying their beneficial oils.

**NUTRITION:** Pumpkin seeds have a high oil content and are good sources of protein, zinc, magnesium, and copper. They

are also a naturally soothing food—they contain large amounts of L-tryptophan, the substance in turkey and milk that makes us sleepy. Studies of whether they might be used to treat anxiety disorders are currently under way.

**NUT EXTRAS:** The word *pumpkin* is derived from *pepon,* the Greek word for "large melon." A long series of linguistic changes later, American colonists came to call the beloved squash pumpkin. The seeds became known also by their Spanish name, *pepitas* ("little seeds"), given to them by the conquistadores in the sixteenth century.

# Sesame Seeds

**ORIGINS:** Written references to the sesame plant date back to 3000 BC. It was first domesticated in either Africa or India. Culinary uses developed later, as native peoples of the Middle East and India began to toast and use the seeds in bread doughs and utilize the oil for cooking. The top five sesame-producing countries today are China, India, Myanmar, Sudan, and Uganda. Three million metric tons or 75 percent of the world's production is grown in these countries. Nowadays sesame is also commercially grown (and machine-harvested) in Texas, California, Louisiana, and Arizona.

**FORMS AND USES:** The seeds of the sesame plant can be purchased hulled, with skins on, or natural. White seeds are hulled, beige are unhulled, and black are available as well. Two kinds of sesame oil are available for purchase: cold-pressed and roasted. Cold-pressed oil is golden in color and bland in flavor and is most frequently used as a cooking oil (over low heat only) or in salad dressings. Roasted sesame oil has an intense sesame flavor and should be used sparingly; it burns easily, so it isn't often used in cooking. It provides a blast of flavor in dressings or for finishing a cooked dish. Sesame seeds can also be purchased as sesame paste or butter, also known as tahini. Sesame products are used in both cooking and baking. A scattering of seeds is seen everywhere as a perky garnish for rolls and other baked goods.

**TASTE, TEXTURE, AND APPEARANCE:** The little sesame seed can be found in a variety of colors, from milky off-white to red and brown to black. Sesame seeds have a very delicate texture and a sweet flavor. However, the lighter-colored seeds provide a less robust and less distinctive flavor, and the darker seeds can have an edge of bitterness, with the black ones tasting smoky and peppery.

**CARE AND KEEPING:** Sesame seeds and their products should have a clean, fresh appearance and no rancid flavor. Store seeds in a cool, dry place for up to 3 months. If refrigerated in an airtight container, seeds can be stored for 6 months. Frozen seeds can be stored for as long as a year. Oil in tahini often separates from the body and must be stirred back in before use. Roasted oil should be refrigerated after opening, and simply processed oil must be checked every few months for rancidity.

**NUTRITION:** Sesame seeds are composed of 44 percent to 60 percent oil and 25 percent protein. One ounce of hulled seeds has 6 grams of protein, 3.7 grams of fiber, and 14 grams of monounsaturated and polyunsaturated fat. The calcium content of sesame seeds is higher than that of milk, as 1 tablespoon of unhulled sesame seeds provides 87.8 milligrams of calcium. These little seeds are also packed with B vitamins, including folic acid, and iron, magnesium, and potassium. Sesame seeds contain vitamin E, which is a potential cancer preventative and proven to improve heart health, and phytosterols, agents that can reduce cholesterol.

**NUT EXTRAS:** Sesame seeds grow huddled in a pod until ripe. Then the pod bursts dramatically, scattering the seeds, which can then be gathered. This biological process seems to have inspired the phrase "open sesame," the magical incantation that gave access to Ali Baba's mythical cave.

# Sunflower Seeds

**ORIGINS:** When Europeans first arrived on the shores of the Americas, they were greeted with the round bright face of the sunflower. The seeds were a source of native food, and the stems were used as building materials. The plants were transported to Europe in the sixteenth century. Peter the Great, the Russian ruler from 1672 to 1725, traveled to Holland and was the first to take sunflowers to his native land, where the seeds were devoured as a snack and the plants were quickly cultivated for their oil. Sunflower cultivation rapidly expanded

*Sunflower seeds and Turkish windblown pistacios*

when the Russian Orthodox Church left sunflower seed oil off its list of fats forbidden during Lent and Advent. Sunflower oil was one of the few fats acceptable to the church during this season of fasting, and Russia soon became the world's foremost producer of sunflower seeds to meet demand for the oil. By the end of the nineteenth century, Russian immigrants had reintroduced high-yield sunflowers to their original soil in the United States. Production in the United States had not caught on commercially, but Russian immigrants scattered sunflower seeds throughout the Midwest and West and created an industry. Sunflowers are currently grown in many states, predominantly North Dakota, South Dakota, Minnesota, and Kansas.

**FORMS AND USES:** Sunflower seeds are available for snacking in the shell and for cooking and baking out of the shell. They may be raw or roasted. Sunflower seeds are processed into butter, a boon to those with peanut allergies. They are also pressed for their oil.

**TASTE, TEXTURE, AND APPEARANCE:** Sunflower seeds are mild and slightly nutty. The flavor is reminiscent of that of the Jerusalem artichoke, a knobby vegetable belonging to the same genus, *Helianthus*. The texture of the seeds before they are toasted is firm but tender, and while they are not greasy, their oil content is apparent.

**CARE AND KEEPING:** The teardrop-shaped shells of sunflower seeds are grayish green, black, or striped black and white in color. They should be firm, not limp. If shelled, the pale gray seeds should be uniform in color and almost crisp. Yellowing is an indication of rancidity. Like most nuts and seeds, sunflower seeds are best kept in an airtight container in the refrigerator for up 6 months. Long storage should be in the freezer, where cold temperatures will not affect texture or flavor.

**NUTRITION:** Sunflower seeds are a great source of vitamin E, and ¼ cup per day can provide over 90 percent of the recommended daily intake of vitamin E. Phytosterols, the plant-based compounds that can help lower LDL cholesterol, are abundant in sunflower seeds (as they are in pistachios). Sunflower seeds are chock-full of magnesium, a mineral responsible for regulating muscle and nerve spasms, and as a result can help control such different conditions as high blood pressure and asthma. One quarter of a cup of sunflower seeds provides over 30 percent of a day's magnesium requirement. Selenium, another beneficial mineral, is abundant in sunflower seeds and is believed to deter cancer cell growth; again, ¼ cup of sunflower seeds provides over 30 percent of the daily nutritional requirement.

**NUT EXTRAS:** The Latin name of the sunflower, *Helianthus annuus*, is a direct reflection of the flower's bright appearance. *Helios* is the Greek word for "sun," and *anthos* means "flower." The sunflower's brilliant yellow petals are like the sun's rays, surrounding a dark, seed-filled center. The sunflower has symbolized innocence, hope, and light, and it is easy to see why.

# Walnuts

**ORIGINS:** Walnuts are a kind of Everynut and very recipe-friendly. They grow almost everywhere and are indigenous to Asia, Europe, and North and South America. The common walnut that is widely available today—one of fifteen species in the genus *Juglans*—probably originated in the region that now includes Iran, Iraq, Afghanistan, and Turkey. By far the most common walnut is known as the Persian or English walnut. Though walnuts were not indigenous to England, they were well known there by the late 1500s. It was probably English colonists who transported walnuts to what is now the United States. Later, Spanish missionaries carried them to California, where they found an ideal growing environment. Today 99 percent of the walnuts in the United States are grown in California.

**FORMS AND USES:** Walnuts are used in a range of recipes from savory to sweet. They are a good substitute in recipes that call for hazelnuts or pecans, or almost any other kind of nut. They do not need any special preparations, such as blanching. Though there are many varieties of walnut and all are edible, those available in grocery stores are the common walnut, the familiar nut with a large, bumpy shell that's easy to crack and a nutmeat inside that has lots of bumps and ridges. Walnuts are available shelled or unshelled, roasted or unroasted, and whole, halved, chopped, or ground. They are also pressed for their oil.

**TASTE, TEXTURE, AND APPEARANCE:** H-shaped walnuts are crisp yet not terribly hard (softer than raw almonds, for example), with a bumpy surface. They have a mild yet pleasingly nutty flavor. They are sweet with a slightly bitter aftertaste.

**CARE AND KEEPING:** Whether shelled or unshelled, walnuts should be stored airtight in a cool, dry place. When purchasing shelled walnuts, look for unbroken nuts with no musty odor. Their color should be uniform and beige, with no black spots. Walnuts in the shell will keep at room temperature for 1 year. Shelled walnuts can be stored up to 6 months in the refrigerator or freezer. Walnuts should always be allowed to come to room temperature (which happens fairly quickly) before they are chopped or ground, however, or they will turn into a paste in an instant.

**NUTRITION:** Walnuts are rich in thiamin, vitamin B$_6$, folate, iron, magnesium, phosphorus, and zinc. They are also packed with omega-3 fatty acids, and a few ounces of walnuts contain 7 grams of fiber. The U.S. Food and Drug Administration claims that including 1½ ounces of walnuts in one's daily diet reduces the risk of heart disease. The nuts are now being studied for their ability to prevent type 2 diabetes in women.

**NUT EXTRAS:** Black walnuts, which are indigenous to the United States, are a highly prized type of nut with a more pronounced flavor than common walnuts. Walnut oil is frequently used in France; it is delicious in vinaigrettes, where it is usually combined with olive oil to mute its strong flavor. It is also often added to bread and pastry recipes that have walnuts to heighten the walnut flavor.

# About the Recipes: Measuring, Toasting, Chopping, Seasoning

# Measuring Nuts

Nuts and seeds may be measured by either volume or weight. Volume measures how much space an ingredient takes up and is done in solid round measuring cups. Fill the cup with the nuts and give it a little shake—this will help nestle the nuts and give an accurate measurement. Alternatively, weights are a precise way to ensure correct measurement. A digital kitchen scale is perfect for this. All of our recipes give both types of measurements for each nut or seed, and we have rounded the measurements up or down to the closest quarter of an ounce.

# Toasting Nuts

The deep fragrant flavor of nuts and seeds is brought to the fore when they are toasted. Toasting releases the essential oils in nuts and seeds, creating flavors that are just a step up from those that are not. The texture will also change, making the nuts crunchier and crisper. We are avid toasters, and begin most every recipe by getting out the sheet pan and preheating the oven, maximizing flavor and texture before we begin to cook or bake.

Toasting is a quick process. Preheat your oven to 350°F. Line a rimmed sheet pan with parchment paper, this will make clean up a snap. Scatter your nuts onto the pan in a single layer and bake for 10 minutes. Pine nuts and macadamias will toast faster, in about 5 minutes, because of their high fat content. Give the nuts a stir with a high heat spatula or a wooden spoon every 2 to 3 minutes to ensure even browning. The nuts are done when they are golden brown. You will learn to tell when they are done by their fragrance; a warm, toasty smell will fill your kitchen. Over-toasting will ruin the nuts, and you will need to discard them and start again. A watchful eye is key. Allow the pan to cool on a rack, lift the parchment paper, and pour the nuts into your recipe. Your pan will just need a quick wipe, and your recipe results will be a bit more flavorful.

When we don't want to turn on the oven, we toast nuts and seeds on the stovetop, also with great results. Heat a large skillet over medium heat, and add your nuts or seeds in a single layer. Give them a stir every minute or so, and be careful to keep them moving so they don't over-brown. A single layer of nuts in a skillet is fewer than what fits in sheet pans, so this is fine for smaller batches.

We toast as we go, repeating each time we use nuts in a recipe. The essential oils that have been coaxed out of the toasted nuts will fade rapidly with storage, losing the benefit of the process. The little bit of extra time it takes to toast is well worth the enhanced flavorful results.

# Chopping Nuts

We like to purchase shelled nuts in the largest sizes available, and then chop them up before we use them. Wholes and halves tend to be of better quality. Less of their surface area is exposed to the air, keeping them fresher longer. Chopping requires a clean, stable cutting board and a large, sharp chef's knife. Place the required nuts

| 1 CUP OF: | OUNCES | GRAMS |
|---|---|---|
| **ALMONDS** | | |
| Whole | 5 | 142 |
| Slivered | 4.5 | 128 |
| Sliced | 4 | 113 |
| MARCONA ALMONDS | 4 | 113 |
| BRAZIL NUTS | 5 | 142 |
| **COCONUT** | | |
| Sweetened | 4 | 113 |
| Unsweetened | 3 | 85 |
| CASHEWS | 5 | 142 |
| **CHESTNUTS** | | |
| Whole | 6 | 170 |
| Crumbled | 6 | 170 |
| HAZELNUTS | 5 | 142 |
| MACADAMIA | 5 | 142 |
| PECANS | 4 | 113 |
| PISTACHIOS | 5 | 142 |
| PINE NUTS | 5 | 142 |
| PEANUTS | 5 | 142 |
| WALNUTS | 3.5 | 99 |
| POPPY SEEDS | 5 | 142 |
| SESAME SEEDS | 5 | 142 |
| PUMPKIN SEEDS | 5.5 | 156 |
| SUNFLOWER SEEDS | 5 | 142 |

| OUNCE TO GRAM CONVERSION | |
|---|---|
| ¼ OUNCE | = 7 GRAMS |
| ½ OUNCE | = 14 GRAMS |
| 1 OUNCE | = 28.35 GRAMS |
| 4 OUNCES | = 113 GRAMS |
| 8 OUNCES | = 227 GRAMS |
| 16 OUNCES (1 POUND) | = 454 GRAMS |

on the board and with a rocking motion, keeping the tip of the knife on the board, chop away. Remove the chopped nuts, and start a new batch if necessary.

How much each batch of nuts needs to be chopped is described in the recipes. Coarsely chopped means that the processed pieces should be large and irregular, with each nut piece at least cut in half. Chopped nuts are about half the size of coarsely chopped nuts, about a quarter of the size of the original. Keep going for finely chopped nuts. These are small pieces, about ⅛ inch.

Any chopping of nuts will leave a powdery residue on your cutting board. We scoop this up and add it to the recipe. We like the texture of these stray little sandy bits. An alternative is to put the nuts and their scrappy remains into a medium strainer and shake out the residue. That can get stirred into a cup of yogurt or sprinkled on a bowl of cereal, while the bigger pieces get measured and added to the recipe.

When a recipe calls for ground nuts, a food processor is necessary for the job. Place the nuts in the bowl of the processor with the metal blade. Pulse 15 to 20 times, until the nuts are in tiny powdery pieces, looking like a coarse flour. If you go too far and over-process, the finely chopped nuts can turn into nut butter, and that can't take the place of ground nuts. When in doubt, err on the side of under-doing it.

Sliced and slivered nuts need to be purchased in those forms. Even the most precise knife skills can't shape these pieces like industrial equipment can.

# Salt and Pepper

Seasoning a dish is a personal act. It is difficult to tell someone how much salt and pepper goes in a dish, since everyone has a different desire for salt and pepper. Recipes in many books merely say season to taste. Throughout our book, we based the seasoning on our palates. If you follow our guidelines in each recipe you will create a balanced, flavorful dish. If your taste runs to things a little more salty or less spicy, feel free to adjust the seasoning to your taste. Always start with small amounts, you can easily add more.

Nuts can be purchased either salted or unsalted. Salted nuts taste great when popped in your mouth, but they will alter the flavor of a recipe. Every recipe in this collection, unless noted as in a few desserts, relies on unsalted nuts.

*Clockwise from top: Sesame Cashews (page 42); Southern Macadamia Nuts (page 51); Ancho Chile–Orange–Roasted Peanuts (page 53); Bourbon Pecans (page 46); Triple-Ginger Almonds (page 47)*

CHAPTER 1

# Nibbles

# Nuts and Bolts of Nibbles

**The inherent nutritional value of nuts and seeds makes them an ideal** snack by themselves, but when seasoned or when baked into something crisp and crunchy, such as a cracker, their properties shine. They are often eaten out of hand, on the run between meals, or late at night when just a little nosh is necessary.

In America, the appearance of salted, spiced, or roasted nuts on bar tops dates back a mere one hundred years—a blink of an eye in the lengthy history of nuts as a snack. Inexpensive and heavily salted bar nuts encourage patrons to quench their thirst as they munch. We're not snobs, but we like to think of our selection of spiced nuts as more than an impetus to imbibe—they are appetizer sparkers, satisfying snacks, and delicious in their own right.

We imagine that for as long as there have been people who have eaten nuts, there have been travelers who keep nuts in their pockets for sustenance as they cross foreign lands. Nuts can be seasoned and cooked in many different ways; however, we have found that their flavors are best showcased when they reflect the culinary traditions of their regional roots.

Many of the nibbles in this chapter, whether nuts, shortbread, or crackers, are baked. A roll or a stack of 12-by-18-inch sheets of parchment paper is an investment that will pay generous returns in the form of time saved. Parchment makes any baking pan nonstick and reduces cleanup time.

All the recipes in this chapter can be prepared ahead, making them ideal for sneak-up cravings. Most have a very short preparation and cooking time, which makes them even easier to keep on hand. Store them all in airtight plastic containers or in an airtight bag.

We are delighted that nuts pair so beautifully with cheese, and that increased interest in domestic artisanal and imported cheeses has grown along with our fascination with them. In this chapter we make suggestions for nut and cheese combinations when appropriate. There are no hard and fast rules about what nut matches best with what cheese, and our suggestions are just that. The wide world of cheese is even broader than that of nuts, and only your imagination can limit the combinations. Experiment, and eat what tastes good to you.

Keep cracker dough on hand for any snack emergency. This ready-set-go mentality will have you prepared for any gathering. Think of recipes in this section as savory icebox cookies: they can be made ahead, rolled into neat little logs, and refrigerated or frozen to be prepared as a fresh snack at a moment's notice. Even the dough for Whole Wheat–Sesame Crisps on page 62 can be rolled and cut in advance for last-minute baking. Another nice thing about icebox crackers: you can decide how many or how few to bake at a time. Leave the rest of the dough well wrapped and refrigerated for up to 2 days or frozen for up to 2 months.

Even the Dukka Chips (page 64) are simple to prepare; they may not be slice-and-bake crackers but they are made from packaged tortillas. As with the seasoned nuts, we have offered suggestions for cheese pairings with a few of the crackers. Some crackers have cheese incorporated in the dough, for these recipes, a pairing is unnecessary.

Sweet, salty, and spicy—these are the characteristics of the modern nut snack. Make them, store them, share them, and eat them. Most of all, enjoy them.

# Honey-Roasted Mixed Nuts

As native New Yorkers, we have a soft spot in our hearts for the sweet roasted nuts that vendors sell on streetcorners. We were inspired to create this version with honey in addition to the expected sugar. Honey intensifies the flavor and helps the sugar crisply coat the nuts. It reminds us of the most favored part of teiglach, the Rosh Hashanah dessert that crowned Cara's family's table during the New Year celebration. Golden crisp balls of dough were mounded in a pie pan, and tucked into just a few crevices were honey-roasted hazelnuts. The nuts were a treasured treat, plucked from their hiding places before the teiglach was eaten. Just a little pulled tail of honey would remain, along with a bit of stickiness on the hunter's fingers. We know these sweets will be as heartwarming as the teiglach hazelnuts of Cara's childhood.

PREPARATION TIME: *5 minutes*
BAKING TIME: *25 to 30 minutes*
MAKES: *5 cups*
EQUIPMENT: *1 rimmed baking sheet lined with parchment paper and lightly coated with nonstick spray*

⅓ cup honey

¼ cup packed light brown sugar

2 teaspoons ground cinnamon

2 teaspoons kosher salt

1 teaspoon freshly ground black pepper

1 cup (3½ ounces) walnut pieces

1 cup (5 ounces) whole almonds

1 cup (5 ounces) blanched hazelnuts

1 cup (5 ounces) pistachios

1 cup (5 ounces) Brazil nuts

2 tablespoons granulated sugar

1. Preheat the oven to 325°F.
2. Stir the honey, brown sugar, cinnamon, 1 teaspoon salt, and the pepper together in a large saucepan, place over medium heat, and bring to a boil. Remove from the heat and stir in all the nuts, mixing them until all sides are coated and the honey mixture is slightly thickened. Spoon the nuts evenly onto the prepared pan, leaving any leftover honey mixture in the bottom of the saucepan.
3. Bake the nuts for 10 minutes. Pull them out of the oven and, using a wooden spoon or a heatproof spatula, give them a quick stir. This will help the nuts cook evenly and help prevent them from sticking to one another. Return them to the oven and continue to bake until the nuts are golden brown and the honey is fragrant, about 20 minutes more. Stir the nuts two or three times during this final baking. The honey will start to darken and caramelize quickly toward the end of baking. The darker it is, the more you need to watch it, as a diligent eye can prevent the nuts from darkening too much.

4. Remove the nuts from the oven and quickly toss them with the remaining 1 teaspoon salt and the granulated sugar. Briefly cool in the pan on a rack. Pull the nuts apart with a fork while they are cooling but still a little warm, to prevent them from sticking together. A few clusters that remain will add to the textural appeal. The nuts can be stored in an airtight container for up to 1 week.

# Sesame Cashews

This Asian-inspired snack features a double whammy: two favorites from the vast nut and seed repertoire, sesame seeds and cashews. Here the nuts are stirred into a sesame and beaten egg-white mixture, which hardens and glistens around the cashews during baking to create a flavorful, crunchy coating. The coating may seem a little fussy, but the crust it creates is unbeatable. *(See photo page 36.)*

PREPARATION TIME: *5 minutes*
BAKING TIME: *20 to 25 minutes*
MAKES: *3 cups*
EQUIPMENT: *1 rimmed baking sheet lined with parchment paper and lightly coated with nonstick spray*

| | |
|---|---|
| 1 egg white | 1 teaspoon ground ginger |
| 1 tablespoon tahini | 1 teaspoon five-spice powder (see Note) |
| 1 tablespoon soy sauce | 3 cups (15 ounces) roasted cashews |
| 2 tablespoons sugar | ½ cup (2½ ounces) white sesame seeds |
| 1 tablespoon roasted sesame oil | 1 teaspoon kosher salt |

1. Preheat the oven to 300°F.
2. Combine the egg white, tahini, soy sauce, sugar, sesame oil, ginger, and five-spice powder in a bowl and whisk to combine. Add the cashews and stir to coat evenly.
3. Sprinkle ¼ cup sesame seeds evenly over the parchment on the prepared pan. Pour the nuts on top of the seeds and spread them evenly with a spatula, making sure they don't touch each other. Sprinkle the remaining ¼ cup sesame seeds over the cashews. Bake them for 20 to 25 minutes, until the nuts are shiny and the sesame seeds are golden. Halfway through the baking, remove the nuts from the oven and very gently flip them, using a wooden spoon or heatproof spatula. Be careful: too much stirring will cause the sesame seeds and coating to slip off the cashews.
4. Remove the nuts from the oven and sprinkle them with the salt. Cool the pan on a wire rack, separating the nuts with a fork if necessary as they cool. The nuts can be stored in an airtight container for up to 1 week.

**NOTE:** Five-spice powder can be purchased in the spice section of any supermarket. You'll be drawn to its slightly floral complexity. It delivers nuanced flavor, with hints of cinnamon, clove, star anise, and fennel and a spicy bite of pepper underneath it all. While it is always made from a balance of spices, the proportions of these tastes vary from region to region throughout China. Choose one that piques your interest.

# Tea-Smoked Almonds

Using a traditional Chinese tea smoking technique is so easy we couldn't resist trying it with nuts. For thousands of years this simple method has been used to preserve duck and fish while imparting a mild yet distinctive flavor. Although there is no need to preserve almonds, we thought the smoky flavor would be a natural match with them. This process uses uncooked rice, sugar, and tea to pass on a subtle smoldering flavor to the almonds. Different teas will impart different flavors to the smoke, and you will be able to detect a distinct undertone with each one you try. A well-ventilated kitchen is a must here. While much of the smoke is contained during cooking, wisps can find their way out of the edges or escape when you lift the lid. As the smoking mixture heats on the stove, the brown sugar begins to melt and bubble along with the tea. Don't get carried away and turn up the heat to hurry the process; you are looking for the sugar to melt, not burn.

PREPARATION TIME: *5 minutes*
COOKING TIME: *20 minutes*
MAKES: *3 cups*
EQUIPMENT: *1 large lidded saucepan or wok; 1 steamer basket*

3 cups (15 ounces) blanched whole almonds

1 cup long-grain white rice

Zest of 1 orange, removed in strips with a vegetable peeler, with no pith

½ cup packed light brown sugar

¼ cup loose Earl Grey, China black, or jasmine tea leaves

1. Place the almonds in a steamer basket that can nestle in a wok, or into a perforated insert that fits snugly into a large heavy-bottomed saucepan. Line the inside of either with heavy-duty aluminum foil. Put the uncooked rice and the orange zest in the bottom of the lined wok or saucepan. Sprinkle the brown sugar and then the tea on top of the rice. This is the mixture that will provide the smoke that will infuse the almonds.

2. Place the steamer basket or perforated insert into the wok or saucepan above the smoking mixture, and cover.

3. Place the pan over medium heat until the sugar starts to melt and the tea begins to smoke, about 3 minutes. Make sure the fan in your kitchen is on and the pot stays tightly closed at all times, because this process creates a great deal of smoke.

4. Once the sugar begins to melt, make sure the lid is on tight and smoke the almonds for 5 minutes. A deep, strong, sweet smell of cooking sugar will mix with the wafting tea smoke. Remove the pan from the heat and let it stand with the lid closed for another 10 minutes, until the smoke subsides and the pan cools.

*continued*

5. Take the lid off the pan and, using oven mitts if necessary, carefully remove the steamer. The almonds will be dark and burnished, with a slight orange hue. Transfer the nuts to a rimmed baking sheet. Using a rubber spatula, spread them evenly in a single layer and cool. Smoked nuts can be stored in an airtight container for up to 1 week.

# Sweet and Salty Walnuts

Sweet and salty: even just the words together please us. We were delighted when chefs began to combine these complementary flavors, and this dessert trend has great benefits in the world of nuts. It's all about balance, and we think we've found it. Our go-to nut for this kind of treatment is walnuts. All those wrinkles are just crevices that trap the sweet and salty goodness and hold it tight. But we are just as happy to make this with pecans—they are not quite as wrinkly and not quite as intense, but they have an addictive quality of their own. Eat all you want of these by themselves, or toss them with any leafy green salad.

PREPARATION TIME: *5 minutes*
BAKING TIME: *18 to 20 minutes*
MAKES: *4 cups*
EQUIPMENT: *1 rimmed baking sheet lined with parchment paper and lightly coated with nonstick spray*

**4 tablespoons sugar**

**3 tablespoons canola oil**

**4 cups (14 ounces) walnut halves**

**2 teaspoons kosher salt**

1. Preheat the oven to 300°F.
2. In a small saucepan, mix together the sugar, 3 tablespoons water, and the oil and bring to a boil over medium heat. Cook until the sugar is fully melted, about 2 minutes.
3. Place the walnuts in a large bowl and pour in the syrup. Toss to coat the nuts completely.
4. Transfer the walnuts to the prepared pan and bake until they take on a light golden color and the coating has a glazed appearance, 18 to 20 minutes. During the baking, take them out of the oven 2 or 3 times to stir so they bake evenly.
5. Remove the walnuts from the oven and immediately toss them with the salt. Cool the nuts completely in the pan on a wire rack. The walnuts can be stored in an airtight container for up to 1 week.

CHEESE CHOICE: These simply seasoned walnuts pair well with a salty Parmesan or Pecorino cheese. A milder match may be found with a chèvre, or a rich Saint André.

# Bourbon Pecans

Every year during the 1930s, Cara's great-uncle Sam ran a chartered train from Chicago to the Kentucky Derby. The high rollers on this trip expected luxurious meals in the train's formal dining car. These bourbon pecans are based on one of the snacks they nibbled along the way. The recipe dates to a time before regional American cooking was a hot topic. Today this combination of two southern specialties—bourbon and pecans—seems as natural to us as it must have been to the cooks on that train way back when. Use the best Kentucky bourbon you can, such as Maker's Mark, because you can really taste it here. *(See photo page 36.)*

PREPARATION TIME: *5 minutes*
COOKING TIME: *10 minutes*
MAKES: *3 cups*
EQUIPMENT: *1 rimmed baking sheet lined with parchment paper and lightly coated with nonstick spray*

½ cup sugar

½ cup Kentucky bourbon

2 tablespoons light corn syrup

3 cups (12 ounces) pecan halves, toasted

1 teaspoon crushed red pepper flakes

1 teaspoon kosher salt

1. Mix the sugar, bourbon, corn syrup, and pecans in a medium saucepan. Cook them over medium heat, stirring constantly with a spoon or a heatproof spatula. When the mixture begins to boil, the evaporating bourbon will have a sweet, deep, oaky aroma. As the mixture cooks, the bubbles will pop more slowly and eventually most of the liquid will evaporate. The sugar will caramelize and stick to the nuts. This whole process takes about 10 minutes.

2. Remove the pan from the heat and stir in the red pepper flakes and salt while the nuts are still hot.

3. Transfer the nuts to the prepared pan. Pull them apart with a fork while still warm and then cool completely. Store pecans in an airtight container for up to a week.

VARIATION: *Bourbon Bacon Pecans*
Add ½ pound thick slab bacon, cooked, drained, and chopped into ¼-inch pieces. Stir the bacon in with the red pepper flakes and salt in step 2. These must be eaten the day they are prepared, because of the perishable nature of the bacon.

CHEESE CHOICE: The rich Bourbon pecans taste great when paired with an extra-sharp cheddar cheese or a bit milder aged Gouda.

# Triple-Ginger Almonds

Too much ginger has never been an issue for us: the more we use, the happier we are. Putting three forms of it together to season almonds seems just right: fresh ginger for its brightness, candied ginger for its sweetness, and powdered ginger for its warmth, rounding it all off with a peppery bite. Try using kitchen shears or a lightly greased chef's knife to cut the crystallized ginger, which will keep the ginger from piling up and clustering as you work. *(See photo page 36.)*

PREPARATION TIME: *5 minutes*
COOKING TIME: *35 to 40 minutes*
MAKES: *3 cups*
EQUIPMENT: *1 rimmed baking sheet lined with parchment paper and lightly coated with nonstick spray*

1 cup sugar

3 tablespoons finely grated fresh ginger

4 teaspoons ground ginger

1 teaspoon kosher salt

3 cups (15 ounces) whole almonds

1 cup (4 ounces) finely chopped crystallized ginger

1. Stir the sugar, ½ cup water, and the fresh ginger together in a medium skillet and bring to a boil over high heat. The sugar syrup will be clear and bubble up from the bottom. Continue to boil for 3 minutes, then remove the skillet from the heat. Cover and allow the ginger to steep in the syrup. In just 15 minutes, the ginger will infuse the syrup with a pure, vivid, robust flavor. Using a fine-mesh sieve, strain the syrup into a bowl; discard the ginger.

2. Return the syrup to the skillet, place over medium heat, and bring back to a boil. Whisk in the ground ginger and salt. Stir in the almonds.

3. Continue cooking over medium heat for about 15 minutes stirring constantly with a heatproof spatula. The syrup will stick to the almonds and reduce. When a small amount of liquid remains in the bottom of the pan, stir in the crystallized ginger. Eventually no syrup will remain, and the sugar adhering to the nuts will begin to crystallize.

4. When the nuts have been coated completely with sugar and have whitened and crystallized, continue cooking for about 5 minutes to remelt and caramelize the sugar. The sugar from the crystallized ginger will also melt, and the nuts and ginger will stick together nicely. Scrape the nuts evenly onto the prepared pan and cool. Using two forks, separate them, being careful to leave the ginger intact. The cooled almonds can be stored in an airtight container for up to 1 week.

Peanut Caramel Corn (page 49)

# Peanut Caramel Corn

Slightly reminiscent of Cracker Jacks, this peanut-laced popcorn can easily move from ballgame to boardroom. When we were kids, commercial Cracker Jacks were always a disappointment because of their sparse supply of peanuts. Here our prize is peanuts in abundance. Adding a little baking soda to the caramel at the end lightens the mix and gives it a slight, airy lift before it hardens on the popcorn and peanuts. This is best on the day it is prepared.

PREPARATION TIME: *5 minutes*
COOKING TIME: *30 to 35 minutes*
MAKES: *8 cups*
EQUIPMENT: *2 rimmed baking sheets lined with parchment paper and lightly coated with nonstick spray; a candy thermometer*

| | |
|---|---|
| **8 cups freshly popped popcorn** | **½ cup honey** |
| **2 cups (10 ounces) roasted salted peanuts** | **3 tablespoons unsalted butter** |
| **¾ cup packed light brown sugar** | **1 tablespoon vanilla extract** |
| **½ cup granulated sugar** | **½ teaspoon baking soda** |

1. Place the popcorn in a large bowl and toss with the peanuts. Set aside.
2. Stir the brown sugar, granulated sugar, honey, and butter together in a small saucepan. Cover the pan and bring to a boil over medium heat. The steam generated by covering the pan will wash down any sugar crystals that form on the sides, enabling the creation of a smooth caramel. Carefully remove the lid and insert a candy thermometer into the syrup. Boil until the temperature reads 260°F, 15 to 20 minutes. Keep an eye on the syrup to make sure it doesn't scorch or boil up too high. Remove the pan from the heat, stand back, and stir in the vanilla and baking soda (the syrup will foam up when you add these ingredients).
3. Immediately pour the hot caramel syrup over the popcorn and peanuts. Stir quickly but gently with a lightly greased spatula until the popcorn and nuts are coated evenly. Spread on the prepared pans and use a fork to separate the popcorn as much as possible while it is still warm. Set aside to cool. The popcorn softens as it absorbs the caramel and needs to dry thoroughly to recrisp. Use immediately; storage will cause the caramel to become tacky.

*continued*

VARIATION: *Maple-Sunflower Caramel Corn*
Substitute 2 cups (10 ounces) sunflower seeds for the peanuts and grade B maple syrup for
the honey.

---

TIPS: *Working with Caramel and Syrups*

- A good candy thermometer with large, easy-to-read numbers is essential. A syrup or caramel can change dramatically when overcooked or undercooked by a few degrees.

- Choose a heavy, stable pan that will conduct heat evenly. We like to use either a copper pot or a stainless steel pot with a copper core lining because of their ability to conduct heat evenly. Because of the high heat and length of time required to cook syrups, using a thin pan or one that conducts heat unevenly can easily lead to scorched caramel.

- Exercise caution around caramels and syrups. They are extremely hot.

- The temperature of a boiling caramel or syrup may seem to creep up slowly at first, but once the water has evaporated, it can climb quickly. Keep an eye on boiling caramel or syrup at all times. Lower the heat slightly toward the end of cooking to prevent it from getting too hot too fast.

- After removing the caramel or syrup from the heat, cool it quickly by dipping the bottom of the pot in a bowl of ice-cold water for 10 seconds. This stops the residual cooking process and prevents the caramel from getting too dark.

---

# Southern Macadamia Nuts

The barbecue sauce that bathes these macadamia nuts is made by "juicing" an onion to add flavor. We've learned that we don't like the little brown bits left behind from finely diced onions, and the liquid adds tang without texture. It's also a great backdrop for all the spices that add flavor to the sauce, and it is a technique that works. We've made barbecue sauce this way for years and have most often used it to finish chicken on the backyard grill. Tossing it with macadamia nuts was an inspired and happy surprise. The round richness of the nuts and the sauce together are finger-lickin' good! *(See photo page 36.)*

PREPARATION TIME: *15 minutes*
BAKING TIME: *20 to 25 minutes*
MAKES: *4 cups*
EQUIPMENT: *1 rimmed baking sheet lined with parchment paper*

| | |
|---|---|
| 1 small onion, quartered | 2 teaspoons chile powder |
| 1 tablespoon unsalted butter | 1 teaspoon ground ginger |
| 2 tablespoons tomato paste | ½ teaspoon cayenne pepper |
| 2 tablespoons molasses | ½ teaspoon freshly ground black pepper |
| 1 tablespoon honey | 2½ teaspoons kosher salt |
| 1 teaspoon Tabasco sauce | 4 cups (20 ounces) macadamia nuts |

1. Preheat the oven to 300°F.
2. Pulse the onion and ¼ cup water in the work bowl of a food processor for about 2 minutes, until the onion is pureed. Using a fine-mesh sieve, strain the mixture, reserving about ½ cup of the liquid in a bowl and discarding the thick onion pulp.
3. Combine the onion liquid, butter, tomato paste, molasses, honey, and Tabasco sauce in a medium saucepan and warm over low heat. Stir in the spices and 1½ teaspoons of the salt and heat gently for just a minute or two as the sauce thickens slightly.
4. Remove the pan from the heat and stir in the macadamia nuts until they are well coated. Transfer the nuts onto the prepared pan using a slotted spoon. Bake, stirring 2 or 3 times, until the nuts are deep red and the coating is dry, 20 to 25 minutes. Remove the nuts from the oven and sprinkle with the remaining 1 teaspoon of salt. Cool completely on a wire rack. The macadamias can be stored in an airtight container for up to 1 week.

*Platter of nuts, fruit, and cheeses*

# Ancho Chile–Orange–Roasted Peanuts

Peanuts pop with well-rounded, smooth flavor, and smoky ancho chiles add just the right amount of spicy counterpoint for an addictive snack. Unsalted dry-roasted peanuts are available in every supermarket. While they may be tasty on their own, the combination of sprightly citrus and deep-flavored ancho chiles will turn the commonplace into a snack with a little warmth and a bit of sweetness. Whole dried anchos keep best in your cupboard and you can remove the seeds to grind them for this recipe, but the ease of using powder to coat these peanuts makes the purchase worthwhile. If you use the pre-ground powder, make sure the label says "ancho." Anchos have a more robust, smokier flavor than your average chile powder. *(See photo page 36.)*

PREPARATION TIME: *5 minutes*
BAKING TIME: *20 to 25 minutes*
MAKES: *3 cups*
EQUIPMENT: *1 rimmed baking sheet lined with parchment paper*

2 tablespoons olive oil

2 tablespoons ancho chile powder

1 tablespoon sugar

2 teaspoons cumin seeds, toasted and ground

1 teaspoon kosher salt

½ teaspoon cayenne pepper

3 cups (15 ounces) dry-roasted peanuts

1 tablespoon freshly grated orange zest

1. Preheat the oven to 300°F.
2. Heat the oil in a large skillet over medium heat for about 2 minutes, until it begins to shimmer and ripple. Add the chile powder, sugar, cumin, salt, and cayenne and stir frequently with a spatula until the oil and the spices are well combined, forming a smooth paste, 2 more minutes.
3. Add the peanuts and orange zest to the spice paste, turn off the heat, and stir until all the nuts are entirely coated. Pour the nuts evenly onto the prepared pan. Bake them until the coating is dry, about 25 minutes. After about 10 minutes, use a heatproof spatula to push the nuts gently around the pan to ensure even baking. Repeat this process 2 or 3 more times during baking. When the nuts are done, they will darken slightly and become a little shiny.
4. Scoop the peanuts with a spoon onto a clean pan, spread them apart, and let them cool completely. They may lose a little of their sheen as they cool. The nuts can be stored in an airtight container for up to 1 week.

CHEESE CHOICE: These robust nuts taste great with a mild counterpoint of Queso Fresco.

# Cheddar-Hazelnut Crackers

Start with a very sharp cheddar when you plan to make these. The bright tang and little edge of an aged cheese will balance perfectly with the robust hazelnuts. Double your cheddar pleasure and serve a crumbly hunk of the same cheese when you eat them. These are versatile, and we make them all year, but they are at their best with fall fruits such as crisp apples, juicy pears, and luscious figs.

PREPARATION TIME: *30 minutes, plus 2 hours to chill*
BAKING TIME: *20 minutes for 2 sheets*
MAKES: *50 crackers*
EQUIPMENT: *2 rimmed baking sheets lined with parchment paper*

1 cup all-purpose flour

1 cup (3½ ounces) hazelnut flour

½ teaspoon salt

1 stick (8 tablespoons) unsalted butter, chilled and cut into ½-inch pieces

1 cup (4 ounces) grated extra-sharp cheddar cheese (use the largest holes of a box grater)

1 large egg yolk

½ cup (2½ ounces) coarsely chopped hazelnuts

1. Place the flours, salt, and butter in the work bowl of a food processor and process for about 30 seconds, until the mixture is the texture of coarse cornmeal. (Be sure the butter stays cold and is cut into small pieces, so the crackers will be crumbly and tender.) You can tell it is ready when you rub a tiny amount between your fingers and it feels cool and gritty. No visible pieces of the butter will remain.

2. Add the cheddar cheese and process quickly to combine, about 10 seconds. The mixture will begin to moisten and adhere to itself, gathering together in a shaggy, shapeless cluster. Add the egg yolk and pulse for 15 seconds, just until the mixture forms a ball. Overprocessing will cause the dough to become too warm and make the crackers tough.

3. Turn the dough out onto a lightly floured surface. Scatter the hazelnuts over the dough and knead gently until they are blended throughout. If your hands are sticking to the dough, lightly flour them. Adding the hazelnuts after the dough forms allows the nut chunks to remain large and helps prevent overworking the dough. Divide the dough in half and roll each half into a cylinder about 7 inches long.

4. Wrap each piece of dough in parchment or wax paper and chill for at least 2 hours, until firm enough to slice, or up to 2 days. For longer storage, wrap the dough in plastic wrap and freeze for up to 3 months.

5. When ready to bake, preheat the oven to 350°F.

6. Unwrap the dough, trim the ends, and cut each cylinder into ¼-inch slices. Arrange the slices on the prepared pans, leaving about 1 inch between them. Bake until the tops of the crackers are lightly golden and the hazelnuts are a deep beige, about 20 minutes. The crackers will smell like a fresh grilled cheese sandwich, with a hint of crisp nuttiness.

7. Cool the crackers on the pans on wire racks. Repeat as needed with the remaining dough and cooled pans until all the crackers are baked, or freeze the dough for future use. Serve the cooled crackers immediately or store them in an airtight container for up to 3 days.

# Pecan-Stilton Crackers

Although Stilton has a pungent flavor, you can use any moist blue cheese, such as Maytag or gorgonzola, in this recipe. These crackers make a great accompaniment to seasonal roasted fruit. In the fall pears are a perfect complement, and in the summer nectarines, peaches, or plums can do the trick. Slice any of these fruits and cook them briefly in a little butter or olive oil. Sprinkle slightly underripe fruit with a teaspoon or two of sugar before sautéing to improve its flavor and tenderness. Cool the fruit to room temperature and top each cracker with a slice. Add a dollop of crème fraîche and a bit of finely chopped chives and you have an elegant appetizer with very little work. Unadorned, these crackers make a great snack any time.

PREPARATION TIME: *30 minutes, plus 2 hours to chill*
BAKING TIME: *20 minutes for 2 sheets*
MAKES: *50 crackers*
EQUIPMENT: *2 rimmed baking sheets lined with parchment paper*

**2 cups all-purpose flour**

**1 stick (8 tablespoons) unsalted butter, chilled and cut into ½-inch pieces**

**1 cup (4 ounces) crumbled Stilton or other assertive blue cheese, chilled**

**1 cup (4 ounces) finely chopped pecans**

1. Process the flour and butter in the work bowl of a food processor for about 30 seconds, until the mixture is the texture of coarse cornmeal. You can tell it is ready when you rub a tiny amount between your fingers and it feels cool and gritty. No visible pieces of butter will remain.

2. Add the Stilton and pulse repeatedly until the dough forms a ball, about 30 seconds. The cheese will add enough moisture to hold the dough together without any liquid or egg. It is also salty enough to enliven the flavor without adding any salt.

3. Turn the dough out onto a lightly floured surface and divide it in half. Roll each half into a cylinder about 7 inches long. The dough will be a little bit sticky, but it is easy to handle. You can dust some flour on your hands or just use parchment paper to manipulate the dough. Place a sheet of parchment paper or wax paper on the counter and scatter ½ cup chopped pecans over it. Roll 1 piece of dough in the pecans to coat the outside. Repeat with the remaining ½ cup pecans and the second piece of dough.

4. Wrap each piece of dough in parchment paper or wax paper and chill for at least 2 hours, until firm enough to slice, or up to 2 days. For longer storage, wrap the dough in plastic wrap and freeze for up to 3 months.

5. When ready to bake, preheat the oven to 350°F.

6. Unwrap the chilled dough, trim the ends, and cut as many ¼-inch slices as you like. Arrange the slices on the prepared pans, leaving 1 inch between them. Bake until the tops of the crackers are smooth and golden, 18 to 20 minutes. The chopped pecan edges will darken a little. Just make sure to take the crackers out of the oven before they turn a deep brown, because a minute or two of overbaking will leave you with crackers that are not really burned but have a slightly harsh edge. The crackers will seem slightly soft when they come out of the oven but should be set enough to maintain their shape when moved.

7. Cool the crackers on the pans on wire racks. Repeat as needed with the remaining dough and cooled pans until all the crackers are baked, or freeze the dough for future use. Serve the cooled crackers immediately or store them in an airtight container for up to 3 days.

# Pistachio-Lemon Coins

Careful baking enables bright green pistachios to shine in these savory crackers. For years we have baked sweet pistachio lemon icebox cookies and biscotti. Those recipes led us to this savory, thyme-infused variation, and we love the result: an herbal, green-flecked, crumbly snack, delicious on its own or with a variety of cheeses. Overbaking will turn the verdant nuts brown, so keep an eye on them. We prefer stone-ground cornmeal for its crunchy texture and rustic flavor. It can be used interchangeably with standard supermarket brands.

PREPARATION TIME: *30 minutes, plus 2 hours to chill*
BAKING TIME: *15 minutes for 2 sheets*
MAKES: *50 crackers*
EQUIPMENT: *2 rimmed baking sheets lined with parchment paper*

1½ cups all-purpose flour

½ cup stone-ground yellow cornmeal

2 teaspoons freshly chopped thyme, woody stems removed

2 teaspoons salt

1 stick (8 tablespoons) unsalted butter, chilled and cut into ½-inch pieces

2 large eggs

1 tablespoon freshly squeezed lemon juice

2 teaspoons freshly grated lemon zest

¾ cup (3¾ ounces) coarsely chopped pistachios

1. Pulse the flour, cornmeal, thyme, and salt in the work bowl of a food processor to mix. Add the cold butter and pulse repeatedly, about 30 seconds, just until the mixture has a coarse, crumbly texture. No visible pieces of butter will remain, and the mixture should still feel cool to the touch. Whisk the eggs, lemon juice, and zest together in a small bowl. Pour the liquid into the food processor and pulse just until the dough forms a loose ball around the blade, 10 more seconds.

2. Turn the dough onto a lightly floured surface. Scatter the pistachios over it and knead gently until they are blended throughout the dough.

3. Divide the dough in half. Working quickly, roll each half into a cylinder about 7 inches long. If the dough remains cool, handling it will be easy. Wrap the logs in parchment paper or wax paper. Chill for at least 2 hours, until firm enough to slice, or up to 2 days. For longer storage, wrap the dough tightly in plastic wrap and freeze for up to 3 months.

4. When ready to bake, preheat the oven to 350°F.

5. Unwrap the chilled dough, trim the ends, and cut as many ¼-inch slices as you like. Arrange the slices on the prepared pans, leaving 1 inch between them. Bake until the edges of the crackers are lightly browned and the tops are beginning to turn golden, about 15 minutes. A watchful eye will keep the pistachios green and prevent overbaking. The piquant combination of lemon and thyme will perfume the kitchen. The crackers may feel a little soft when they are done, but they will firm up as they cool.

6. Cool the crackers on the pans on wire racks. Repeat as needed with the remaining dough and cooled pans until all the crackers are baked, or freeze the dough for future use. Serve the cooled crackers immediately or store them in an airtight container for up to 3 days.

CHEESE CHOICE: These crackers taste great with a slightly salty feta cheese on the side. A fresh ricotta stirred with a drop of honey would make a delicious but slightly milder pair.

# Gruyère-Poppy Pinwheels

These crackers are a visual delight, a tight swirl of dark blue poppy filling wrapped inside a cheesy blanket. The nutty flavor of Gruyère helps the poppy seeds shine. Like many of the doughs for our crackers, the dough for these can be prepared, frozen, and then baked as needed. Many poppy-seed fillings call for grinding the seeds before using them. This seems to make the seeds more absorbent if they are cooked in a liquid, but it's not a necessary step here. We prefer to use the seeds whole in this recipe, as they yield a filling with a sandier texture than ground seeds do. While all nuts and seeds need to be fresh for optimum flavor, poppy seeds are particularly prone to rancidity. Taste a few of your seeds before you begin. There is no salvaging old or spoiled seeds; throw them out and purchase fresh ones.

PREPARATION TIME: *50 minutes, plus 3 hours to chill*
BAKING TIME: *20 minutes for 2 sheets*
MAKES: *40 crackers*
EQUIPMENT: *2 rimmed baking sheets lined with parchment paper*

### FOR THE DOUGH

2 cups all-purpose flour

1½ teaspoons sugar

½ teaspoon salt

1½ sticks (12 tablespoons) unsalted butter, chilled and cut into ½-inch pieces

1 cup (4 ounces) freshly grated Gruyère cheese

1 large egg

1 large egg yolk

¼ cup whole milk

### FOR THE POPPY FILLING

1 tablespoon olive oil

1 small onion, finely chopped

1 cup (5 ounces) poppy seeds

¾ cup (3 ounces) freshly grated Gruyère cheese

### FOR FINISHING

1 egg white, lightly beaten

1. Make the dough: Pulse the flour, sugar, and salt in the work bowl of a food processor until blended, about 5 seconds. Add the cold butter and process continuously for 30 seconds, until the mixture is the texture of coarse cornmeal. The dough will feel cool and sandy when it is ready. Add the cheese and process to combine, about 10 seconds. Add the egg, egg yolk, and milk and pulse with 2 or 3 short bursts, only until the dry ingredients are moistened. The dough won't form a ball but will stick together if it is squeezed. Place the dough on a lightly floured surface and pat it into a square about 1 inch thick. Wrap it and chill for about 1 hour or until the dough is firm.

2. While the dough is chilling, prepare the filling: Heat the oil in a small skillet over medium heat, add the onion, and cook, stirring occasionally, until it is translucent but not brown, about 7 minutes. Scrape the onion into a small bowl and cool. Stir in the poppy seeds and cheese. Set aside. The filling can be made a day in advance and chilled.

3. Roll the dough out on a lightly floured surface to a 10-by-15-inch rectangle. Place the dough on the counter with one of the 15-inch sides closest to you. Brush the surface with the beaten egg white and sprinkle the filling evenly over it, leaving a ½-inch border along the side closest to you and the 15-inch border farthest away.

4. Beginning at the 15-inch side farthest from you, fold the bare dough over the filling and then roll the dough into a tight cylinder. The exposed edge of dough nearest to you will adhere to the cylinder to seal it closed. Gently roll the entire log back and forth to elongate slightly, to about 16 inches. Cut the log in half, wrap both halves tightly in parchment paper, and chill for 2 hours or overnight, until the dough is firm enough to slice.

5. When ready to bake, preheat the oven to 350°F.

6. Trim the ends and slice the dough into ⅜-inch thick pieces. Place the slices 2 inches apart on the prepared pans. Bake until the crackers spread out slightly and the edges are lightly colored, about 20 minutes. As the crackers bake, the cheese in the filling may melt and ooze out ever so slightly, and that is fine. Most of the cheese will remain inside, and the bit that comes out will be toasty and crisp when the baking is finished.

7. Cool the crackers on the pans on wire racks. Repeat as needed with the remaining dough and cooled pans until all the crackers are baked, or freeze the dough for future use. Serve the cooled crackers immediately or store them in an airtight container for up to 3 days.

# Whole Wheat–Sesame Crisps

Combining whole wheat flour with all-purpose flour does more than increase the nutrients in this recipe. The whole wheat flour imparts a nuttiness of its own which works with the sesame oil and sesame seeds to produce a robust, earthy flavor. While there is a little resting time for the dough, the mixing method could not be quicker or easier. It takes just two bowls, a whisk, and a spatula, but the results are crunchy and wonderfully complex.

PREPARATION TIME: *15 minutes, plus 30 minutes to rest*
BAKING TIME: *15 to 18 minutes for 2 sheets*
MAKES: *50 crackers*
EQUIPMENT: *2 rimmed baking sheets lined with parchment paper*

4 large eggs

2 tablespoons olive oil

1 tablespoon roasted sesame oil

1½ cups all-purpose flour

¾ cup whole wheat flour

1 cup (5 ounces) sesame seeds

1½ teaspoons salt

1 teaspoon sugar

1 teaspoon baking powder

1. Whisk the eggs, olive oil, and sesame oil together in a large bowl. In a separate bowl, stir together the flours, sesame seeds, salt, sugar, and baking powder.
2. Gradually add the dry ingredients to the egg mixture while stirring with a spatula or a wooden spoon. The dough should be moist and soft but not sticky. If it is not smooth, turn the dough out onto a lightly floured surface and knead slightly. It should cohere quickly, without the addition of much flour. Cover the dough, either in the bowl or on the countertop, with plastic wrap and let rest for 30 minutes.
3. Preheat the oven to 350°F.
4. Divide the rested dough in half and work with one piece at a time. Roll the dough on a clean, lightly floured work surface into a rough square about 10 by 10 inches and ⅛-inch thick. Using a pizza wheel, cut into 2-inch squares and place the squares on a prepared pan, leaving about 1 inch between the squares. Use an offset spatula to transfer the squares to the pan.
5. Using the tines of a fork, pierce each square all over. Bake until the crisps are golden brown, 15 to 18 minutes. The tablespoon of roasted sesame oil is just enough to create an enticing, deep, toasty aroma as they bake.
6. Cool the crackers on the pans on wire racks. Repeat as needed with the remaining dough and cooled pans until all the crackers are baked, or freeze the dough for future use. Serve the cooled crackers immediately or store them in an airtight container for up to 3 days.

*From top: Whole Wheat–Sesame Crisps (page 62);*
*Dukka Chips (page 64)*

# Dukka Chips

Purchasing tortillas makes these a snap to prepare—we just provide the flavoring for the blank canvas. Dukka is a traditional Egyptian condiment found on kitchen tables throughout the Middle East. It's sprinkled on just about everything and used as a dip when mixed with yogurt. Like other home-based dishes, there are as many variations of dukka as there are cooks who make it. Our version is more than an Egyptian original; it showcases an array of nuts and seeds from around the world. It's important to note that if these chips need to travel, pack them tightly, keep them flat, and wrap them well. The topping will loosen if the chips get bumped or tossed, so treat them with care.

PREPARATION TIME: *25 minutes*
BAKING TIME: *12 to 15 minutes for 2 sheets*
MAKES: *64 chips*
EQUIPMENT: *2 rimmed baking sheets lined with parchment paper*

½ cup (2½ ounces) sesame seeds

¼ cup (1¼ ounces) chopped Brazil nuts

¼ cup (1¼ ounces) chopped hazelnuts

4 tablespoons (¾ ounce) unsweetened coconut flakes

2 tablespoons (½ ounce) sunflower seeds

¼ cup coriander seeds, toasted and lightly crushed

2 tablespoons cumin seeds

1 teaspoon kosher salt

1 teaspoon ground cinnamon

½ teaspoon cayenne pepper

8 corn or whole wheat tortillas, approximately 8 inches in diameter

3 tablespoons olive oil

1. Preheat the oven to 350°F.
2. Combine the sesame seeds, Brazil nuts, hazelnuts, coconut, sunflower seeds, coriander seeds, and cumin seeds in a small mixing bowl and toss. Transfer to one prepared pan and toast in the oven for about 10 minutes. The mixture is ready when it is slightly browned and the warm smell of spices fills the kitchen. Remove the mixture from the oven and allow it to cool completely.
3. Working in small batches, process the cooled nut-spice mixture in a spice grinder or food processor until finely ground, about 30 seconds. If the mixture is still warm when it is processed, the nuts will become oily and pasty, so be sure to cool it thoroughly first. Leave the parchment paper on the pans to reuse in step 4. Pour the ground mixture into a bowl. Add the salt, cinnamon, and cayenne and stir together. Divide the dukka in half; use one half now and refrigerate the other half (it will keep in an airtight container for up to 1 month).

4. Place 2 tortillas on each of the prepared pans. Brush each tortilla lightly with olive oil and sprinkle with 2 tablespoons of dukka. Cut each tortilla into eight wedges using a pizza wheel. Bake for 12 to 15 minutes, until the spice is fragrant and the edges of each wedge have a hint of color and a slight curl like an ancient parchment. Cool on the pans on racks. Repeat the process on the cooled pans with the remaining dukka and tortillas. Serve the chips at room temperature. If there are any leftovers, store them flat in an airtight container for up to 2 days.

# Walnut-Parmesan Shortbread

Shortbreads are traditional Scottish baked goods, but their character belies their name. They are not breads but rather buttery, crumbly-crisp cookies with little more than butter, sugar, and flour in their roster of ingredients. The substitution of savory ingredients for sweet ones creates a different species of shortbread altogether, like this version, which keeps the expected texture of sweet shortbread but takes on added flavor thanks to the Parmesan cheese and ground walnuts. These are excellent when served with cheeses or soups or alone.

PREPARATION TIME: *30 minutes, plus 1 hour to chill*
BAKING TIME: *20 minutes for 2 sheets*
MAKES: *96 shortbreads*
EQUIPMENT: *2 rimmed baking sheets lined with parchment paper*

1½ cups all-purpose flour

1¼ cups (4½ ounces) finely chopped walnuts

1½ teaspoons sugar

1 teaspoon salt

1½ sticks (12 tablespoons) unsalted butter, softened

2 large eggs

¾ cup (1 ounce) freshly grated Parmesan cheese

1. Place ¼ cup flour, ¾ cup walnuts, and the sugar in the work bowl of a food processor and pulse repeatedly for 1 minute, until the nuts are finely ground. The flour will coat the nuts as they are pulsed and prevent them from getting oily. Add the remaining 1¼ cups flour and the salt and pulse just until blended. Set this mixture aside.

2. In the bowl of a standing mixer fitted with the paddle attachment, cream the butter on low speed until soft, about 1 minute. Turn the mixer up to medium high and continue to beat until the butter is lightened in color and texture, about 5 minutes. The light yellow butter will turn to an almost strawlike off-white when it is creamed enough, and the air that has been added during this beating will turn the butter almost puffy. Stop the mixer and, using a rubber spatula, scrape down the sides of the bowl.

3. Add half of the flour-and-nut mixture to the lightened butter and mix slowly to combine. Add the eggs and mix again, just until combined. Stop the mixer, scrape down the sides, and return the mixer to low speed.

4. Add the Parmesan with the remaining flour-and-nut mixture and allow the paddle to rotate slowly until all the ingredients are combined, about 1 minute. Remove the bowl from the mixer and, using the spatula, stir the remaining ½ cup walnuts into the dough. Divide the dough in half, flatten each half into a disk, wrap each piece in plastic wrap, and chill until ready to use, at least 1 hour, until firm, but as long as overnight.

5. When you are ready to bake the shortbreads, preheat the oven to 325°F.

6. On a lightly floured surface, roll 1 piece of the dough to ¼-inch thick. As you roll, lift the dough just slightly or run an offset spatula between the dough and the surface to prevent it from sticking. Using a 1½-inch round cutter lightly dipped in flour, cut circles and carefully place them on the prepared pans, about 1 inch apart. Gently press the scraps together, chill briefly, and reroll. Try to use only the tiniest amount of flour when you reroll the dough, as additional flour will make the crackers tougher, and tender is the goal.

7. Bake the shortbreads until the tops are barely colored and the edges are lightly browned, about 20 minutes. You will smell the cheese as the shortbreads begin to take on color. Don't allow the bottoms to darken too much; a fully brown color indicates overbaking.

8. Cool the shortbreads on the pans on racks. Repeat as needed with the remaining dough and cooled pans until all the shortbreads are baked, or freeze the dough for future use. The shortbreads can be stored between layers of wax paper or parchment paper in an airtight container for up to 1 week.

# Pine Nut–Rosemary Disks

Nut-laced savory shortbreads make great pre-meal nibbles. Pine nuts and rosemary are a natural combination—both evoke the aroma of an evergreen forest. Adding cornmeal gives you a little extra crunch to go with the buttery bite of shortbread, and stone-ground rather than regularly processed cornmeal delivers a satisfyingly coarse texture. Using yolks instead of whole eggs will give the baked crackers a slightly burnished veneer, just a bit darker than whole eggs would.

PREPARATION TIME: *25 minutes, plus 1 hour to chill*
BAKING TIME: *20 to 25 minutes for 2 sheets*
MAKES: *75 shortbreads*
EQUIPMENT: *2 rimmed baking sheets lined with parchment paper*

2 cups all-purpose flour

½ cup stone-ground cornmeal

1 teaspoon sugar

1½ teaspoons salt

1½ sticks (12 tablespoons) unsalted butter, softened

¾ cup (3¾ ounces) coarsely chopped pine nuts

1 tablespoon freshly chopped rosemary, woody stems removed

1 large egg

2 large egg yolks

1. In a medium bowl, mix the flour, cornmeal, sugar, and salt. Set aside.

2. In the bowl of a standing mixer fitted with the paddle attachment, cream the butter on low speed until smooth and softened, about 1 minute. Turn up the speed of the mixer to medium high and beat the butter until light, about 5 more minutes. As the butter beats, it will become both lighter in color, an almost off-white hue rather than gold, and lighter in texture, both creamy and smooth.

3. Turn the mixer to low and add half the flour-and-cornmeal mixture. Mix just until the dry ingredients are incorporated and add the pine nuts, rosemary, and egg yolks. Stop the mixer and, using a rubber spatula, scrape down the sides. Restart the mixer on low speed and add the remainder of the flour-and-cornmeal mixture. Beat until just mixed, less than 1 minute.

4. Remove the dough from the mixer and divide it in half. If the dough seems a bit dry, gently press it together with your hands. If it is still too dry, add 1 or 2 teaspoons of cold water. Flatten each piece on a lightly floured surface and wrap it in plastic wrap. Chill for at least 1 hour, or until you are ready to bake. The disks of dough can stay wrapped airtight overnight in the refrigerator.

5. When you are ready to bake, preheat the oven to 325°F.

6. Unwrap one piece of dough and roll it out to ¼-inch thick on a lightly floured surface. Using a 1½-inch round cutter lightly dipped in flour, cut circles and carefully place them on the prepared pans about 1 inch apart. Gently press the scraps together, chill briefly, and reroll. Try to use a minimal amount of flour when you reroll the dough, as additional flour will make the shortbreads tougher, and tender is the goal.

7. Bake until the shortbreads are golden, 20 to 25 minutes. They will be dotted with darker flecks, but these pieces of pine nuts should remain a deep golden brown and not get burned. Fragrant rosemary will dominate all other smells as the shortbreads bake.

8. Cool the shortbreads on the pans on a rack. Repeat as needed with the remaining dough and cooled pans until all the shortbreads are baked, or freeze the dough for future use. The shortbreads can be stored between layers of wax paper in an airtight container for up to 1 week.

CHEESE CHOICE: Match these crackers with any mild soft cheese such as Camembert or Brie.

*Clockwise from top: Black Bean Hummus with Peanuts (page 77); Pistachio Raita (page 86); Walnut–Red Pepper Spread (page 73); Dukka Chips (page 64); Whole Wheat–Sesame Crisps (page 62)*

CHAPTER 2

# Dip It

# Nuts and Bolts of Dips and Spreads

**The dips and spreads that follow are diverse, simple to prepare, and** great to make ahead for family and casual entertaining. Their flavors and textures come from around the world. We have included savory dips that make great starters, and we serve them with breads, crackers, and raw or blanched vegetables. Also, there are a few sweet spreads that are fruit-dunking friendly and make sparkling dessert toppers. We have made suggestions of what we enjoy best with these dips, but you really can serve them with anything you choose. Many of the crackers from the Nibbles chapter make great companions, and a few bowls of dips with crackers at their sides made a delicious small meal.

The prep-ahead nature of these dips and spreads makes them perfect for anyone who opens the refrigerator door looking for a little something. Most can be kept airtight in the refrigerator for 3 days or so, waiting to be scooped and savored.

The thickness of a dip depends a bit on personal preference. We enjoy our dips with a fairly thick consistency, but sometimes a few days in the refrigerator will cause a dip to thicken too much even for us. If you want to thin a dip that you've just pulled from the refrigerator, give it a brisk stir, and gradually stir in cold water, tablespoon by tablespoon, until you reach your desired consistency. Taste for seasoning and add a bit of salt and pepper if needed.

A dip can also be made thinner when you prepare it, by adding a little more of the liquid that is used in the recipe, whether it is the reserved liquid from a can of beans, juice, or water.

# Walnut–Red Pepper Spread
## MUHAMMARA

Rich with walnuts and flavored with pomegranate molasses, this Syrian spread comes from Mary Tutunjian, Andrea's grandmother. Many variations of this spread can be found throughout the Middle East, and it is a popular meze, or appetizer, to serve before the main meal. Mary always made her muhammara with crisp scarlet peppers. We have chosen to roast our peppers instead of using them uncooked, because we have found that roasting them adds a smoky flavor and creates a smoother dip. The final flavor is reminiscent of Mary's original, with its magical rich-tart undertones of pomegranate molasses and toasted walnuts. If you take a shortcut and use jarred roasted peppers, the result will be less favorable; however, if you must, you will need to add up to ½ cup of plain breadcrumbs to absorb the extra moisture. This dip has sneaked into other parts of our culinary repertoire, and thinned with a little extra olive oil has become a fabulous dressing for chicken salad. *(See photo page 70.)*

PREPARATION TIME: *15 minutes, plus 2 hours to chill*
MAKES: *4 cups*

### FOR THE SPREAD

2¼ cups (8 ounces) walnut pieces, toasted

2 pounds (about 5) red bell peppers, roasted, skinned, and seeded (see box page 74)

¼ cup extra-virgin olive oil

¼ cup pomegranate molasses

2 tablespoons freshly squeezed lemon juice

1 teaspoon ground cumin

½ teaspoon kosher salt

½ teaspoon sugar

### FOR SERVING

Ground cumin

Pine nuts, toasted

Pita bread, cut into triangles

1. Pulse the walnuts in the work bowl of a food processor 6 or 7 times, until they are roughly chopped. Add the roasted peppers and pulse to a chunky paste, about 15 seconds. Add the remaining ingredients and pulse until just combined, about 30 seconds. The walnuts absorb liquid and will act as a thickening agent, but overprocessing will cause the spread to liquefy and become too thin. The combination of the red peppers, the brown walnuts, and the garnet-hued pomegranate molasses will create a warm terra-cotta-colored mixture with a chunky texture and rich flavor. Season with salt to taste.

*continued*

2. Scrape the spread into a serving dish, cover, and chill for at least 2 hours. Or seal it in an airtight container and refrigerate for up to 3 days.

3. Just before serving, sprinkle with a large pinch of cumin and a few toasted pine nuts. Serve with the pita triangles on the side.

---

### Roasting Peppers

Once you have eaten a freshly roasted pepper, you will never buy jarred ones again. The smoky flavor is certainly worth the small amount of effort required.

Peppers can be roasted under a broiler, directly over a gas burner, or on a gas or charcoal grill. Wash the peppers and wipe them dry. Place the cleaned peppers on a roasting pan if using the broiler or directly over the flame of a gas burner or grill.

Regardless of where you are roasting the peppers, the method stays the same: Rotate and flip each pepper as one side becomes blackened, until the entire pepper looks burned. (If the peppers are not charred enough, the skins will not come off easily.) After roasting, place the peppers in a bowl and cover it with a lid or plastic wrap, or place them in a paper bag and roll the top closed. This process allows the peppers to steam a little, releasing the charred skin from the flesh. After about 20 minutes, or when the peppers are cool enough to handle, pull out the cores by the stems, peel off the skins, and remove the seeds. You can use the back of a knife or a paper towel to remove some of the black pieces that remain. Do not rinse the peppers, as you would be rinsing off the flavor. It is okay if a little bit of charred skin adheres.

# Hummus

When Andrea was young, long before she went to culinary school, she would take the train from Manhattan to visit her grandmother in Brooklyn. A quick cooking lesson was often on the agenda, and one of the first things she learned to make was hummus. One fall day the musky smell of cooked beans filled the tiny kitchen on Eighty-seventh Street. Ingredients were lined up on the counter in glass jars. Mugs from the cupboard were clustered around them, and Andrea quickly learned that these were her grandmother's measuring cups. Chickpeas, tahini, cumin, and citric acid were among the ingredients that filled the mugs or her grandmother's cupped hands as Andrea scribbled notes. During the lesson her grandmother explained in her broken English that there was no such thing as a food processor in the old country, so everything had to be mashed and mixed by hand. She chuckled and said that sometimes now she even used canned beans, and her husband, George, didn't notice the difference. At the end of the lesson, Andrea's grandmother pulled open a drawer, handed her two fifty-dollar bills, and told her to buy a food processor. She packed up the glass jars filled with spices along with some of the freshly prepared hummus and sent Andrea back home on the train. The spices have been replaced many times, but the jars are still in Andrea's home. This recipe is a version of Mary Tutunjian's using precise measurements.

PREPARATION TIME: *15 minutes, plus 2 hours to chill*
MAKES: *2 cups*

### FOR THE HUMMUS

2 cloves garlic

3 cups cooked chickpeas (see box page 76), or two 15-ounce cans, drained and rinsed. Reserve ½ cup cooking liquid or liquid from the cans.

⅓ cup tahini

1½ teaspoons ground cumin

1 teaspoon citric acid (see Note)

2 tablespoons extra-virgin olive oil

1½ teaspoons kosher salt

### FOR SERVING

White sesame seeds, toasted

Black sesame seeds

Pita bread, cut into triangles, or plain crackers

1. In the work bowl of a food processor pulse the garlic repeatedly until finely chopped, about 15 seconds.
2. Add the chickpeas and puree until very smooth, about 2 or 3 minutes. The chickpeas will form a paste with small chunks. Slowly add a couple of tablespoons of the reserved liquid while the machine is running, until the mixture becomes smooth.

*continued*

3. Add the tahini, cumin, citric acid, olive oil, and salt and process well, again until very smooth. This may take a minute or two, but be patient and don't worry: the mixture cannot be overprocessed.

4. If the spread is too thick for your liking, add more of the reserved liquid, 1 tablespoon at a time, until the desired consistency is achieved. Hummus should be smooth, creamy, and barely thick enough for a spoon to stand straight up in. Season with salt to taste.

5. Chill the hummus for at least 2 hours or up to 3 days in a tightly sealed container. When ready to serve, sprinkle with the sesame seeds and serve with pita triangles or crackers.

NOTE: Citric acid, also known as lemon salt or sour salt, can be found in Middle Eastern food stores. It is used instead of lemon juice in many Syrian dishes. It is also used for pickling and canning. If you cannot find citric acid, substitute 3 tablespoons strained lemon juice for each teaspoon of citric acid.

## Cooking Dried Beans

Place 2½ cups (1 pound) dried beans in a large bowl and cover with cold water; set aside overnight. Drain and rinse, then place in a medium saucepan and cover with enough clean cold water to reach 2 or 3 three inches above the bean line. Add 2 teaspoons kosher salt and bring to a boil over medium heat. Lower the heat until the water is simmering and cook the beans until tender, at least 1 hour. The cooking time will vary depending on the size, dryness, and variety of the beans, anywhere between 1 and 3 hours. Check the beans while they are cooking and make sure that they are always covered with simmering water. If the water has evaporated, add more to cover and keep cooking. Strain, and reserve the cooking liquid if the recipe calls for it. Properly cooked beans will be tender when tasted, with their skins still clinging to them.

# Black Bean Hummus with Peanuts

In this 1960s-style recipe, inspired by the first wave of natural-food cookbooks, black beans stand in for chickpeas and peanut butter substitutes for tahini. When Cara was in college, she belonged to a food co-op in which students took turns cooking dinner for a dormitory. She prepared this hummus often as one of her appetizers, relying on pantry standards tucked away in the basement kitchen. Nothing could taste better than this earthy preparation after a long day in the library. Fast-forward a few years and this dish is still a huge hit. We love the slightly spicier version with the optional cayenne pepper. *(See photo page 70.)*

PREPARATION TIME: *15 minutes, plus 2 hours to chill*
MAKES: *2 cups*

### FOR THE HUMMUS

½ cup (2½ ounces) roasted peanuts

3 cloves garlic

3 cups cooked black beans (see box page 76), or two 15-ounce cans, drained and rinsed. Reserve ½ cup cooking liquid or liquid from the cans.

¼ cup freshly chopped cilantro

½ cup chunky natural peanut butter

1½ teaspoons ground cumin

1½ teaspoons ground coriander

3 tablespoons freshly squeezed lemon juice

3 tablespoons extra-virgin olive oil

1½ teaspoons kosher salt

½ teaspoon freshly ground black pepper

½ teaspoon cayenne pepper (optional)

### FOR SERVING

¼ cup (1¼ ounces) chopped roasted peanuts

Pita bread cut into triangles and toasted

1. Process the peanuts and garlic in the work bowl of a food processor until finely chopped, about 30 seconds. Add the beans and cilantro and process until very smooth and slightly lightened in color, about 2 minutes. The dark beans will be transformed into a rich purplish gray paste. Add the remaining ingredients, including the cayenne if you like, and process well, again until very smooth, about 2 minutes.

2. If the hummus is too thick, add some of the reserved liquid, 1 tablespoon at a time, until the desired consistency is achieved. Season with salt and pepper to taste. The hummus should be thick enough to spread on the pita and hold its shape.

3. Chill in a well-sealed container for at least 2 hours or up to 3 days. When ready to serve, stir in the remaining ¼ cup of peanuts. Bring to room temperature 30 minutes before serving. Serve with pita triangles.

# Tomato-Almond Tapenade

Tapenade is a thick spread that is typically made from the bounty of southern France: ripe olives, capers, and olive oil. It is traditionally made by hand in a mortar with a pestle, but our modern food processors have made the laborious chopping simple. The addition of almonds and sun-dried tomatoes is our personal take on this recipe. The almonds add a welcome toasty crunch and are a perfect fit with the other sunny Provençal ingredients. Rinsing the capers will help tame the saltiness. We love eating this with a mild goat cheese served on the side to add a bit of tangy creaminess.

PREPARATION TIME: *15 minutes, plus 2 hours to chill*
MAKES: *3 cups*

1 cup (3 ounces) sun-dried tomatoes, rehydrated (see box below)

1 cup (4½ ounces) slivered almonds, toasted

2 cloves garlic

1½ cups pitted black Kalamata olives

⅓ cup freshly chopped flat-leaf parsley

2 tablespoons drained capers, rinsed

2 tablespoons freshly chopped basil

⅓ cup extra-virgin olive oil

¼ cup balsamic vinegar

1 teaspoon kosher salt

½ teaspoon freshly ground black pepper

FOR SERVING

Thinly sliced and lightly toasted baguette

1. In the work bowl of a food processor, process the sun-dried tomatoes, almonds, and garlic until finely chopped, about 1 minute. Add the olives, parsley, capers, and basil. Pulse about 10 times, or until the mixture is roughly chopped. Transfer to a medium bowl and stir in the olive oil and vinegar. The spread will be almost black, with flecks of red and gold. Season with the salt and pepper.
2. Chill for at least 2 hours or up to 3 days in a tightly sealed container. Bring to room temperature 30 minutes before serving. Serve with the toasted slices of baguette.

---

### *Rehydrating Dried Tomatoes*

To rehydrate sun-dried tomatoes, place them in a small saucepan and pour in enough cold water to cover. Bring to a boil over high heat and remove from the heat immediately. Allow the tomatoes to stand for 5 minutes, then drain.

# Crab-Coconut Dip

In 1962 Cara first tasted her mother's clam dip, which seemed very exotic back then. By the time she was ten, she was preparing it herself and had realized that the key to clam dip success was using room-temperature cream cheese: cold cream cheese always stuck to the blender. Over thirty years later, that childhood recipe was transformed into this striking dip. Creamy white with specks of green and pink, it has a flavor that is far from its inspiration, and it is repeatedly requested by many of Cara's catering clients. The marriage of crab and coconut is like an unexpected tropical paradise—cool and tempting.

PREPARATION TIME: *20 minutes, plus 2 hours to chill*
MAKES: *3 cups*

½ pound cream cheese, softened and cut into 6 pieces

¼ cup unsweetened coconut milk

2 tablespoons freshly chopped chives

1 tablespoon freshly chopped mint

1 pound fresh lump crabmeat

¾ cup (2¼ ounces) unsweetened coconut flakes, toasted

1 teaspoon kosher salt

½ teaspoon freshly ground black pepper

FOR SERVING

Snow peas, strings removed

Radishes

1. In the bowl of a food processor, puree the cream cheese, coconut milk, chives, and mint until smooth, about 1 minute. Stop the processor and scrape down the sides using a rubber spatula once or twice, to ensure even mixing.

2. Break up the crabmeat in a large bowl, making sure there are no remaining bits of cartilage or shell. It is best to do this with your hands, but try to keep the chunks of crab intact. Mix well with the coconut. Gently stir in the cream cheese–coconut milk mixture and season with the salt and pepper.

3. Chill the dip until firm, at least 2 hours or up to 3 days in a well-sealed container. We serve the dip straight from the refrigerator, with crunchy snow peas and snappy radishes.

# Pumpkin Seed Guacamole

When the Spanish first arrived on the shores of Mexico, they were introduced to the countless foodstuffs that were native to the Americas. The Aztecs, who lived throughout the region, had been combining their indigenous ingredients, and one of their dishes was called ahuaca-mulli. A combination of two domesticated fruits, avocado and tomato, guacamole is still made in a similar way and has become a worldwide favorite. Pumpkin seeds were also a staple of the Aztecs, as squashes of all kinds were first domesticated in the Americas. Adding them to guacamole seems logical, as a homage to one of America's first regional cuisines. Hass avocados turn from pebbled green to heavily black when ripe and change from firm to just yielding to the touch when ready. *(See photo page 276.)*

PREPARATION TIME: *20 minutes*
MAKES: *2 to 3 cups*

3 ripe Hass avocados

¼ cup freshly squeezed lime juice

3 plum tomatoes, seeded and finely chopped

1 small white onion, finely chopped

¾ cup (4 ounces) coarsely chopped pumpkin seeds, toasted

¼ cup freshly chopped cilantro

1 jalapeño pepper, seeded and finely chopped

2 cloves garlic, finely chopped

1½ teaspoons kosher salt

½ teaspoon freshly ground black pepper

FOR SERVING

Tortilla chips

1. Using a sharp knife and starting at the stem end of the avocados, cut through the skin and flesh down to the pit. Work the knife around the pit to cut each avocado in half. Twist the avocado halves to separate them and remove the pit. Using a spoon, scoop the flesh from the skin into a medium bowl. Mash the avocados until they are a thick verdant puree with some small bits remaining. We often use a potato masher to make guacamole; its broad grid makes quick work of the necessary squashing. If you don't have one, a fork will do the job.

2. Stir in the lime juice, then gently stir in the tomatoes, onion, pumpkin seeds, cilantro, jalapeño, and garlic. Avocados turn brown when they are exposed to oxygen, so your best bet for keeping them green is to add an acid—lime juice—and make the guacamole as close to serving time as possible.

3. Season with the salt and pepper and serve immediately or refrigerate for no more than an hour in an airtight container with plastic wrap directly on the surface of the dip. Serve with the tortilla chips or Vegan Black Bean and Pecan Tostada Stacks (page 277).

# Spicy Peanut Dip

Peanut dip is thought to have originated in Thailand, but many Southeast Asian cuisines feature ground nut sauces as dips and accompaniments. What's known to Americans as peanut dip is quite different from its Southeast Asian roots. The elaborate sauces that include curry paste and coconut milk have been set aside here. A bit salty, a little sweet, and with a hint of heat, this dip is a straightforward Americanized version. With a nod to its Asian roots, we make it when we crave the seductive balance of those flavors.

PREPARATION TIME: *10 minutes, plus 2 hours to chill*
MAKES: *1¾ cups*

One ½-inch piece fresh ginger, sliced

2 cloves garlic

1 cup smooth natural peanut butter

3 tablespoons freshly squeezed lemon juice

2 tablespoons light soy sauce

1 tablespoon packed light brown sugar

1 teaspoon chili paste, preferably sambal oelek (available in the international food section of most supermarkets)

FOR SERVING

½ cup (2½ ounces) coarsely chopped roasted peanuts

Peeled sliced jicama or peeled sliced carrots

1. Process the ginger and garlic in the work bowl of a food processor until finely chopped, about 30 seconds. Add the peanut butter, lemon juice, soy sauce, brown sugar, and chili paste. Process the mixture until smooth and thickened, about 2 minutes. Stop the processor and scrape down the sides of the bowl using a spatula, as needed. With the food processor running, add up to ½ cup hot water 1 tablespoon at a time, adding enough to make a dip that holds its shape and is not too thin. The dip should be slightly thick and resemble stirred sour cream.

2. Chill for at least 2 hours or up to 3 days in a well-sealed container. Allow the dip to come to room temperature 30 minutes before serving and stir well. Fold in the chopped peanuts and serve with the vegetables.

# Curried Cashew-Eggplant Dip

Piercing the skin of an eggplant is essential before roasting, as the skin is like a taut balloon and the vegetable can explode if the steam does not find a way to escape. Cara's grandmother neglected this step once, and the ensuing explosion blew the oven door open and rocked the house. The cleanup was horrific as well, with eggplant pulp plastered to the walls and floor. If eggplant is well handled, the smoky flavor that results from proper roasting adds depth and dimension to this mildly spicy, curry-tinged dip.

PREPARATION TIME: *30 minutes, plus 45 minutes to roast the eggplant and 2 hours to chill*
MAKES: *3 cups*

1 large eggplant (about 1½ pounds)

2 tablespoons olive oil

1 medium onion, chopped

1 clove garlic, finely chopped

1 tablespoon curry powder

1 cup (5 ounces) roasted cashews

½ cup nonfat Greek yogurt

¼ cup freshly chopped cilantro

2 teaspoons kosher salt

½ teaspoon freshly ground black pepper

FOR SERVING

Flat bread or pita, cut into triangles and toasted

1. Preheat the oven to 400°F.
2. Place the eggplant in a small roasting pan and prick the skin with the tines of a fork in several places to allow the steam to escape while roasting. Roast for 40 to 45 minutes, until the eggplant is soft and tender. Set it aside to cool. A properly cooked eggplant will collapse, and a little brown liquid will seep out. This step can be done a day ahead; just wrap the eggplant with its juices in a plastic bag and refrigerate it.
3. Heat the oil in a medium skillet over low heat. Add the onion and garlic and cook, stirring occasionally, until soft, about 5 minutes. Stir in the curry power and cook, stirring, until the spice absorbs the oil, coats the onion and garlic, and slightly sticks to the pan, about 5 minutes. Set the mixture aside to cool.
4. Chop the cashews roughly in the work bowl of a food processor. Add the onion mixture and process 5 seconds, until combined.
5. Cut the cooled eggplant in half lengthwise and scoop the flesh from the skin into the work bowl. Pulse the ingredients together briefly, 2 or 3 times, being careful not to overprocess, or the eggplant will liquefy. Transfer to a medium bowl and fold in the yogurt and cilantro. Season with the salt and pepper.
6. Chill in a well-sealed container for at least 2 hours or up to 3 days. Bring the dip to room temperature 30 minutes before serving. Serve with flat bread or pita.

# Vegetarian "Chopped Liver"

Cara's first memory of eating real chopped liver on perfectly fresh rye bread is of the day her family moved to their new Long Island home. As healthy eating became a way of life, her family replaced true chopped liver with this vegetarian substitute. It is so delicious that it has become a Jewish holiday staple at Cara's house and at most of her clients' homes. Quarts and quarts of it are packed into the refrigerators before the holidays, and many a frantic call is made to order more. Some refer to it as a vegetable pâté, but we prefer to call it as it seems, a mock or modernized, healthier version of its schmaltz-filled ancestor. Both the mushrooms and the walnuts provide the deep brown color expected in chopped chicken liver, and easily fool the eye. Don't hesitate to use frozen peas; slightly overcooking them darkens their color, adding to the chopped-liver illusion.

PREPARATION TIME: *35 to 45 minutes, plus 2 hours to chill*
MAKES: *2 cups*

2 tablespoons canola oil

1 large onion, cut in half and thinly sliced

2 teaspoons kosher salt

1 cup sliced button mushrooms

1 cup fresh or frozen peas

1 cup (3½ ounces) walnut pieces

2 large eggs, hard-boiled

½ teaspoon freshly ground black pepper

FOR SERVING

Matzoh crackers or sliced rye bread

1. Heat the oil in a medium skillet over low heat. Add the onion, season with 1 teaspoon of salt, and cook, stirring occasionally, until golden brown, 15 to 20 minutes. It will take that long to caramelize the onion and cook it to a deep color that reveals its characteristic flavor. Keep the heat low, move the slices occasionally in the pan, and have patience.

2. Add the mushrooms and cook, stirring occasionally, until the mushrooms soften and release their liquid, about 5 minutes. Add the peas, cover the skillet, and cook the mixture for an additional 5 minutes, or until the peas are cooked through. Overcooking the peas won't hurt here; a dull green pea color will help duplicate the look of liver. Remove from the heat and cool.

3. Roughly chop the walnuts in the work bowl of a food processor. Add the cooled vegetables and process until a thick paste forms, about 45 seconds. Remove the mixture from the bowl and set it aside. Without cleaning the bowl, process the eggs until they are roughly chopped, about 10 seconds. Fold them into the vegetable mixture.

4. Season with the remaining teaspoon of salt and the pepper and chill for at least 3 hours or up to 3 days in a well-sealed container. Bring to room temperature 30 minutes before serving. Serve with matzoh crackers or freshly sliced rye bread.

# Artichoke-Almond Spread

Almonds and artichokes stand in for eggplant in this rustic spread similar to caponata, a Sicilian sweet-and-sour dip. Artichokes, which are a lot easier to work with than they look, are a member of the thistle group of the sunflower family. Most grown in this country come from Monterey, California. When purchasing artichokes, large or small, look for full, firm vegetables without any yellow or brown spots. Baby artichokes, available in early spring, have smooth sides and need very little trimming; they are completely edible, as the choke hasn't had a chance to develop. Fresh are best, but we have made this successfully with frozen artichoke hearts. Artichokes in the can are packed in brine, which would add an unwanted saltiness, so stick with fresh or frozen.

PREPARATION TIME: *40 to 45 minutes*
MAKES: *4 cups*

¼ cup olive oil

1 medium onion, finely chopped

3 cloves garlic, finely chopped

1½ pounds cooked fresh baby artichokes (see box page 85) or frozen, thawed

One 15-ounce can diced tomatoes, drained

¼ cup Spanish or Italian green olives, pitted and chopped

2 tablespoons drained capers, rinsed

2 tablespoons red wine vinegar

1 tablespoon sugar

1½ teaspoons kosher salt

½ teaspoon freshly ground black pepper

¾ cup (3½ ounces) chopped slivered almonds, toasted

2 tablespoons freshly chopped basil

FOR SERVING

Thinly sliced baguette

1. Heat the olive oil in a deep skillet over low heat. Add the onion and garlic and cook, stirring occasionally, until softened, fragrant, and translucent, about 5 to 10 minutes.
2. Add the artichokes and the tomatoes and cook an additional 5 minutes. Stir in the olives, capers, vinegar, and sugar and continue cooking for 5 more minutes.
3. Season the mixture with the salt and pepper. Remove from the heat and stir in the almonds and basil. Serve the spread warm, right after it is prepared, or cold, with slices of baguette. It can be made up to 2 days in advance. Refrigerate in a well-sealed container and serve as is or warm it for a few minutes over low heat in a small saucepan, stirring frequently.

## Preparing Baby Artichokes

To prepare baby artichokes, remove the outermost row of petals by inserting a stainless steel knife blade behind each petal and pulling it away from the base. Trim off the top ½ inch or so of the artichoke. Pare away the outer skin of the base and any stem left. Cut the trimmed artichokes into quarters and immediately place them in a bowl of ice water acidified with lemon juice, which will keep them from turning brown.

Remove the artichokes from the ice water, place them into a medium saucepan, and cover with fresh water. Bring to a boil over medium-high heat and cook for about 10 minutes, until they are tender. Drain well before using.

# Pistachio Raita

Raita is a Indian yogurt condiment often mixed with fruits, nuts, or vegetables. It is served as a dip or sauce to accompany a meal, but it also makes an excellent breakfast or snack. Pistachio Raita has its own yin-and-yang flavors. The nuts are mild, and the hot jalapeño and cool yogurt balance each other. Feel free to use only one jalapeño if you prefer a less spicy dip, but we find that the mild yogurt tones the peppery edge. *(See photo page 70.)*

PREPARATION TIME: *15 minutes, plus 2 hours to chill*
MAKES: *2 ½ cups*

1 tablespoon olive oil

2 teaspoons ground cumin

1 teaspoon ground coriander

2 jalapeño peppers, seeded and finely chopped

2 cups (10 ounces) pistachios, toasted and finely ground

1 cup freshly chopped cilantro

1 cup nonfat Greek yogurt

2 tablespoons freshly squeezed lime juice

2 tablespoons honey

6 scallions, white and green parts, thinly sliced

1 teaspoon kosher salt

½ teaspoon freshly ground black pepper

FOR SERVING

Pita or naan bread

1. Heat the oil in a medium skillet over medium heat. Add the cumin, coriander, and jalapeños. Cook, stirring, until a paste is formed, about 1 minute. Continue cooking until the paste is sizzling and fragrant, about 5 minutes. Remove from the heat and set aside to cool.

2. Mix the pistachios, cilantro, yogurt, lime juice, honey, and scallions in a medium bowl until well combined.

3. Stir the cooled spices into the yogurt-pistachio mixture. Season with the salt and pepper. The raita should be the consistency of sour cream. If it is thicker, stir in 1 tablespoon of water at a time to thin. Chill for 2 hours before serving with pita or naan bread. The raita can be stored up to 3 days in an airtight container in the refrigerator.

# Creamy Crunchy Nut Butter Dip

This dip is deceptive; it tastes so rich that it is hard to believe it is made just of low fat yogurt and nut butter. We add a touch of sweetener and a hint of vanilla, and it is the perfect after-school snack. Tart apples and salty pretzels are our favorite things to dip in, but a hunk of banana or a crisp cranberry-pistachio biscotto (see page 325) are also delightful. We like to make this with our homemade nut butter, but when pressed, we've had nearly equal success with commercial natural butters.

PREPARATION TIME: *5 minutes*
MAKES: *3 cups*

2 cups reduced fat Greek yogurt

1 cup natural nut butter—almond, peanut, or cashew (see box page 88)

4 tablespoons maple syrup or honey

1 tablespoon vanilla extract

½ cup (2½ ounces) chopped nuts (almonds, peanuts, or cashews)

FOR SERVING

Sliced apples or bananas

Combine the yogurt and the nut butter in a small mixing bowl and stir well. Mix in the maple syrup, vanilla, and nuts and serve immediately with apples and bananas. Wrap any leftovers in an airtight container and refrigerate for up to 1 week.

# HOMEMADE NUT BUTTER

With all of the nut butters now available commercially, we first hesitated when we thought about making our own. What's the point, if we can buy them? The point, we found, is that they are simple to prepare and delicious to eat. They can be whirled in a food processor at a moment's notice, and their freshness is incomparable. We make them in small quantities, add the amount of salt that we like, and keep them refrigerated. They are gone within the week. Almond, cashew, hazelnut, and peanut are our favorites. All of these nuts have enough fat in them to make a puree or butter, but we've added a tiny bit of oil to the recipe to proverbially grease the wheels of progress, and make it a quicker process. These butters can be used interchangeably with any other nut butter labeled "natural."

PREPARATION TIME: *15 minutes*
MAKES: *1 cup*

2 cups (10 ounces) nuts, toasted (almonds, peanuts, hazelnuts, or cashews)

1 to 2 teaspoons nut or canola oil

¼ teaspoon salt (optional)

1. In the work bowl of a food processor, grind the nuts for 3 minutes, then stop the processor to add 1 teaspoon of oil and the salt. Scrape down the sides of the work bowl and continue processing for another 3 to 5 minutes, until the nut butter is as smooth or chunky as you like. Some of the nuts will take longer than others. If the nut butter still appears too dry to spread, add the additional teaspoon of nut oil and continue processing for 2 to 3 minutes more.

2. Serve the nut butter on bread or toast, or use in Creamy Crunchy Nut Butter Dip (page 87). Store the nut butter in an airtight container in the refrigerator for up to one week.

# Chocolate-Hazelnut Spread

We were introduced to this yummy spread in Israel while working in a kibbutz kitchen that fed hundreds every day. As a volunteer, Cara was put to work peeling vegetables, chopping fruit, and cleaning just-laid eggs. One of the bonuses of this job was making "Nutella" by the bucketful, gallons at a time. Although the kitchen set out four full meals a day (hardworking kibbutzniks eat two breakfasts, one early, before work begins, and the next a few hours later), this hazelnut-and-chocolate spread was available whenever a hungry resident stepped through the kitchen's back door, past the big bins of just-picked grapefruit. Spread on fruit or bread, it can transform a ho-hum snack into a sweet treat. Drop a dollop on our Hazelnut–Sour Cream Waffles (page 130) or any waffle or pancake and breakfast just gets better. The commercial version is now widely available, but the ease of preparing it at home will have you making it by the tubful too.

PREPARATION TIME: *30 minutes*
MAKES: *2 cups*

2 cups (10 ounces) blanched hazelnuts, toasted

1 cup confectioners' sugar

⅓ cup Dutch process cocoa powder (see box page 90)

2 tablespoons hazelnut oil or canola oil

1 teaspoon vanilla extract

½ teaspoon salt

FOR SERVING

Strawberries, bananas, or apples

Slices of toast, pancakes, or waffles

1. In the work bowl of a food processor, process the hazelnuts until a paste forms, about 2 minutes. Stop the processor, scrape down the sides of the bowl with a spatula, and continue to process for 3 minutes. The hazelnuts will have the texture of sand, with a little remaining graininess.
2. Add the confectioners' sugar and cocoa and pulse until everything is well mixed, about 1 minute. Drizzle in the oil and add the vanilla and salt. Process until the spread is smooth (except for a little bit of visible hazelnut), about 5 minutes. Using a spatula, place it in a clean airtight container and refrigerate for up to 1 month.

## Cocoa Powder

Cocoa powders can be divided into two simple categories, Dutch process and natural. Both are made from pulverized cacao beans, but the Dutch process variety takes a potassium bath before grinding. The addition of potassium, an alkali, neutralizes the acid in the cocoa, producing cocoa powder that is dark and complex. In baking, natural powders are often used with baking soda, balancing the natural acidity with an introduced alkali. Natural powders are lighter and fruitier than Dutched ones.

# Almond Romesco

A Catalonian classic, romesco has dozens of variations. Some feature roasted peppers, while others combine peppers and tomatoes. Sometimes day-old bread is added for thickening. What they all have in common is the inclusion of nuts. Variations showcase almonds or hazelnuts, and either, or a combination of both, will do the trick. Any kind of romesco has a deep, earthy flavor and a slightly rough texture. It is a sauce of the countryside and of the people, made from locally abundant ingredients. Commonly served at room temperature, romesco pairs perfectly with the foods of the Spanish countryside, brimming in a bowl beside simple grilled fish or chicken. We love it spread on almost anything and serve it as we would hummus or guacamole.

PREPARATION TIME: *1 hour*
MAKES: *2 cups*

4 large ripe tomatoes, cut in half, cored, and seeded

1 red pepper, stems and seeds removed, cut into strips

½ cup olive oil

4 cloves garlic, chopped

1 cup (4½ ounces) slivered almonds, or ½ cup almonds and ½ cup chopped hazelnuts

1 slice day-old bread, cut into rough cubes

3 tablespoons sherry vinegar or red wine vinegar

1 teaspoon kosher salt

½ teaspoon freshly ground black pepper

FOR SERVING

Simply prepared chicken or fish

Raw carrots, cucumbers, or celery

1. Preheat the oven to 375°F.

2. In a medium bowl, toss the tomatoes and red pepper with 2 tablespoons olive oil. Pour them into a roasting pan and bake for 30 minutes. The tomatoes and pepper will soften, and the skins will shrink and wrinkle a bit. Let them cool until you can handle them and slip off the skins. Set aside.

3. In a small skillet, heat 2 more tablespoons oil over medium heat. Add the garlic and the nuts, stir carefully, and cook, allowing the garlic to toast a bit, for 2 or 3 minutes. Add the cubes of stale bread and cook until the edges of the bread look crisp and the garlic is soft and fragrant, about 5 minutes. Allow this mixture to cool for 5 minutes.

*continued*

4. Place the nut mixture in the work bowl of a food processor and process until the mixture is finely chopped but has not been pureed to a paste, about 30 seconds. Add the tomatoes and peppers and process for 10 seconds to mix well. This sauce will look dry and a bit chunky. Add the vinegar and pulse 3 to 5 times, just to combine, about 5 seconds. While the processor is running, drizzle in the remaining 4 tablespoons olive oil. A thick, chunky, deep red spread with flecks of tan will result. Season with the salt and pepper. Serve alongside chicken or fish, or with any vegetables. Store the romesco in an airtight container in the refrigerator for up to 1 week. This sauce can be served cold or at room temperature.

# Skordalia

Just a taste of garlicky skordalia can transport you to the islands of Greece, where this spread is as native as whitewashed homes, ancient ruins, and ocean breezes. Everyday ingredients are whipped together to create an otherworldly dip. Pine nuts or almonds would work in this dish, but the rustic flavor of toasted walnuts balances perfectly with the edgy and slightly aggressive garlic. Don't hesitate to leave some chunky pieces of potato in the mix. Skordalia was prepared for thousands of years before the invention of the food processor, and roughly hand-mashed potatoes provide the most interesting and authentic texture. Our Greek friends traditionally serve it on Palm Sunday with salt cod; it is equally delicious and eaten all year with raw vegetables, lamb, or any other meat. We piggyback the preparation of this dip with the preparation of mashed potatoes, boiling a few extra spuds and setting them aside for this purpose.

PREPARATION TIME: *1 hour*
MAKES: *3 cups*

5 medium Yukon Gold potatoes (about 2 pounds)

1 tablespoon plus 1 teaspoon kosher salt

3 cloves garlic

½ cup (1¼ ounces) walnut pieces, toasted

2 tablespoons white wine vinegar

2 tablespoons freshly squeezed lemon juice

½ cup extra-virgin olive oil

½ teaspoon freshly ground black pepper

FOR SERVING

Raw carrots, cucumbers, or celery

Simply prepared lamb or salt cod

1. Place the potatoes in a medium saucepan and cover with cold water. Add 1 tablespoon kosher salt and bring to a boil over high heat. Lower the heat and simmer until the potatoes are soft, about 35 minutes. The potatoes are done when a sharp knife slips through them with no resistance. Drain them and allow them to cool. Peel them and place them in a medium bowl.

2. Using the tines of a large fork, the back of wooden spoon, or a potato masher, mash the potatoes until they are mostly smooth.

3. In the work bowl of a food processor, process the garlic and walnuts until roughly chopped, about 10 to 15 seconds. Add the vinegar and lemon juice and pulse 2 or 3 times, just to mix. With the processor running, slowly drizzle in the olive oil. The

*continued*

chopped walnuts will keep the olive oil in suspension, creating a smooth and pale emulsification. Scrape the walnut mixture into the bowl with the mashed potatoes and stir and fold until combined. Season the skordalia with the remaining 1 teaspoon salt and the pepper. There is a seductive beauty in eating this while the potatoes are freshly mashed and ever so slightly warm, but we can't resist it when cooled as well. It can be refrigerated in an airtight container for 2 or 3 days. After removing from the refrigerator, allow the skordalia to come to room temperature and, if needed, stir in 1 tablespoon of olive oil to loosen the mixture. Serve as an accompaniment to raw vegetables or simply prepared meat or fish.

# Walnut Tarator

Like its vivid red Spanish cousin romesco, pale Turkish tarator has many variations. And like romesco, it has a long, long history of home preparation. Tarator is a simple and straightforward dip, great as one among many for a party. Its lack of complexity calls for the best ingredients, for the basis of its flavor lies in them. While walnuts are frequently chosen for tarator, some Turkish families use almonds or sesame seeds. Whatever nut you select, freshness is paramount.

PREPARATION TIME: *15 minutes*
MAKES: *1 cup*

1½ cups (5¼ ounces) walnut pieces, toasted

2 cloves garlic

1 slice day-old white bread

3 tablespoons red wine vinegar

¼ cup olive oil

½ teaspoon kosher salt

¼ teaspoon freshly ground black pepper

FOR SERVING

Cucumber spears

Turkish flatbread

1. In the work bowl of a food processor, pulse the walnuts and garlic until finely chopped, about 15 to 20 seconds. Meanwhile, place the bread in a small bowl and cover it with cold water to soak. After a few minutes, the bread will absorb the water and appear spongy. Pour off the water and squeeze the bread to remove any excess. Add the soaked bread to the walnut mixture in the food processor and let it spin for 2 minutes, until very smooth. Add the vinegar and continue to mix for an additional 10 seconds.

2. While the processor is still running, slowly drizzle in the olive oil. The tarator will thicken and turn the color of straw as the olive oil emulsifies with the walnut paste. Season with the salt and pepper. Serve with crisp cucumber spears or Turkish flatbread. Tarator can be stored in an airtight container in the refrigerator for 3 or 4 days.

# Macadamia-Mango Salsa

Whether served with chips, crackers, or toasted baguette slices, this salsa is bright and refreshing. Not only is it a great starter, but it is a wonderful sauce for grilled salmon, chicken, or any burger (see Red Lentil–Cashew Sliders, page 269, or Black Bean and Pumpkin Seed Burgers, page 270). The richness from the roasted macadamia nuts and the sweetness from the mangoes balance perfectly with the bite of the cilantro and lime juice. This is another quick and easy recipe to prepare, and one we are confident you will add to every party menu. Just be sure to make enough!

PREPARATION TIME: *15 minutes, plus 1 hour to chill*
MAKES: *2 cups*

2 ripe mangoes, peeled, pitted, and cut into ½-inch dice

4 plum tomatoes, seeded and cut into ½-inch dice

¾ cup finely chopped red onions

1½ cups (7½ ounces) coarsely chopped macadamia nuts

2 tablespoon freshly squeezed lime juice

2 tablespoons packed light brown sugar

¼ cup freshly chopped cilantro

1 teaspoon kosher salt

½ teaspoon freshly ground black pepper

FOR SERVING
Tortilla chips

Toss all the ingredients together in a medium bowl and chill for at least 1 hour or up to 3 days prior to serving. Serve chilled with tortilla chips.

# Coconut Chutney

We created this coconut chutney as an accompaniment to the Keema Matar on page 205. But once we tasted it we were hooked and realized what a great dip this was on its own. Simple and straightforward, a touch spicy and really creamy, with just a hint of the exotic, it goes wonderfully with crudités and crackers. If you gradually add the coconut milk as you make it, you can control the final texture of the dip. We add enough coconut milk to make a creamy creation as thick as Greek yogurt, stiff enough to stick to anything you choose to dip in it. *(See photo page 204.)*

PREPARATION TIME: *15 minutes, plus 1 hour to chill*
MAKES: *2 cups*

1½–2 cups coconut milk

1 cup (3 ounces) unsweetened coconut flakes

1 tablespoon freshly grated ginger

2 cloves garlic, finely chopped

¼ cup freshly chopped cilantro

½ teaspoon crushed red pepper flakes, plus more for finishing

3 tablespoons packed light brown sugar

1 tablespoon freshly squeezed lime juice

½ teaspoon kosher salt

FOR SERVING

Pita or naan

1. Combine all the ingredients in a blender, starting with 1½ cups coconut milk, and blend to mix well, 2 to 3 minutes.
2. To create a thinner dip, add the remaining coconut milk, 1 tablespoon at a time, blending until the desired texture is achieved.
3. Chill for at least 1 hour, and sprinkle the chutney with a few red pepper flakes before serving.

*Syrian "Meatballs" with Pumpkin Seeds (page 101)*
*served with tzatziki (page 102)*

# Nuts and Bolts of Little Bites

**When you're faced with a small group of guests or a holiday horde of** family, the morsels in this chapter are lifesavers. Little bites, by our definition, are savory individual treats that stimulate your appetite before dinner. A combination of several of these treats can substitute for a meal, and they are all perfect for a cocktail party. In fact, all these bites were created with parties in mind; they complement cocktails and kick-start any gathering.

This chapter is a collection of recipes for individual treats that can be plattered and set out to serve in a buffet or more formally plated and "butlered," or passed around. Little bites are the best way to whet the appetite of your guests at a gathering. Choose treats that feature eclectic flavors, add a few dips or spreads, and tastes from around the world will be at your fingertips. Think about preparing these in advance; many have instructions for freezing and reheating. Currently many of our catering clients forgo a formal dinner and substitute a large variety of appetizers. Guests are always delighted!

# Syrian "Meatballs" with Pumpkin Seeds
## PUMPKIN KIBBEH

Kibbeh is a Middle Eastern dish with many regional variations. In its most recognized preparation, kibbeh is made with ground lamb, either raw or cooked, and is mixed with bulgur wheat. The abundance of pumpkins—a gourd that grew throughout the region— and the need to create a meatless, Lenten-friendly version of kibbeh led to this variation centuries ago. Throughout her childhood and to this day, some variation of kibbeh is served at Andrea's aunt Rosemary Skaff's home at every holiday meal. This pumpkin version is always an anticipated favorite. We have seen pumpkin kibbeh shaped into balls and fried, and we have seen it baked flat in a pan, but we prefer it hand molded into small football shapes and simply baked. No fuss with frying, and they are the perfect size for a little bite. *(See photo page 98.)*

PREPARATION TIME: *1 hour*
BAKING TIME: *30 minutes*
MAKES: *16 to 18 "meatballs"*
EQUIPMENT: *1 rimmed baking sheet, lightly brushed with olive oil*

1 cup finely ground bulgur

2 tablespoons olive oil, plus more for finishing

1 medium onion, cut into ¼-inch dice

1 clove garlic, finely chopped

1¾ cups (one 15-ounce can) pumpkin puree

½ cup plain breadcrumbs

1 teaspoon kosher salt

½ teaspoon freshly ground black pepper

¼ teaspoon ground cinnamon

¼ teaspoon allspice

### FOR THE FILLING

1 cup (5 ounces) chopped pine nuts, lightly toasted

½ cup (2¾ ounces) chopped pumpkin seeds, lightly toasted

2 cups packed baby spinach

¼ cup freshly chopped flat-leaf parsley

3 tablespoons freshly squeezed lemon juice

1½ teaspoons kosher salt

1½ teaspoons coriander seeds, toasted and ground

1 teaspoon cumin seeds, toasted and ground

½ teaspoon freshly ground black pepper

### FOR SERVING

Pistachio Raita (page 86) or tzatziki (see Note)

*continued*

1. Preheat the oven to 350°F.
2. Place the bulgur in a small bowl and add 1 cup cold water. Allow the bulgur to soak until all the water is absorbed, about 30 minutes.
3. While the bulgur is soaking, heat the oil in a medium skillet over medium heat. Add the onion and garlic and cook, stirring occasionally, until translucent, about 5 minutes. Add the pumpkin and breadcrumbs and cook, stirring, until fragrant, about 5 minutes.
4. Place the pumpkin mixture in a work bowl of a food processor and add the bulgar, salt, pepper, cinnamon, and allspice. Process until well mixed and no visible pieces of onion remain, about 1 minute. Transfer to a bowl and set aside.
5. Make the filling: Place all the ingredients in the work bowl of a food processor and process continuously for about 30 seconds until mixture is finely chopped. Set aside.
6. To assemble the "meatballs," dip your hands in cold water; do not dry. The moisture will keep the batter from sticking to your hands while you shape the balls. Take 2 tablespoons (about 2 ounces) of the pumpkin mixture and round it into a ball. Make a hole in the sphere with your finger and fill it with ½ teaspoon of the filling. Seal the ball and mold it into an oval about 2½ inches long, with slightly tapered ends like a tiny football. Place it on the prepared pan and repeat with remaining pumpkin mixture and filling.
7. Drizzle the footballs with olive oil and bake for 30 minutes, until golden brown and firm. Serve hot, directly from the oven. Store leftovers well wrapped in the refrigerator for up to 3 days. Reheat pumpkin "meatballs" on a rimmed baking sheet covered with aluminum foil in a 325°F oven for 20 minutes, until warmed through.

VARIATION: *Baked Layered Pumpkin Kibbeh*

If you are pressed for time and can't hand form the kibbeh, consider baking it as you would lasagna. Double the pumpkin-bulgur mixture and lay half of it in a lightly oiled 9-by-13-inch pan. Spread the filling on top, and finish with the remaining pumpkin-bulgur mixture. Using a large knife, score the top ¼ inch deep in a diamond pattern. Scatter ¼ cup of pine nuts, press them down slightly, and drizzle 2 tablespoons of olive oil over the top. Bake in a 350°F preheated oven for 45 minutes until firm and golden.

NOTE: Tzatziki is a traditional yogurt cucumber sauce served with many Middle Eastern dishes. Stir together 2 cups Greek yogurt with 2 teaspoons finely chopped garlic. Add to it ½ cup peeled, seeded, and chopped cucumber, 1 tablespoon chopped fresh mint, and 1 tablespoon freshly squeezed lemon juice. Season with salt and pepper to taste. Store the sauce in the refrigerator in an airtight container for up to 3 days.

# Parsley-Sunflower Mini-Frittata

Andrea's Syrian grandmother prepared a version of this omelet in a special stovetop copper pan that resembled an egg poacher. Oil was gently heated in each of its seven spherical indentations. When the egg mixture was added, it sizzled until the edges browned and crisped. The fragrant egg quickly set and was then flipped until cooked through, producing a light yet solid texture. Because this unusual pan is rarely found, we have modified the recipe to call for muffin tins.

PREPARATION TIME: *30 minutes*
BAKING TIME: *15 to 20 minutes for 2 tins*
MAKES: *40 mini-frittatas*
EQUIPMENT: *Two 12-cup muffin tins, lightly coated with nonstick spray*

2 tablespoons olive oil

2 medium onions, finely chopped

2 cloves garlic, finely chopped

12 large eggs

1 bunch flat-leaf parsley, cleaned, tough stems removed, and chopped

1 tablespoon finely chopped mint

1 teaspoon kosher salt

½ teaspoon freshly ground black pepper

1 cup (5 ounces) crumbled feta cheese

½ cup (2½ ounces) sunflower seeds

1. Preheat the oven to 350°F.
2. Heat the olive oil in a large skillet over medium heat. Add the onions and cook, stirring occasionally, until softened and translucent, about 5 minutes. Add the garlic and cook for 2 minutes more. Set aside to cool.
3. Whisk the eggs with the parsley, mint, salt, and pepper in a large bowl. Stir in the cooled onions and garlic.
4. Ladle 1 tablespoon of the egg mixture into each cup. When the tin is filled, strew some of the feta and sunflower seeds evenly over the egg mixture. Bake until the mini-frittatas begin to brown and the filling is set, 15 to 20 minutes.
5. Cool the mini-frittatas in the tin on a rack. Gently remove them by running a sharp knife around the sides and lifting them out carefully. Wipe the inside of the cooled muffin tins clean, re-coat them with nonstick spray, and repeat with the remaining frittata mixture, feta, and sunflower seeds. Serve warm or at room temperature.

# Crisp Almond Crab Cakes

Crab cakes are an American specialty as old as Colonial times. New World settlers found our shores teaming with crabs and created countless recipes to make use of them. Now crabs are a bit scarcer and their sweet flesh is at a premium. Crab cakes combine the luxury of crab meat with the practicality of a filler that makes their cost more reasonable. We love our crab cakes chock full of crab, with just the smallest bit of matzoh meal, which is super-absorbent and sops up any extra liquid while binding the vegetables and crab together. The almond crust browns beautifully when lightly sautéed, creating a crispy exterior that contrasts with the creamy interior.

PREPARATION TIME: *30 minutes*
COOKING TIME: *25 minutes*
MAKES: *24 crab cakes*
EQUIPMENT: *1 rimmed baking sheet lined with parchment paper*

1 medium onion, chopped

1 red bell pepper, seeded and chopped

2 cloves garlic, chopped

1 pound lump crabmeat, picked over to remove any shell

2 large eggs, lightly beaten

½ cup matzoh meal

2 tablespoons mayonnaise

1 tablespoon Dijon mustard

1 tablespoon kosher salt

½ teaspoon freshly ground black pepper

2 cups (8 ounces) sliced almonds

½ cup canola oil

1. Process the onion, pepper, and garlic in the work bowl of a food processor until finely chopped, about 30 seconds.

2. Transfer to a mixing bowl and add the crab. Gently stir in the eggs, matzoh meal, mayonnaise, and mustard and season with the salt and pepper. Be careful not to overmix, or the crabmeat will shred. Use immediately, or transfer to an airtight container and refrigerate for up to 24 hours.

3. Clean the work bowl of the food processor and process the almonds until they are finely chopped, about 15 seconds. Spread them out in an even layer on a shallow plate. Take a heaping tablespoon of the crabcake mixture and shape it into a 1½-inch disk. Repeat with the remaining crab mixture. Dredge each crab cake in almonds on both sides. Arrange the cakes in a single layer on the prepared pan until ready to fry. The crab cakes can be formed up to several hours in advance, covered in plastic wrap, and refrigerated.

4. Heat ¼ cup oil in a medium skillet over high heat until shimmering. Slip 6 crab cakes into the skillet. Fry, turning once with tongs, until golden brown on both sides, about 3 minutes per side. Be careful not to overbrown the almonds. Drain the crab cakes on paper towels and repeat with the remaining cakes. During frying, bits of almond and crab cake will fall off and darken. When this happens, carefully pour off the oil and replace it with the remaining clean oil. Heat again before continuing to fry.

5. Serve the crab cakes warm. They can be prepared up to 1 day in advance and stored in the refrigerator in an airtight container. Reheat them in a 300°F oven for approximately 10 minutes before serving.

Crunchy Coconut Shrimp with Ginger Dipping Sauce
(page 107)

# Crunchy Coconut Shrimp with Ginger Dipping Sauce

We've always believed that coconut-crusted shrimp are ubiquitous; they can be found in fast-food restaurants, catering halls, and frozen food isles. But after several catering clients asked for them, we decided to give them a try and upgrade them. We have set aside our fear of deep frying to make these, because frying is the only method that can produce a crisp coconut exterior. Use the largest shrimp you can—we prefer shrimp sized under 15 per pound. They are easy to clean and stay juicy when they are cooked. Try your best to keep the oil at the correct temperature: too hot and the shrimp will darken too quickly, before the insides are cooked, and too cool and the shrimp will be soggy. Some of the coconut will drop off as the shrimp cook and remain in the oil, darkening as you go. Those dark bits can stick to the following batch of shrimp, leaving blackened specks on the golden crust. We try to finish the batch before that excess affects our cooking shrimp, and we generally do. Pull the cooked shrimp out of the oil with a slotted spoon, drop them onto a stack of paper towels for a second, then put them on a platter and serve them piping hot.

PREPARATION TIME: *25 to 30 minutes*
COOKING TIME: *25 to 30 minutes*
MAKES: *30 pieces*
EQUIPMENT: *A deep-fry thermometer; 1 rimmed baking sheet lined with paper towels*

FOR THE GINGER DIPPING SAUCE

1 cup white vinegar

¾ cup packed light brown sugar

2 tablespoons freshly grated ginger

2 tablespoons freshly squeezed lime juice

1 teaspoon finely chopped garlic

1 teaspoon red chili paste

¼ cup cornstarch dissolved in ¼ cup water

FOR THE COCONUT SHRIMP

1 large egg

1 cup seltzer

1 cup all-purpose flour

1 teaspoon curry powder

1 teaspoon kosher salt

2 cups (6 ounces) unsweetened coconut flakes

2 pounds (about 32) jumbo shrimp, shelled and deveined

3 to 4 cups canola oil

*continued*

1. Make the dipping sauce: Combine the vinegar, brown sugar, ½ cup water, and the ginger, lime juice, garlic, and chili paste in a small saucepan. Bring to a boil over medium heat. Add the cornstarch-water mixture and continue to boil until the mixture thickens, about 3 minutes. Remove from the heat and cover.

2. Prepare the batter: Beat the egg and seltzer in a medium bowl. Sift the flour, curry powder, and salt into the egg mixture and stir well to combine. The batter may have some lumps, but that is fine.

3. Scatter the coconut evenly on a rimmed baking sheet. One by one, hold a shrimp by the tail and dip it into the batter, allowing the excess to drip back into the bowl. Roll the coated shrimp in the coconut and set aside. Preheat the oven to 300°F.

4. Heat the oil in a deep-sided medium saucepan over medium-high heat until the temperature reaches 350°F on the thermometer. Working in batches of 6, carefully slip the coated shrimp into the oil and fry, turning once with tongs, until golden and cooked through, about 4 minutes. While you are frying, check the temperature every 3 to 5 minutes and regulate the heat under the pan to keep it as close to 350°F as possible, so the shrimp will stay crunchy. When each batch is finished, place the shrimp on the paper towel–lined baking sheet and keep warm in the oven until all the shrimp are cooked. Serve hot, with the dipping sauce on the side.

# Savory Poppy-Onion Hamantaschen

Hamantaschen, named for the villain Haman and said to resemble his hat, are triangular treats filled with a variety of sweet centers. They are traditionally served during the Jewish holiday of Purim, the celebration of Queen Esther's protection of the Jewish people in Persia 3,000 years ago. Current celebrations include distributing treats such as hamantaschen, helping the poor, reading the story of Esther, and dressing up in costumes. When Cara was a young girl, her award-winning Purim costume was not that of Esther, which most girls longed to wear, but that of a hamantaschen, which her father made for her. This is a savory adaptation of the classic hamantaschen served at Purim.

PREPARATION TIME: *1 hour, plus 2 hours to chill*
BAKING TIME: *15 to 20 minutes for 2 sheets*
MAKES: *24 hamantaschen*
EQUIPMENT: *3 rimmed baking sheets lined with parchment paper*

## FOR THE CREAM CHEESE DOUGH

1 stick (8 tablespoons) unsalted butter, softened

4 ounces cream cheese, softened

1 tablespoon sugar

1 egg yolk

¼ teaspoon salt

2 cups all-purpose flour

## FOR THE FILLING

1½ cups (7½ ounces) poppy seeds

¾ cup whole milk

1 tablespoon sugar

2 tablespoons olive oil

1 large onion, finely chopped

1½ teaspoons kosher salt

½ teaspoon freshly ground black pepper

## FOR FINISHING

1 egg lightly beaten with a pinch of salt

1. In the bowl of a standing mixer fitted with the paddle attachment, beat the butter, cream cheese, and sugar on medium speed until light and fluffy, about 5 minutes. Beat in the egg yolk and salt just until mixed, 30 seconds. Scrape down the sides of the bowl to make sure the dough is well mixed. Add the flour and mix only until incorporated. Wrap the dough in plastic wrap and refrigerate until firm, at least 2 hours or overnight.

2. While the dough is chilling, prepare the filling: in a small spice grinder or the work bowl of a food processor, grind the poppy seeds. Transfer the seeds to a small saucepan; add the milk and sugar and cook over low heat until thickened, stirring occasionally, 20 to 30 minutes.

*continued*

3. Warm the oil in a medium skillet over medium heat until hot. Add the onion and cook until it is lightly colored, about 10 minutes.

4. Combine the cooked onion with the poppy seed–milk mixture and season with the salt and pepper. Cool completely before using. The filling can be made up to 3 days in advance, if well wrapped and chilled.

5. When ready to bake, preheat the oven to 350°F.

6. To form the hamantaschen, remove half the dough from the refrigerator and place it on a lightly floured surface. Roll the dough to a ⅛-inch thickness. Using a 3-inch round cookie cutter, cut out circles and place them next to each other without touching on the prepared pans. Repeat with the remaining half of the dough. Gently knead the scraps into a ball and chill to use later. Reroll the reserved scraps only once, or the dough will toughen.

7. Lightly brush the tops of the circles with beaten egg, and drop a scant tablespoon of filling in the center of each circle. Fold the sides over the filling in three places, leaving an exposed center in the shape of a triangle. The sides should not overlap but just touch. Where they meet, pinch the corners together to ensure that the hamantaschen stay closed.

8. Brush the tops of the hamantaschen with beaten egg and bake until golden, 15 to 20 minutes. Serve slightly warm or at room temperature. Store in an airtight container for up to 3 days.

# Ham and Cheese Rugelach

Rugelach, the well-known Jewish pastry, are crescent-shaped cookies typically filled with spiced nuts and dried fruits and covered with cinnamon sugar. The rich pastry dough that was originally prepared with sour cream. American ingenuity changed sour cream to cream cheese, and creative cooks made the most of any available ingredients for fillings. We have substituted savory fillings for the more frequently found sweet centers. The way they are formed stays the same, but these rich crescents make fabulous hors d'oeuvres.

PREPARATION TIME: *45 minutes, plus 2 hours to chill the dough*
BAKING TIME: *15 to 20 minutes for 2 sheets*
MAKES: *48 rugelach*
EQUIPMENT: *2 rimmed baking sheets lined with parchment paper*

**Cream Cheese Dough (page 109)**

**4 tablespoons whole grain mustard**

**½ cup (2½ ounces) finely chopped pistachios**

**½ cup (1¾ ounces) finely chopped walnuts**

**1 cup (4 ounces) freshly grated Gruyère cheese**

**½ cup (2½ ounces) finely chopped smoked ham, such as black forest**

**4 teaspoons freshly chopped thyme**

**1 egg beaten with a pinch of salt**

1. Preheat the oven to 350°F.

2. Prepare the dough as directed on page 109 and divide it into 4 equal pieces. Working with 1 piece at a time, roll the dough out on a lightly floured surface to a 10-inch circle.

3. Make sure the dough isn't sticking to your surface. If it is, gently lift the dough with an offset spatula and lightly flour the surface underneath. Spread 1 tablespoon mustard over the dough to within ⅓ inch of the edge. Mix the pistachios and walnuts together in a small bowl. Sprinkle ¼ cup nuts, ¼ cup cheese, ⅛ cup ham, and 1 teaspoon thyme over the mustard.

4. Using a pizza wheel, divide the circle into 4 wedges. Then cut each wedge into 3 equal triangular pieces. Starting from the outside (wide) edge, tightly roll each piece. Bend the two ends inward slightly to form a crescent shape and place on a prepared pan. Repeat with the remaining dough and filling.

5. Brush each rugelach lightly with the egg wash. Bake until golden, about 20 minutes. The rugelach are irresistible when served warm. Store leftovers refrigerated in an airtight container for 2 days. Reheat in a 325°F oven for 10 minutes.

6. Baked rugelach can be frozen, wrapped airtight between layers of parchment paper, for up to 3 months. Defrost the rugelach in a 325°F oven for about 20 minutes.

*Poppy-Coated Scallops (page 113)*

# Poppy-Coated Scallops

Scallops are one of the easiest shellfish to cook, and we love it that they require so little cleaning and quick cooking. The art of the preparation, then, is in the shopping. First, choose sea scallops that are labeled "dry," which means that they have not been soaked in a preservative. Next, make sure they are just the right size for a little bite; about 15 to a pound will give you 1-ounce pieces. Find the hard little muscle that clings to the side of each scallop and gently remove it with your fingers, and you are ready to cook. The poppy seeds make a deep, crunchy crust that contrasts beautifully with the creamy white interior. We've been known to undercook the scallops ever so slightly and refrigerate them to serve later at a catered event. Reheat them in a single layer on a rimmed baking sheet for 5 minutes and they should be perfect.

PREPARATION TIME: *10 minutes*
COOKING TIME: *15 to 20 minutes*
MAKES: *30 pieces*

1 cup panko breadcrumbs

⅓ cup (1½ ounces) poppy seeds

1 tablespoon finely grated lemon zest

1 teaspoon plus a pinch kosher salt

½ teaspoon freshly ground black pepper

3 large egg whites

2 pounds dry sea scallops

½ cup canola oil

1. Mix the panko, poppy seeds, lemon zest, 1 teaspoon salt, and the pepper in a shallow bowl. In a separate bowl, whip the egg whites and the pinch of salt with a fork until they loosen.

2. One at a time, dip the scallops into the egg whites, allowing the excess to drip back into the bowl. Roll each scallop in the poppy seed mixture to coat. Line the scallops up in a single layer on a rimmed baking sheet.

3. Pour enough of the oil into a medium skillet to cover the bottom in a thin layer. Heat over medium heat until rippling. Slip 6 scallops into the pan and cook, turning once with tongs, until lightly browned on both sides, about 2 minutes per side. Repeat with the remaining scallops. Serve warm. (Cooked scallops can be kept warm on the baking sheet in a 200°F oven while you cook the remaining scallops.)

# Tuna Confit with White Beans, Pine Nuts, and Basil

Making a confit, generally a salted meat or fish that is cooked slowly in fat, is a process of preservation. Confits were created before refrigeration, in an effort to preserve foods that had short shelf lives. Originally they were used to keep duck or goose meat, but in modern kitchens fish is cooked this way. This confit can be sliced and served on pieces of toasted baguette, topped with the white bean and pine nut salad. Given its nature, the tuna can be made up to a week ahead, but we save the bean salad preparation for the day before we serve it. An overnight stay helps meld the flavors of the salad.

PREPARATION TIME: *1 hour 15 minutes, plus 1 hour to cool*
MAKES: *32 pieces*
EQUIPMENT: *A deep-fry thermometer*

### FOR THE CONFIT

3 cups olive oil

2 sprigs rosemary

2 sprigs thyme

2 bay leaves

6 black peppercorns, cracked

2 tablespoons kosher salt

Zest of 1 lemon, julienned

1 large onion, cut in half and sliced

1 pound very fresh tuna, at least 1-inch thick

### FOR THE SALAD

2 cups cooked cannellini or navy beans (see page 76), or one 15-ounce can, drained and rinsed

4 plum tomatoes, cut in half, seeded, and cut into ½-inch dice

6 scallions, white and green parts, thinly sliced

¼ cup chopped Niçoise olives

¼ cup chiffonade of basil leaves (see box page 115)

1 tablespoon freshly chopped thyme leaves

½ cup (2½ ounces) pine nuts, toasted

⅓ cup extra-virgin olive oil

2 tablespoons red wine vinegar

1 teaspoon kosher salt

½ teaspoon freshly ground black pepper

### FOR FINISHING

1 large baguette, sliced into 32 pieces and toasted

1. Prepare the confit: Place all the ingredients except the tuna in a heavy-bottomed pot such as a Dutch oven. Using the thermometer, slowly cook over medium heat until the olive oil reaches 145°F. Adjust the heat as needed to hold the oil at this temperature for 15 minutes. After 15 minutes, turn the heat off and let the oil cool for 30 minutes. After

the oil has steeped, return it to the heat and add the tuna to the pot. Make sure it is entirely covered with the oil; if it is not, add more oil until it is. Over low heat, bring the oil up to 145°F again. Remove the pot from the heat and allow the tuna to cook in the heated oil for 5 to 10 more minutes. Check the tuna for doneness—it should be cooked through and remain slightly pink in the middle. Remove the tuna from the oil, wrap it in plastic wrap, and refrigerate it. Allow the oil to cool separately. When the oil is cool, place the tuna in a large glass container and strain the aromatic oil over it through a fine-mesh sieve to cover. Discard the solids. Cover the immersed tuna and refrigerate it for up to a week.

2. To prepare the salad, place the beans, tomatoes, scallions, olives, basil, thyme, and pine nuts in a medium bowl. In a separate small bowl, whisk the olive oil into the vinegar. Pour this over the bean mixture and season with the salt and pepper.

3. When ready to serve, slice the tuna against the grain into ⅓-inch slices and cut each slice in half. Place 1 slice on a piece of baguette. Top with a small spoonful of bean salad. Serve at room temperature.

---

## Chiffonade

*Chiffonade* is a fancy way of saying herbs or leafy vegetables cut into strips. To cut chiffonade efficiently and neatly, stack up the leaves you wish to cut, roll them into a cylinder, and then slice them into ribbons. When you unfurl the results, you'll have a nice pile of evenly sized slices.

*Upside-Down Cranberry-Pistachio Muffins*
(page 119)

# Morning Glory

# Nuts and Bolts of Morning Glory

**Common wisdom says that breakfast is the most important meal of the** day, and we're pretty sure it's true. Nuts and seeds not only lend richness and flavor to traditional breakfast baked goods, they are packed with fiber, leaving you satisfied until lunchtime. We've learned to cook with them as well as bake for breakfast, adding them to savory dishes as well as sweet.

While all the items in this chapter are generally served for breakfast, most of them are welcome at any time of day. We prepare scones the night before we need them, wrap them in plastic on a baking pan, and pop them in the oven for the next day's tea. Like their breakfast buddies, muffins, they taste best on the day they are baked. Donna's Kichen Sink Granola (page 135) gets gobbled as a midnight snack. We've never lost our childhood love of a pancake supper. Clearly, breakfast is not just for breakfast any more. Nuts and seeds make breakfast great any time of day.

# Upside-Down Cranberry-Pistachio Muffins

Making these muffins is loads of fun. To ensure that the miniature crowns of nuts and berries atop them stay in place and intact when you flip them over, use paper liners in your muffin tins and coat the papers lightly with nonstick spray before adding the nuts and compote. The silky green color is slightly obscured by the bright garnet cranberries, but one bite and you'll know the pistachios are there. The compote is spectacular by itself. We even serve it with pancakes or waffles instead of syrup. For a super-indulgent treat, eat it with a bowl of vanilla ice cream. *(See photo page 116.)*

PREPARATION TIME: *30 minutes*
BAKING TIME: *15 to 20 minutes*
MAKES: *18 muffins*
EQUIPMENT: *One 12-cup muffin tin and one 6-cup muffin tin lined with paper liners, liners and pans lightly coated with nonstick spray (see box page 120)*

FOR THE CRANBERRY COMPOTE

One 12-ounce bag fresh cranberries

½ cup sugar

½ cup freshly squeezed orange juice

1½ teaspoons freshly grated orange zest

FOR THE MUFFINS

2 cups all-purpose flour

¼ cup sugar

1 tablespoon baking powder

½ teaspoon salt

1 cup whole milk

1 stick (8 tablespoons) unsalted butter, melted

2 large eggs

1 teaspoon vanilla extract

1½ teaspoons freshly grated orange zest

1½ cups (7½ ounces) coarsely chopped pistachios

1. Preheat the oven to 400°F.
2. Make the cranberry compote: Combine the cranberries, sugar, orange juice, and zest in a medium saucepan and bring to a boil over high heat. Lower the heat to medium and cook, stirring often, until the cranberries have burst and the compote begins to thicken, about 10 minutes. Set aside to cool.
3. Make the muffins: Stir the flour, sugar, baking powder, and salt together in a large mixing bowl. Whisk the milk, melted butter, eggs, vanilla, and orange zest together in a separate bowl. Fold the egg mixture into the dry ingredients with a rubber spatula just until the dry ingredients are moistened. Do not overmix.

*continued*

4. Sprinkle a tablespoon of pistachios in the bottom of each prepared liner. Spoon 2 table-spoons of the cranberry compote over the pistachios. Spoon the muffin batter over the cranberries so that each liner is slightly less than two-thirds full. Since these muffins are served upside-down, filling the liners a little less than you do with other muffins will avoid a large crown on the top after they have risen, so be careful not to overfill the liners. Bake until the muffins are well risen and firm when lightly pressed and a tooth-pick inserted into the center of a muffin comes out clean, 15 to 20 minutes. Do not insert the toothpick too far, or you may reach the cranberry compote and get an inaccurate reading of doneness.

5. Allow the muffins to cool completely in the tins on racks. Remove them from the tins, peel off the paper liners, and serve them upside-down on a plate or platter.

## Muffin Pan Sizes

At first glance most muffin pans look the same, a tin with 6 or 12 cups, waiting to be lined, filled, and baked. We have learned that there are real differences in cup size, and the volume that a cup can hold not only will affect the size of each muffin (or cupcake) but will determine the number of muffins baked. We have seen pans that have cups with 2-ounce, 3-ounce and 4-ounce capacities. All of our recipes are sized for 3-ounce cups—we find them not too small, not too large, and just right!

# Carrot-Sunflower Muffins

These earthy, nutritious muffins are a simpler spin on this chapter's namesake, morning-glory muffins. Much like morning glories, they celebrate the sweetness and glowing color of carrots as well as the satisfying toothsomeness of nuts and seeds. However, what sets these muffins apart is the central role in which they cast sunflower seeds. Instead of playing just one part among many, here sunflower seeds are given the lead, tying the muffins together with their rich flavor, vitamin boost, and crispy crunch.

PREPARATION TIME: *25 minutes*
BAKING TIME: *15 to 20 minutes*
MAKES: *18 muffins*
EQUIPMENT: *One 12-cup muffin tin and one 6-cup muffin tin lightly coated with nonstick spray and lined with paper liners (see box page 120)*

| | |
|---|---|
| 1 cup all-purpose flour | ¼ cup honey |
| 1 cup whole wheat flour | ¼ cup packed light brown sugar |
| 1 tablespoon baking powder | 2 large eggs |
| 1 teaspoon ground ginger | 1 teaspoon vanilla extract |
| ¼ teaspoon salt | 1 cup (4 ounces) shredded carrots |
| ¾ cup whole milk | ¾ cup (3¾ ounces) sunflower seeds |
| ½ cup vegetable oil | |

1. Preheat the oven to 400°F.
2. Stir the all-purpose flour, whole wheat flour, baking powder, ginger, and salt together in a large mixing bowl.
3. Whisk the milk, oil, honey, brown sugar, eggs, and vanilla together in a separate bowl. Gently stir the egg mixture into the dry ingredients with a rubber spatula until the batter is streaky. Add the carrots and ½ cup sunflower seeds and fold just until the dry ingredients are moistened. Do not overmix.
4. Spoon the batter into the paper liners, dividing it evenly; each liner should be about two-thirds full. Sprinkle the remaining ¼ cup sunflower seeds on top. Bake until the muffins are well risen and firm when lightly pressed and a toothpick inserted into the center of a muffin comes out clean, 15 to 20 minutes.
5. Cool in the tins on racks and serve at room temperature. Store the muffins in an airtight container.

# Golden Banana–Brazil Nut Muffins

We are always excited when our fruit bowls have a bunch of overripe bananas, just begging us to fire up the oven and bake. The tropical affinity of bananas and Brazil nuts makes them an obvious baking duo. Too often bakers reach for walnuts or pecans for their banana breads and muffins. This recipe reminds us all to explore the flavor and depth of Brazil nuts instead. If you have more ripe bananas than needed for this recipe, try peeling, wrapping, and then freezing them for a future use.

PREPARATION TIME: *25 minutes*
BAKING TIME: *15 to 20 minutes*
MAKES: *18 muffins*
EQUIPMENT: *One 12-cup muffin tin and one 6-cup muffin tin, lightly coated with nonstick spray and lined with paper liners (see box page 120)*

2 cups all-purpose flour

⅔ cup packed light brown sugar

1 tablespoon baking powder

1 teaspoon ground cinnamon

¼ teaspoon salt

¾ cup whole milk

1 stick (8 tablespoons) unsalted butter, melted

2 large eggs

1 teaspoon vanilla extract

1 cup mashed banana (about 2 very ripe bananas)

1 cup (5 ounces) coarsely chopped Brazil nuts, lightly toasted

4 teaspoons granulated sugar

1. Preheat the oven to 400°F.

2. Stir together the flour, brown sugar, baking powder, cinnamon, and salt in a large mixing bowl.

3. Whisk the milk, melted butter, eggs, and vanilla together in a separate bowl. Fold the egg mixture into the dry ingredients with a rubber spatula until the batter is streaky. Add the mashed bananas and ½ cup Brazil nuts and fold just until the dry ingredients are moistened. Do not overmix.

4. Spoon the batter into the paper liners, dividing it evenly; each liner should be about three-quarters full. Sprinkle ¼ teaspoon granulated sugar and some of the remaining ½ cup Brazil nuts over each muffin. Bake until the muffins are well risen and firm when lightly pressed and a toothpick inserted into the center of a muffin comes out clean, 15 to 20 minutes.

5. Cool in the tins on racks and serve at room temperature. Store the muffins in an airtight container.

# Pecan-Date Muffins

One of the delights of Cara's childhood was a visit to the Chock full o'Nuts Café with her grandmother. Her grandmother's favorite lunch was a date-and-walnut-bread sandwich with a cream cheese filling. Cara remembers watching carefully as her grandmother invariably licked up every crumb from her plate with a moistened finger, commenting on the indulgent combination of the sweet, crunchy, and creamy ingredients. We've made these muffins with that sandwich in mind, substituting pecans for walnuts. Feel free to eat them with a schmear of cream cheese to evoke times past, like Proust, with a bite of a baked treat.

PREPARATION TIME: *20 minutes*
BAKING TIME: *15 to 20 minutes*
MAKES: *18 muffins*
EQUIPMENT: *One 12-cup muffin tin and one 6-cup muffin tin, lightly coated with nonstick spray and lined with paper liners (see box page 120)*

1 cup chopped dates

2 cups all-purpose flour

¼ cup packed dark brown sugar

1 tablespoon baking powder

¼ teaspoon salt

1 stick (8 tablespoons) unsalted butter, melted

2 large eggs

4 tablespoons molasses

2 tablespoons dark rum

1 teaspoon freshly grated orange zest

1¼ cups (5 ounces) coarsely chopped pecans

1. Preheat the oven to 400°F.
2. Bring ¾ cup water and the dates to a boil in a small saucepan over medium heat. Set aside to cool.
3. Stir the flour, brown sugar, baking powder, and salt together in a large mixing bowl.
4. Whisk the melted butter, eggs, molasses, and dark rum together in a separate bowl. Fold the egg mixture into the dry ingredients with a rubber spatula until the batter is streaky. Add the dates with all the water, the orange zest, and the pecans and fold just until the dry ingredients are moistened. Do not overmix.
5. Spoon the batter into the paper liners, dividing it evenly; each liner should be about three-quarters full. Bake until the muffins are well risen and firm when lightly pressed and a toothpick inserted into the center of a muffin comes out clean, 15 to 20 minutes.
6. Cool in the tins on racks and serve at room temperature. Store the muffins in an airtight container.

# Orange-Hazelnut Scones

Scones were first baked in seventeenth-century Scotland. Those scones were simple yeast-raised griddle cakes. Over the years, the recipe has evolved. In the process, scones have become available worldwide and have been baked with every possible combination of ingredients. These scones have beautiful color and texture. We find that a handful of chopped candied orange peel, with its bittersweet flavor, makes a nice addition to many sweet baked goods. Here the slightly bitter peel is the perfect foil for hazelnuts, both chopped and in flour form. These are delicious plain or spread with a little sweet butter and orange marmalade.

PREPARATION TIME: *20 minutes*
BAKING TIME: *15 to 18 minutes*
MAKES: *18 scones*
EQUIPMENT: *1 rimmed baking sheet lined with parchment paper*

1½ cups all-purpose flour

½ cup whole wheat flour

½ cup (1¾ ounces) hazelnut flour

¼ cup sugar

4 teaspoons baking powder

¼ teaspoon salt

¾ stick (6 tablespoons) unsalted butter, chilled and cut into small pieces

1 cup (5 ounces) coarsely chopped hazelnuts

¼ cup finely chopped candied orange peel

¾ cup buttermilk

1 large egg

1 to 2 tablespoons whole milk

1. Preheat the oven to 400°F.
2. Stir the all-purpose flour, whole wheat flour, hazelnut flour, sugar, baking powder, and salt together in a large mixing bowl. Carefully rub the butter into the dry ingredients with your fingertips until no visible pieces remain. Stir in the hazelnuts and candied orange peel.
3. Whisk the buttermilk and egg together in a separate bowl and fold into the dry ingredients, using a rubber spatula. After the dry ingredients are fully moistened, mix the dough by hand for 30 seconds.
4. Transfer the dough to a lightly floured work surface. Flour the top lightly and press or gently roll the dough into a ½-inch-thick square. Using a 2½-inch round cutter dipped in flour, cut circles from the dough and place them on the prepared baking sheet, spacing them 1 inch apart. Gently press together the scraps and reroll the dough. Cut

as many rounds as possible from the rerolled dough and add them to the baking sheet. Discard any dough scraps left from cutting the second batch.

5. Brush the tops of the scones with milk. Bake until they are golden and well risen, 10 to 15 minutes. Serve immediately. Scones are best the day they are baked but can be split and toasted the following day, or refreshed in a 350°F oven for 5 minutes.

# Pumpkin Spice Scones

Crisp weather, scarlet leaves, and bright orange pumpkins always welcome us to fall. Pumpkins are a great ingredient to bake with, but turning them from their fibrous squash selves into a smooth puree is a labor of love. Instead we place the vibrant orbs on our porches, admire their seasonal charm, and open a can of pumpkin puree. Canned pumpkin puree is a boon to bakers: it adds nutrients and texture, color and body, and is a great time-saver. These scones are flavored with pumpkin's favorite spices, cinnamon, nutmeg, and ginger. They are a sort of inside-out scone, combining the flesh of the pumpkin with its nutritious seeds. You don't have to wait until fall to bake these; you will find canned pumpkin all year round in the supermarket. The flavor may evoke the autumn, but we have been known to bake a batch in summer, anticipating the season.

PREPARATION TIME: *20 minutes*
BAKING TIME: *15 to 18 minutes*
MAKES: *18 scones*
EQUIPMENT: *1 rimmed baking sheet lined with parchment paper*

2½ cups all-purpose flour

½ cup packed light brown sugar

2 teaspoons baking powder

½ teaspoon baking soda

1 teaspoon ground cinnamon

½ teaspoon salt

½ teaspoon ground ginger

¼ teaspoon freshly grated nutmeg

⅛ teaspoon ground cloves

1½ sticks (12 tablespoons) unsalted butter, chilled and cut into small pieces

1 cup (4 ounces) golden raisins

¾ cup (4 ounces) pumpkin seeds

½ cup canned pumpkin puree

1 cup heavy cream

FOR FINISHING

¼ cup heavy cream

¼ cup (1¼ ounces) pumpkin seeds

3 teaspoons cinnamon

4 tablespoons granulated sugar

1. Preheat the oven to 400°F.

2. Stir the flour, brown sugar, baking powder, baking soda, cinnamon, salt, ginger, nutmeg, and cloves together in a large mixing bowl. Carefully rub the butter into the dry ingredients with your fingertips until no visible pieces remain. Stir in the raisins and pumpkin seeds.

3. Whisk the pumpkin puree and 1 cup cream together in a separate bowl, then fold them into the dry ingredients, using a rubber spatula. After the dry ingredients are fully moistened, mix the dough by hand for an additional 30 seconds.

4. Scoop up the dough with a 3- or 4-ounce ice cream scoop or spoon and drop each scoop onto the prepared pan, spacing the scones 2 inches apart.

5. To finish before baking: Using a pastry brush, paint the top of the scones with the cream. Strew the pumpkin seeds on top. Mix the cinnamon with the granulated sugar in a small bowl, then sprinkle on top of the scones.

6. Bake until the scones are golden and well risen, 15 to 18 minutes. Scones are best served immediately, but they will keep for up to 1 day if well wrapped. Refresh them for 5 minutes in a 350°F oven, or split them and toast them.

*Pecan Crème Brûlée French Toast (page 129)*

# Pecan Crème Brûlée French Toast

Brunch has always been a favorite meal of ours, and it's often overlooked when people choose to entertain. We love the not-too-early, not-too-late, lazy-day feel it gives, and it always has an air of informality, which we prefer when cooking for guests. Plus you can offer both savory and sweet foods for brunch, tempting everyone's palate. Pecan Crème Brûlée French Toast falls into the sweet category. Unlike true crème brûlée, in which a crust of crunchy sweetness gilds the top, here the gooey sweetness covers the bottom of the dish. Our crunch comes from the pecans, the perfect foil for soft, soaked challah. This is a great way to use day-old bread with no loss of quality.

PREPARATION TIME: *10 minutes, plus overnight to chill*
BAKING TIME: *35 to 40 minutes*
MAKES: *6 to 8 servings*
EQUIPMENT: *One 10-inch gratin dish*

6 tablespoons (¾ stick) unsalted butter

1 cup packed light brown sugar

2 tablespoons light corn syrup

1 tablespoon canola oil

½ cup (2 ounces) chopped pecans

1 medium loaf challah, cut into 1-inch-thick slices

6 large eggs

1¾ cups whole milk

2 teaspoons vanilla extract

½ cup (2 ounces) pecan halves

1. In a medium saucepan, combine the butter, brown sugar, and corn syrup and cook over low heat, stirring, until the better melts and the ingredients are well mixed and just a bit bubbly around the edges.
2. Remove the pan from the heat and stir in the oil and chopped pecans. Pour the syrup into the gratin dish.
3. Place the challah slices on top of the pecan syrup in the gratin dish, overlapping them slightly.
4. Beat the eggs in a small bowl. Whisk in the milk and vanilla. Pour this mixture over the challah so the bread can soak up the liquid. Push the challah slices under the liquid until they have absorbed as much as they can.
5. Sprinkle the pecan halves over the top, cover with aluminum foil, and place the dish in the refrigerator to chill overnight. The challah will absorb the maximum amount of liquid, creating a French toast that is evenly cooked.
6. When ready to bake, preheat the oven to 350°F. Bake the dish for 30 to 35 minutes, until the egg mixture is set. Remove the foil and bake for an additional 5 minutes, or until the French toast is golden brown and crusty on the top. Serve warm.

# Hazelnut–Sour Cream Waffles

These are rich, European-style waffles suitable for a Belgian waffle iron if you have one. The batter will work with an American waffle iron too, but the yield will be slightly higher because the waffles will be a little thinner. For toppings, we love them with the classic butter and maple syrup. Or when they are in season, serve with a heaping pile of fresh blackberries, raspberries, or strawberries that have been sliced and tossed with a teaspoon or two of sugar. Ice cream or our Chocolate-Hazelnut Spread (page 89) will turn these tangy breakfast staples into a rich after dinner treat.

PREPARATION TIME: *10 to 15 minutes*
COOKING TIME: *3 to 5 minutes per waffle*
MAKES: *Six 4-inch Belgian waffles, or seven 6-inch standard waffles*
EQUIPMENT: *1 waffle iron, inserts lightly coated with nonstick spray*

1 cup all-purpose flour

1 cup (3½ ounces) hazelnut flour

2 tablespoons packed light brown sugar

2 teaspoons baking powder

½ teaspoon baking soda

¼ teaspoon salt

1 cup sour cream

½ cup whole milk

2 large eggs

½ stick (4 tablespoons) unsalted butter, melted

½ cup (2½ ounces) coarsely chopped hazelnuts, toasted

1. Stir the all-purpose flour, hazelnut flour, brown sugar, baking powder, baking soda, and salt together in a large mixing bowl.
2. Whisk the sour cream, milk, and eggs together in a separate bowl. Fold the liquid mixture into the dry ingredients, using a rubber spatula, scraping as you fold, just until the dry ingredients are moistened. Fold in the melted butter and chopped hazelnuts.
3. Heat the waffle iron and using about ½ cup of batter cook the waffles according to the manufacturer's instructions. Serve each batch of waffles as soon as it is finished.

# Oatmeal-Ginger Almond Pancakes

In 1979 Americans were broadening their culinary horizons, and we were happy to be part of that wave. A recipe appeared in the burgeoning food section of the *New York Times* for pancakes made with cooked oatmeal. They were flavored with fresh ginger and a little white wine and seemed very appealing and exotic. We began to make them, and quickly added almonds to the mix. This is an adaptation of that recipe, which remains to this day yellowed and taped in an old notebook. Its flavors, however, never get old.

PREPARATION TIME: *30 minutes*
COOKING TIME: *15 to 20 minutes total, 4 minutes per 2 pancakes*
MAKES: *Thirty-two 3-inch pancakes*
EQUIPMENT: *1 large skillet or griddle pan*

¾ cup rolled oats

1 tablespoon freshly grated ginger

1¾ cups all-purpose flour

2 tablespoons packed dark brown sugar

2 teaspoons baking powder

½ teaspoon baking soda

¼ teaspoon salt

1½ cups whole milk

½ stick (4 tablespoons) unsalted butter, melted

3 large eggs

½ cup (2 ounces) crushed sliced almonds, toasted

Butter, oil, or vegetable cooking spray

1. Bring 1½ cups water to a boil in a medium saucepan over medium heat. Stir in the oats and ginger and cook, stirring, until the oats have softened and absorbed most of the liquid, about 5 minutes. Set aside to cool.
2. Stir the flour, brown sugar, baking powder, baking soda, and salt together in a large mixing bowl.
3. Whisk the milk, melted butter, eggs, and cooled oatmeal together in a separate bowl until blended. Stir the egg mixture into the dry ingredients just until moistened, then mix in the almonds.
4. Heat the skillet or griddle pan over low to medium heat. Carefully grease the surface of the pan with the butter, oil, or vegetable cooking spray. When the pan is hot, pour about 3 tablespoons of batter per pancake onto it. Cook until the bottom is lacy brown and a few bubbles are breaking on the surface, 1 to 2 minutes. Flip with a spatula and cook until the underside is spotty brown and the pancakes are puffy and cooked through, 1 to 2 minutes. Serve the pancakes immediately as each batch is finished. Wrap any leftovers and refrigerate or freeze them for a future use.

# Puffed Apple-Walnut Pancake

This single large pancake is baked in a skillet in the oven, where it puffs into a beautiful golden dome. Like a soufflé, it is meant to be eaten right out of the oven, as it begins to deflate when you remove it. This was a favorite of Cara's in her grad school days. She and her roommate Weslie would frequently share this pancake on a Sunday morning, usually washed down with an entire pot of coffee between the two of them. Since this is a breakfast dish, it is not overly sweet. If you prefer a little extra sweetness, give the pancake a heavy dusting instead of a light sprinkle of confectioners' sugar.

PREPARATION TIME: *10 minutes*
BAKING TIME: *20 to 25 minutes*
MAKES: *6 servings*

2 tablespoons unsalted butter

2 Granny Smith apples, peeled, cored, cut in half and then cut into ½-inch slices

1 cup (3½ ounces) coarsely chopped walnuts

½ cup raisins

4 large eggs

2 tablespoons granulated sugar

¾ cup whole milk

3 tablespoons canola oil

¾ cup all-purpose flour

¼ teaspoon salt

Confectioners' sugar

1. Preheat the oven to 450°F.
2. Heat the butter in a heavy-bottomed, ovenproof medium skillet over medium heat until foaming. Add the apples and cook, covered, stirring often, until tender, about 5 minutes. Stir in the walnuts and raisins during the last minute of cooking, then remove the pan from the heat.
3. Whisk the eggs, sugar, milk, and oil together in a large mixing bowl while the apples are cooking. Stir in the flour and salt and whisk until smooth. Pour the batter over the cooked apples in the skillet.
4. Place the skillet in the oven and bake until the pancake is well risen and a bit golden around the edges, 20 to 25 minutes.
5. Carefully invert the skillet onto a heavy, heatproof serving plate. To do this, cover the top of the pancake with the plate and hold the plate firmly in place as you grasp the skillet by the handle and invert it and the plate together. If the pan is too heavy (and hot) for you to do this comfortably, let the pancake cool for 10 minutes or so first. Then, using heavy potholders or oven mitts, ignore the handle and position your hands on opposite sides of the skillet. Clamp the plate over the skillet with your hands and invert the pancake onto the plate. Sift confectioners' sugar on top of the pancake. Serve warm.

# Peanut Butter Oatmeal

Cara's Uncle Jacob made oatmeal for breakfast every day, and he would always swirl a heaping tablespoon of peanut butter into the bowl when it was ready to eat. The heat of the cooked cereal would nearly melt the peanut butter, creating tendrils. The habit has trickled down to the next generation and throughout families. It seems such an easy way to combine the flavor and nutrition of peanuts with the heartwarming wholesomeness of cereal. Variations abound. Some top the concoction with a teaspoon of jam, others with chocolate chips or chopped salted peanuts. Andrea's daughter Danielle now makes it every day, all year long, and enjoys it in its simplest and most straightforward form, just oatmeal and peanut butter. Jacob recently passed away, at the age of ninety-one, and we attribute his longevity in part to this early morning habit.

PREPARATION TIME: *10 minutes*
MAKES: *1 to 2 servings*

½ cup whole milk

¾ cup rolled oats

⅛ teaspoon kosher salt

3 tablespoons natural peanut butter

¼ cup (1¼ ounces) coarsely chopped roasted peanuts

1. Bring the milk and 1 cup water to a boil in a small saucepan over medium heat. Stir in the oats and salt. Stir often for about 5 minutes, until the oatmeal is tender. Do not worry if all the liquid has not been absorbed. Continue to stir the oatmeal as it cools: it will thicken and absorb the remainder of the liquid.
2. While the oatmeal is still warm, whisk in the peanut butter. Spoon the cereal into a serving bowl (or bowls) and sprinkle with the chopped peanuts.

# Syrian Cream of Wheat with Walnuts and Raisins
## MAMOUNIEH

Andrea, one of four children, grew up on Long Island. When she was about eight years old, her parents took a rare vacation without her and her siblings. The four of them stayed home and were cared for by their grandparents—half the week by their maternal grandparents and the other half by their paternal grandparents. The arrival of their Syrian paternal grandparents was especially exciting, because those grandparents rarely ventured out of Brooklyn. Andrea's grandmother had long worried that Andrea and the other kids were too skinny, so she took this opportunity to fatten them up. As the siblings recall, Sitto (which translates to "Grandma") woke them very early every day to feed them breakfast, which included an assortment of fresh fruit, yogurt, and soft-cooked eggs. When breakfast was finished, they returned to their rooms and were instructed to rest and get ready for school. When they arrived downstairs the second time, much to their surprise, waiting on the table was breakfast number two. Andrea and her siblings still laugh about this. They have fond memories of Sitto's farina-style cereal, called mamounieh (pronounced *ma-moo-nee-eh*), bursting with cinnamon, raisins, and walnuts—always a round-two selection. Andrea and her siblings asked for it every day. This is a recreation of that buttery Syrian treat.

PREPARATION TIME: *15 minutes*
MAKES: *2 servings*

2 cups whole milk

⅓ cup sugar

⅛ teaspoon kosher salt

3 tablespoons unsalted butter

⅓ cup Cream of Wheat or other farina

½ cup (1¾ ounces) finely chopped walnuts, toasted

½ cup (2 ounces) raisins

¼ teaspoon ground cinnamon

1. Bring the milk, sugar, and salt to a boil in a small saucepan over medium heat. Set aside.

2. Melt the butter in a large saucepan over medium heat and add the farina, stirring constantly to brown it slightly. Gradually add the boiled milk mixture to the farina, stirring constantly with a heat-resistant spatula or wooden spoon. Bring to a boil. Cook according to the instructions on the package (either 2½ or 10 minutes, depending on the type of farina).

3. Remove the mixture from the heat and stir in the walnuts, raisins, and cinnamon. Serve immediately, with a little extra milk for pouring over the top, if desired.

# Donna's Kitchen-Sink Granola

This is the most nut-filled granola we have ever tried, and we love it. The recipe is from Cara's friend Donna Isaacson in California, whose friends all beg for a bag of it whenever she makes it. As Donna has revealed, the key to making this granola is attentive stirring, which prevents it from burning around the edges. Although its most common use is as a hearty breakfast, try it as an ice cream topping. It can't be beat!

PREPARATION TIME: *20 minutes*
BAKING TIME: *25 to 30 minutes*
MAKES: *Twenty-four ½-cup servings*
EQUIPMENT: *2 rimmed baking sheets lightly coated with nonstick spray*

5 cups (1 pound) rolled oats (not instant)

½ cup honey

½ cup maple syrup

1 cup (5 ounces) whole almonds

¾ cup (3 ounces) pecan pieces

½ cup (2¼ ounces) slivered almonds

½ cup (1¾ ounces) walnuts

½ cup (2 ounces) sweetened shredded coconut

½ cup (2¾ ounces) pumpkin seeds

½ cup (2½ ounces) sunflower seeds

¼ cup flaxseeds

⅓ cup wheat germ

¼ cup canola oil

⅔ cup raisins

⅔ cup dried cranberries

½ cup sliced dried apricots

½ cup dried blueberries

1. Preheat the oven to 325°F.
2. Mix the oats, honey, maple syrup, nuts, coconut, seeds, wheat germ, and canola oil in a large bowl and toss well. Make sure all the dry ingredients are evenly coated with the moist ones. Pour the mixture onto the prepared pans and place in the oven. Because this mixture tends to brown quickly on the edges, rotate the pans and stir every 5 minutes or so, making sure it doesn't overbake. Remove from the oven when it is evenly golden brown, 20 to 30 minutes. Allow the granola to cool and pour it into a large, clean bowl.
3. Add the dried fruit and toss well to mix. Store airtight at room temperature for up to 1 month.

# Dave the Baker's Babka

This recipe is loosely based on a recipe given to us by our friend and colleague Michael Schwartz. When Michael was nine years old, he went to Camp Ramah in the Poconos. Every Friday morning the counselors would wake the young boys and walk them to the camp's huge kitchen so they could watch Dave the Baker make babka, which would be served at Shabbat breakfast the next day. The mixers were enormous, and Michael was awestruck by the vast size of them and of all the other kitchen equipment—as well as by the smell of chocolate. Every week Michael watched as Dave took leftover baked goods from the previous seven days and dumped them into a mixer to make the crumb filling for babka. Once Dave casually pulled a plastic ballerina off a leftover birthday cake and threw that in too. This made quite an impression on young Michael!

Fast-forward eight years, and seventeen-year-old Michael was the camp baker's assistant, following Dave's recipe every week as written on a grimy old index card. Dave had retired by then—he was already quite old when Michael was a camper, or so he seemed to a nine-year-old—but another Camp Ramah employee had, after much struggle, convinced Dave to dictate the recipe before he left. Since those days Michael has changed the oil to butter and the water to milk, but other than that, he remains faithful to Dave's recipe. Dave's last name is a mystery—no one ever knew him as anything but Dave the Baker. Still, Michael believes he deserves credit, so we've named this recipe for him. We've tinkered with the recipe a little and eliminated the need for leftover cake to make the filling. Presumably the babka was made at Camp Ramah on Friday morning for religious reasons, but this always tastes better after it has had a chance to sit, so we recommend making it a day in advance.

PREPARATION TIME: *1½ hours, plus 3 hours rising time*
BAKING TIME: *40 to 45 minutes*
MAKES: *2 loaves*
EQUIPMENT: *Two 9-by-5-by-3-inch loaf pans, buttered and lined with parchment paper*

### FOR THE DOUGH

2½ teaspoons (1 envelope) instant dry yeast

1 cup warm (100°F) whole milk

3½ cups all-purpose flour

¼ cup sugar

3 tablespoons unsalted butter, softened

1 tablespoon vanilla extract

1 tablespoon freshly grated orange zest

1 teaspoon salt

1 large egg

1 large egg yolk

5 tablespoons unsalted butter

⅓ cup sugar

6 ounces semisweet chocolate, finely chopped

½ cup (2½ ounces) ground almonds, toasted

¼ cup (2 ounces) raisins soaked in ¼ cup dark rum

½ teaspoon ground cinnamon

3 tablespoons unsalted butter, softened

3 tablespoons sugar

¾ cup all-purpose flour

½ cup (2 ounces) crushed sliced almonds

½ teaspoon ground cinnamon

1 large egg, beaten

1. Make the dough: Sprinkle the yeast over the warm milk in a medium bowl and whisk to dissolve. Stir in 1 cup flour and make sure it is evenly moistened. Cover the bowl and let stand in a warm place until the sponge has risen slightly and is bubbling, 25 to 30 minutes.

2. Put the sugar, butter, vanilla, orange zest, and salt in the bowl of a standing mixer fitted with the paddle attachment. Beat on medium speed until light, about 5 minutes. Add the egg and yolk and beat until combined. Turn the mixer to low and add the remaining 1¼ cups flour, in 3 or 4 additions. Beat in the yeast mixture until incorporated.

3. Scrape the dough into an oiled bowl and turn to coat all sides with oil. Cover the bowl with plastic wrap and let rise in a warm place until the dough has doubled in size, about 1 hour.

4. While the dough is rising, wash and dry the mixer bowl, and prepare the filling and the streusel. For the filling: Heat the butter and sugar in a medium saucepan over low heat. Once the butter is melted and the sugar is dissolved, remove from the heat and stir in the chopped chocolate. Let stand a minute to melt the chocolate, then whisk until smooth. Stir in the almonds, raisins, and cinnamon and set aside.

5. For the streusel: Cream the butter and sugar in the clean bowl of the standing mixer, fitted with the paddle attachment, until light, about 5 minutes. Add the flour, almonds, and cinnamon and beat on low speed until the mixture is crumbly. Set aside. The streusel can be prepared several days in advance and stored in a well-sealed container in the refrigerator.

*continued*

6. Make the babka: Turn the dough out onto a lightly floured work surface and divide in half. Press all the air out of the dough. Let the dough rest, covered with a damp towel, for 15 minutes.

7. Roll each piece of the dough into a rectangle roughly 5 by 10 inches. Divide the filling and distribute equally over the top of each piece, leaving a ½-inch border around the edges. Brush the edges with the beaten egg. Starting with one of the short ends, roll each piece up into a tight cylinder. Grasp each end with one hand and twist the ends in opposite directions (just once).

8. Place the loaves in the prepared pans and cover with oiled plastic wrap. Let them rise in a warm place for 15 minutes. Press some of the air out, very gently, as it begins to rise. This will help eliminate gaps between the filling and the baked dough. Cover the loaves again and let rise until the top almost reaches the top of the pan, about 1 to 1½ hours.

9. While the babka is rising, preheat the oven to 350°F.

10. Brush the top of the risen babka with the remaining beaten egg. Divide the streusel in half and sprinkle over each babka. Bake until golden and well risen, 40 to 45 minutes. Remove the loaves from the pan and transfer to a rack to cool fully before serving. Store leftovers in an airtight bag. Slice and toast them the next day for a great snack.

# Walnut Shakshuka

With its exotic name and exciting flavors, shakshuka makes an easy brunch dish for any group. Eggs can be poached in the savory sauce, or they can be baked in it; the method is your choice. Either way, the tomato and walnut sauce can be made a day ahead and kept refrigerated—just simmer it in a skillet before completing the dish. Or freeze the sauce and have it at the ready for impromptu gatherings; it will keep in an airtight container for up to 3 months. We were introduced to shakshuka by a catering client, who had tried it on a visit to Israel. We added walnuts to the sauce when we recreated it for a celebratory brunch. The walnuts both thicken the sauce a little and add a bit of crunch to the top. Sop up the sauce and egg yolk with warm pita or hunks of baguette. This is an informal dish that begs to be devoured. We pair it with any other dish with flavors of the Middle East or North Africa.

PREPARATION TIME: *40 minutes*
MAKES: *4 servings*

2 tablespoons olive oil

1 large onion, thinly sliced

2 red bell peppers, seeded and thinly sliced

1 jalapeño or other hot pepper, seeded and sliced

2 cloves garlic, finely chopped

1 teaspoon ground cumin

1 teaspoon sweet paprika

½ teaspoon turmeric

¼ teaspoon cayenne pepper

1 cup (3½ ounces) chopped walnuts, toasted

1½ teaspoons kosher salt

One 28-ounce can crushed plum tomatoes

8 large eggs

1. Heat the olive oil in a large skillet over medium heat. Add the onion and red peppers and cook for about 10 minutes, until the vegetables have softened but are not browned. Add the jalapeño and garlic and stir.

2. Add the cumin, paprika, turmeric, and cayenne to the pan and stir until the spices are mixed thoughout the vegetables. Turn the heat to low, stir, and let the spices become fragrant, about 5 minutes. Add ½ cup walnuts, the salt, and the tomatoes. Simmer the sauce for 10 minutes, until just slightly thickened.

3. If you would like to poach the eggs in the sauce on the stovetop, break each one into a cup and slip it into the simmering sauce, evenly spacing the eggs around the skillet, and cover. If you prefer to bake the eggs, preheat the oven to 350°F, place the eggs in the sauce, and put the skillet in the oven. Cook the eggs in the sauce until they are done as you like them; an egg with a slightly runny yolk will take about 5 minutes to cook. Sprinkle the remaining ½ cup walnuts on top of the cooked eggs. Spoon the eggs out to serve, surrounded with lots of sauce.

*Farro-Chickpea Salad with Sunflower Seeds*
*(page 167)*

CHAPTER 5

# In the Soup . . .
# On the Salad

# Nuts and Bolts of Soups and Salads

**Enjoying a soup or a salad that is flavored, fortified, or festooned with nuts** or seeds is a healthy and delicious way to begin a meal. In our soups, nuts and seeds are predominant; they thicken the texture, broaden the taste, and enrich the entire kettle. In the salads, they are the little stars that mostly appear in toasted form to provide crunch and add sparkle. They add body as well to these first courses.

Soups are often prepared with specific nuts according to geography and local custom. Traditionally, many African soups are thickened with peanuts, Spanish soups gain body and flavor from almonds, and many Asian cuisines use coconuts and their milk to add richness as well as flavor. We have touched on all these favorites, and with reference to ethnographic tradition, we have expanded the soup repertoire. Everything a nut can do, it can do in a soup: ground nuts, nut purees, and nut pastes are used as thickeners, nut pieces and crisps add texture (see Crackling Chestnut Bisque, page 143), and nuts' very presence in any form (pastes, pieces, and oils) develops the full flavor of a soup.

One of the beautiful things about soups is their ability to be made ahead without any compromise in quality. After a soup has been chilled and stored in the refrigerator it is a good idea to taste it for salt and pepper when reheating. Don't be surprised if a little bit of additional seasoning perks up your leftovers—cold storage occasionally dampens flavor, and careful readjusting will restore your original balance.

The role of nuts and seeds in salads is somewhat different. Nuts and seeds are usually tossed in at the last minute or sprinkled over a finished salad, adding an element of surprise to every bite. Their appeal lies not only in their flavor and texture, but also in their visual charm. Nut oils can also be an integral ingredient of salad dressings. Often overlooked, walnut, hazelnut, and sesame oils provide roasted richness for a concentrated nut flavor when added to dressings. The lighter oils—peanut, macadamia, and sunflower—add a hint of nuttiness without overpowering the other ingredients.

# Crackling Chestnut Bisque

Certain flavors are as welcome at our Thanksgiving celebration as old friends and family. Chestnuts and fennel are among them. The subtle chestnut and aromatic fennel marry and intertwine and prove that a good soup is greater than the sum of its parts. But don't wait for Thanksgiving. Like other nuts, chestnuts are harvested seasonally but are processed and sold all year long. Vacuum packages and glass jars keep them at the ready. Bisques are rich, smooth soups enriched with a little cream, and this one aptly fits the definition. The "cracklings" are bits of crisply fried chestnut that sit on top of the soup, waiting to be scooped up. The contrast of the crunchy and the smooth can be savored in each bite.

PREPARATION TIME: *15 to 20 minutes*
COOKING TIME: *45 minutes*
MAKES: *12 cups*

2½ cups (15 ounces) peeled chestnuts (see box page 144)

2 tablespoons unsalted butter

2 medium leeks, white part only, sliced

2 large bulbs fennel, trimmed, cored, and chopped (see box page 144)

2 parsnips, peeled and chopped

2 teaspoons kosher salt

2 tablespoons chestnut flour or all-purpose flour

½ cup dry white wine

8 cups chicken stock or vegetable stock

1 cup heavy cream

½ teaspoon freshly ground black pepper

½ teaspoon freshly grated nutmeg

Chestnut Cracklings (page 144)

1. Preheat the oven to 350°F. Place the peeled chestnuts on a rimmed baking sheet lined with aluminum foil. Roast until the chestnuts are fragrant, about 20 minutes.
2. Melt the butter in large saucepan over medium heat. Add the leeks, fennel, parsnips, and 1 teaspoon salt and cook, stirring, until the vegetables are wilted, about 5 minutes.
3. Add the flour to the vegetables and cook, stirring, for 2 minutes. Pour in the wine; the sauce will thicken. Cook, stirring, until very thick, about 5 minutes. Gradually pour in the stock and continue to stir. Add the chestnuts and bring the mixture to a boil. Lower the heat until the soup is simmering and cook for 30 minutes, or until all the ingredients are tender. Remove the soup from the heat. Using a handheld or standard blender (see box page 146), puree the soup until smooth.
4. Return the soup to low heat. Add the cream slowly, then the remaining 1 teaspoon salt and the pepper and nutmeg. Bring the soup to a simmer. To serve, ladle the soup into bowls and sprinkle each serving with 1 teaspoon cracklings. Store any cooled leftovers in a covered airtight container in the refrigerator for up to 3 days. Reheat any quantity of soup over low heat.

# CHESTNUT CRACKLINGS

**2 tablespoons olive oil**

**1 cup (6 ounces) coarsely crumbled chestnuts**

Heat the olive oil in a medium skillet over medium heat until hot, about 1 minute. Add the crumbled chestnuts and cook, stirring, until browned and crisp, about 5 minutes. Remove from the pan and drain on paper towels. The cracklings can be made up to a few hours in advance.

## *Peeling Chestnuts*

Chestnuts are often available in their shells, especially in their prime fall season, October through December. Peeling may seem daunting, the tough shells resistant to pressure, but it is easy to accomplish. First, using the point of a sharp paring knife; cut an "x" through the shell on the flat side of the nut. If the nuts are to be roasted, preheat the oven to 350°F. Place the nuts cut side up on a rimmed baking sheet in a single layer. Roast for 20 to 30 minutes, until the center of the "x" begins to curl and open up. Remove the chestnuts from the oven, and cool. The peels can easily be pulled off after the nuts have cooled. If the nuts are to be used unroasted, use the paring knife to pull away the shell from the center of the cut "x". Alternatively, vacuum-packed bags of chestnuts are available in most supermarkets, and the crumbly nuts are easy to use without the cumbersome peeling.

## *Preparing Fresh Fennel*

Pale green bulbs of fennel, sometimes called anise, add crunch to salads and a subtle licorice flavor to soups. Search out firm, unblemished bulbs that still have some of the stalks and feathery fronds attached. (The fronds, pinched off and coarsely chopped or left whole, make a welcome addition to a mixed green salad or a nice finishing touch for soups.) To prepare fresh fennel, trim the stalks even with the top of the bulb. Put the bulb trimmed side down on a cutting board and cut it in half through the core. If the outer layers are very thick and/or turning brown, pull them off. If not, simply peel the outer layer with a vegetable peeler. Cut out the core and the fennel is ready to slice, dice, or chop.

# West African Peanut Soup

The cargo holds of empty slave ships were filled with the indigenous materials of the Americas on their return trips to Africa, which introduced peanuts to the western shores of that continent. They easily adapted to the hot, moist growing conditions and were incorporated in regional cuisines. Ground peanuts found their way into soups and stews, seasoned in different ways. One of our favorites, from Senegal, is made with a mild curry. This is a great vegan recipe, packed with flavor and protein. There are many different recipes for peanut soup: some are chunky, like a stew; some are pureed; some are even thinned with coconut milk. We choose a smooth soup, but if you prefer the hearty type, just omit pureeing. If you choose to puree the soup and it is too thick for your liking, stir in ½ cup coconut milk.

PREPARATION TIME: *15 to 20 minutes*
COOKING TIME: *30 minutes*
MAKES: *8 cups*

2 tablespoons canola oil

1 large onion, chopped

2 cloves garlic, chopped

1 teaspoon kosher salt

1 tablespoon Madras curry powder

2 tablespoons tomato paste

6 ripe plum tomatoes, seeded and chopped

2 medium sweet potatoes, peeled and chopped

6 cups vegetable stock

1 cup smooth natural peanut butter, stirred well before measuring

1 tablespoon packed light brown sugar

½ teaspoon freshly ground black pepper

FOR SERVING

¼ cup (1¼ ounces) chopped roasted peanuts

6 scallions, white and green parts, thinly sliced

1. Heat the oil in a medium saucepan over medium heat. Add the onion and garlic and season with ½ teaspoon salt. Cook, stirring, until the onion is wilted and translucent, about 5 minutes.

2. Stir in the curry powder and tomato paste. Cook, stirring, until fragrant, about 3 minutes. Add the tomatoes and sweet potatoes and stir, cover with the stock, and bring to a boil. Lower the heat until the liquid is simmering and cook, stirring occasionally, for 15 minutes, or until the tomatoes and sweet potatoes are thoroughly soft.

3. Ladle 1 cup of liquid from the pan into a small stainless steel bowl. Add the peanut butter and whisk until smooth. Whisk the peanut butter mixture into the simmering soup. Cook on low heat for 10 minutes. Stir in the brown sugar and remove the soup from the heat.

*continued*

4. Using a handheld or standard blender (see box below), puree the soup until very smooth. Season with the pepper and the remaining ½ teaspoon salt.

5. To serve, ladle the soup into bowls. Scatter some of the roasted peanuts and scallions over each serving and serve hot. Store any cooled leftovers in a covered airtight container in the refrigerator for up to 3 days. Reheat any quantity of soup over low heat.

### I Wanna Hold Your Handheld Blender

Some finished soups, such as chowders and vegetable soups, are chunky. Others, such a bisques and cream soups, are smooth. Smooth soups can be pureed in a variety of ways—by using an old-fashioned food mill, a food processor, or a blender, or by our preferred method, a handheld blender. You can immerse a handheld blender right in the pot of hot soup, so blending is easy, fast, and clean. Be careful to keep the blade immersed to prevent splashing. Move the blender through the soup so it blends evenly, and continue blending until the soup has reached the consistency you like.

If you don't have a handheld blender, you can puree your soup in batches in a blender or food processor, then transfer it to a clean pot. A blender can safely accommodate more liquid than a food processor can. In either case, make sure the soup has cooled before blending; pureeing hot soup in a blender can blow the top right off. Smaller, cooler batches will help minimize any mess.

Straining pureed soups is sometimes recommended. It may be difficult to pour nut-thickened soups through a sieve without leaving behind most of the finely ground nuts. A little extra pureeing, with or without straining, will provide the creaminess you're looking for without compromising the texture of the soup.

# Spinach, Potato, and Pistachio Soup

This soup reminds us of a Middle Eastern vichyssoise, and we like it as much chilled as we do warm. Redolent of cumin and coriander when it is simmering in the kitchen, it transports us to a world away. If you are planning to serve it chilled, start with 2 tablespoons olive oil instead of butter; a smoother texture will be the result. The spinach is added in the final steps so the soup will stay bright green; adding it earlier would overcook it and change its verdant color into something less vivid. Both the pistachios and the potatoes are thickeners here. If the soup is refrigerated overnight and if you find it too thick, add a little more stock until you reach the desired consistency. *(See photo page 148.)*

PREPARATION TIME: *20 minutes*
COOKING TIME: *35 minutes*
MAKES: *12 cups*

2 tablespoons unsalted butter

3 ribs celery, chopped

2 medium onions, chopped

2 cloves garlic, chopped

3 teaspoons cumin seeds, toasted and ground

½ teaspoon coriander seeds, toasted and ground

2 teaspoons kosher salt

2 pounds all-purpose potatoes, peeled and chopped

8 cups chicken stock or vegetable stock

2 cups (10 ounces) coarsely chopped pistachios, toasted

1 pound baby spinach, washed

1½ cups plain Greek yogurt

½ teaspoon freshly ground pepper

1. Heat the butter in a large saucepan over medium heat until foaming. Add the celery, onions, garlic, cumin, coriander, and 1 teaspoon salt. Cook, stirring occasionally, until the vegetables are translucent and beginning to soften, about 5 minutes.

2. Add the potatoes, stock, and 1¾ cups pistachios. Bring to a boil, then lower the heat until the liquid is simmering. Cook for 30 minutes, or until the potatoes are easily pierced with a fork. Remove the soup from the heat and drop in the spinach. The heat from the soup is enough to cook the spinach.

3. With a handheld or standard blender (see box page 146), puree the soup until very smooth. Whisk in 1 cup yogurt, the remaining 1 teaspoon salt, and the pepper.

4. To serve, ladle the soup into bowls. Spoon a little of the remaining ½ cup yogurt onto each serving and scatter some of the remaining ¼ cup chopped pistachios on top. Store any cooled leftovers in a covered airtight container in the refrigerator for up to 3 days. If you are reheating leftover soup, do not boil. Be sure to use gentle heat to prevent the yogurt from curdling and the spinach from overcooking.

*From top: White Spanish Almond Gazpacho (page 149); Spinach, Potato, and Pistachio Soup (page 147); Chicken–Brazil Nut Soup (page 155)*

# White Spanish Almond Gazpacho

Traveling with two young vegetarian daughters in Spain, a country that enjoys a carnivorous diet, can be a gustatory challenge. When Cara did this, help cropped up in some surprising places, like the cafeteria of the Prado Museum in Madrid, where we found an unusual white gazpacho. This style of gazpacho is nearer to its Andalusian origins than the chilled, chunky, tomato-filled soup we see frequently today. White gazpacho is based on almonds, garlic, and stale bread and has been a staple in Spain since medieval times. Spanish-grown Marcona almonds are typically used for their sweet, delicate flavor. Once a filling meal for the poor, made of readily available ingredients, it is now a showcase for the rich flavor of lightly toasted almonds and roasted garlic. Our version is based on the delightful flavors we found that day in Madrid.

PREPARATION TIME: *1 hour, plus 2 hours to chill*
MAKES: *10 cups*

1 bulb garlic

½ cup extra-virgin olive oil

1½ cups (6 ounces) Marcona almonds or slivered almonds

3 slices white bread, crusts removed

3 cups cold water or white grape juice

2 English cucumbers, peeled, seeded, and chopped

½ pound seedless green grapes, cut in half

¼ cup sherry vinegar

1½ teaspoons kosher salt

½ teaspoon freshly ground black pepper

FOR FINISHING

2 tablespoons freshly chopped chives

reserved almonds and grapes

1. Preheat the oven to 350°F. Cut the top ½ inch or so off the garlic bulb (a serrated knife works well for this). Drizzle the cut part with 1 tablespoon olive oil and loosely wrap the garlic in aluminum foil. Place directly on the bottom rack and bake until the garlic is golden, soft, and tender, about 45 minutes. Unwrap the garlic and cool.

2. While the garlic is roasting, spread the almonds in an even layer on a rimmed baking sheet. Bake on the top rack until just beginning to color, 7 to 10 minutes. Stir them once or twice as they bake so they color evenly. Transfer the almonds to a bowl and cool.

3. Cut the bread into ½-inch cubes. Put them on the baking sheet and bake until lightly toasted, about 10 minutes. Remove the bread from the oven and cool.

4. Place the bread in a large bowl and pour 2 cups water or grape juice over it. Let it stand until the bread is good and soggy, about 30 minutes. The bread will absorb most of the liquid and act as a thickener for the soup. Using grape juice instead of water will yield a slightly sweeter soup, but the texture will be the same.

*continued*

5. Reserve ¼ cup almonds and place the remainder in the work bowl of a food processor. Process until finely ground, about 20 to 30 seconds. Squeeze the pulp from 4 cloves of the roasted garlic and add it to the ground almonds. Continue to process until a thick paste forms, another 20 seconds. (Unused roasted garlic can be refrigerated and saved for another recipe.) Add the cucumbers and continue to process until pureed, 30 seconds more. Reserve ¼ cup grape halves, place the remainder in the work bowl, and process until smooth, about 1 minute. Squeeze the water or juice from the bread and add the bread to the mixture, processing until no large pieces remain, 30 to 45 seconds. The light green soup will resemble the hue of a pale honeydew melon.

6. Pour the soup into a large bowl and whisk in the remaining 3 tablespoons olive oil and the vinegar. Continue to whisk while adding the remaining 1 cup water or grape juice. Season with the salt and pepper and chill for 2 hours or overnight. When ready to serve, ladle into bowls and garnish with the reserved almonds and grapes and the chives. As with all chilled soups, it is a good idea to check the seasonings before serving and add more salt and pepper if necessary. Store any leftovers in a covered airtight container in the refrigerator for up to 3 days.

# Sesame–Chicken Noodle Soup

Time for a spin on an American favorite, chicken noodle soup. This chunky vegetable-laden soup sets an Asian tone with the addition of Napa cabbage, snow peas, miso, and sesame. Soba noodles are made from buckwheat flour, and their earthy flavor is a great match for the trifecta of sesame in this dish: sesame oil, sesame seeds, and sesame paste. While there seems to be a laundry list of ingredients, preparing all the vegetables is worth the effort. This is a meal in a bowl.

PREPARATION TIME: *45 minutes*
COOKING TIME: *30 minutes*
MAKES: *14 cups*

2 tablespoons plus 2 teaspoons kosher salt

8 ounces soba noodles

2 tablespoons roasted sesame oil

1 tablespoon olive oil

4 cups thinly sliced Napa cabbage (about ½ head)

1 cup (3 ounces) stemmed and sliced ¼-inch-thick shiitake mushrooms

2 cloves garlic, chopped

2 tablespoons finely chopped ginger

1 cup (2½ ounces) snow peas, cut into thin strips

1 cup peeled carrots (about 2) cut into thin strips

1 cup thinly sliced cored and seeded red bell peppers (about 1)

8 cups chicken stock or vegetable stock

2 halves or 1 whole boneless chicken breast (about 1 pound), poached, or 1 store-bought rotisserie chicken, boned and skinned

2 tablespoons tahini

3 tablespoons golden miso (see box page 152)

½ teaspoon freshly ground black pepper

FOR SERVING

½ cup chopped scallions, white and green parts

¼ cup freshly chopped cilantro

3 tablespoons (¾ ounce) white sesame seeds, lightly toasted

1. Over high heat, bring 2 quarts cold water to a boil in a large pot. Add 2 tablespoons salt and the soba noodles. Cook until tender but not soft, 4 to 5 minutes; there should be a little bite left to the noodles. Drain the noodles, toss them with 1 tablespoon sesame oil, and set aside.

2. Warm the olive oil and the remaining 1 tablespoon sesame oil over medium heat in a large saucepan. Add the cabbage, mushrooms, garlic, and ginger and season with 1 teaspoon salt. Cook, stirring occasionally, until the cabbage is wilted and the mushrooms

*continued*

are soft, about 4 minutes. Stir in the snow peas, carrots, and bell peppers and cook until the peppers are softened, about 5 minutes. Pour the stock over the vegetables and bring to a boil. Lower the heat until the soup is simmering and cook until the vegetables are tender, about 5 minutes.

3. Meanwhile, slice the chicken on a diagonal into ½-inch strips. Add the chicken to the soup and cook until heated through, about 5 minutes.

4. Whisk the tahini and miso together in a small bowl until smooth. Add 1 cup hot liquid from the soup and whisk together. Pour the tahini mixture into the soup pot and stir until well blended. Add the noodles and season the soup with the remaining 1 teaspoon salt and the pepper or to taste. The broth will be golden brown and thin, just slightly thickened by the miso and tahini. The miso won't completely dissolve in the soup. The liquid may appear slightly separated—just give a good stir, knowing it is the nature of miso to stay suspended in liquid without fully incorporating.

5. To serve, ladle the soup into bowls and scatter some of the scallions, cilantro, and sesame seeds over each serving. Store any cooled leftovers in a covered airtight container in the refrigerator for up to 3 days. Reheat any quantity of soup over low heat.

*The Mysteries of Miso*

Miso is a traditional Japanese soybean product made through a complex process of aging, pasteurization, and fermentation. It has the texture of peanut butter and comes in a variety of colors ranging from light to dark. The lighter colors are used for delicate soups and the darker colors are used for heartier dishes. You can find miso in the refrigerated section of health-food stores or in Asian markets.

# Pumpkin Soup with Spiced Pepitas

Spices long associated with pumpkin pie—cinnamon, nutmeg, and allspice—take a savory turn in this double pumpkin soup. Pumpkin puree is added to the stock in the soup, along with aromatic vegetables and spicy jalapeños. Pumpkin seeds tossed with toasty cumin are used as a garnish. We prefer coconut milk to cream to enrich this soup, as it adds a subtle tropical tone along with less saturated fat and many more vitamins and minerals. A little drizzle of white crème fraîche on top of the soup helps frame the spicy seeds and provides a tangy bite. This soup is great for any meal, from a formal dinner gathering to a tailgate picnic poured from a thermos.

PREPARATION TIME: *30 minutes*
COOKING TIME: *35 minutes*
MAKES: *9 cups*

2 tablespoons unsalted butter

2 large onions, chopped

2 medium carrots, peeled and chopped

2 ribs celery, chopped

2 cloves garlic, finely chopped

2 small jalapeño peppers, seeded and chopped

2 teaspoons kosher salt

5 cups chicken stock or vegetable stock

1¾ cups (15 ounces) canned pumpkin puree

2 cups unsweetened coconut milk

1 teaspoon coriander seeds, toasted and ground

1 teaspoon cumin seeds, toasted and ground

½ teaspoon freshly grated nutmeg

½ teaspoon ground cinnamon

¼ teaspoon ground allspice

2 tablespoons packed light brown sugar

¼ cup (1½ ounces) pumpkin seeds, toasted

½ teaspoon freshly ground black pepper

FOR SERVING

¼ cup crème fraîche, stirred

Spiced Pepitas (page 154)

1. Melt the butter in a large saucepan over medium heat. Add the onions, carrots, celery, garlic, and jalapeños. Season with 1 teaspoon salt and cook, stirring, until the vegetables begin to soften, about 5 minutes. Add the stock, pumpkin puree, coconut milk, and spices. Bring the soup to a boil, stirring occasionally, then lower the heat until the soup is simmering. Cook until the vegetables are very tender, about 30 minutes.

*continued*

2. Stir the brown sugar into the soup. In a blender, puree the toasted pumpkin seeds with 1 cup soup. Pour the mixture back into the soup and stir. Using a handheld or standard blender (see box page 146), puree the soup until smooth. This will help thicken the soup slightly, enough to coat a spoon when it is dipped in.

3. Season the soup with the remaining 1 teaspoon salt and the pepper or to taste.

4. To serve, ladle the soup into bowls. Spoon 1 teaspoon crème fraîche onto each serving and scatter some of the spiced pepitas on top. Store any cooled leftovers in a covered airtight container in the refrigerator for up to 3 days. Reheat any quantity of soup over low heat.

---

## SPICED PEPITAS

1 teaspoon canola oil

¼ cup raw pumpkin seeds (pepitas)

½ teaspoon cumin seeds, toasted and ground

Pinch cayenne pepper

½ teaspoon kosher salt

Heat the oil in a small skillet over medium heat. Add the pumpkin seeds, cumin, cayenne, and salt. Stir until the seeds become fragrant and darken. Remove from the heat and set aside. The pepitas can be made up to 3 days ahead and kept in an airtight container.

# Chicken–Brazil Nut Soup

While sorting through a box of long-stored papers, Cara discovered that her grandfather was a Brazilian citizen, a family fact that had never been discussed. This soup is a kind of homage to her grandparents, a riff on her grandmother's eastern European chicken soup with a South American twist. The Brazil nuts, black beans, jalapeño, and coconut milk alter the expected chicken soup flavors and create a vivid, rich tableau. No need for matzoh balls with this chicken soup—it has body and texture all its own. *(See photo page 148.)*

PREPARATION TIME: *25 minutes*
COOKING TIME: *50 minutes*
MAKES: *12 cups*

2 tablespoons olive oil

1 medium onion, chopped

1 medium carrot, peeled and chopped

1 clove garlic, finely chopped

2 teaspoons freshly grated ginger

2 teaspoons kosher salt

4 plum tomatoes, cored, quartered lengthwise, seeded, and chopped

1 small jalapeño pepper, seeded and chopped

1 red bell pepper, cored, seeded, and chopped

½ cup long-grain white rice

6 cups chicken stock

1½ cups (7½ ounces) coarsely chopped Brazil nuts

2 thick-cut boneless chicken cutlets (12 ounces), poached

1½ cups unsweetened coconut milk

1½ cups cooked black beans (see box page 76), or one 15-ounce can, drained and rinsed

½ cup freshly chopped cilantro

1 tablespoon freshly squeezed lemon juice

½ teaspoon freshly ground black pepper

1. Heat the oil in a large saucepan over medium heat. Stir in the onion, carrots, garlic, and ginger. Season with 1 teaspoon salt and cook, stirring occasionally, until the vegetables begin to soften, about 5 minutes.
2. Add the tomatoes, jalapeño, bell pepper, and rice. Pour in the stock and bring to a boil over high heat, stirring occasionally. Lower the heat until the soup is simmering and cook for 30 minutes, or until the vegetables are soft and the rice is tender.
3. Ladle about 1 cup of the soup into a blender and add ½ cup Brazil nuts. Blend until well combined. Stir the mixture into the soup. The texture will be slightly grainy, but the broth will thicken. The soup will have an undertone of blushed pink from the tomatoes and peppers.

*continued*

4. Add the remaining 1 cup Brazil nuts, the cooked chicken, the coconut milk, and the black beans to the soup. Continue to cook over low heat until everything is heated through, about 15 minutes. Stir in the cilantro and lemon juice and season with the remaining 1 teaspoon salt and the pepper or to taste. Serve immediately. Store any cooled leftovers in a covered airtight container in the refrigerator for up to 3 days. Reheat any quantity of soup over low heat.

# Cauliflower-Cashew Chowder

Chowders are chunky, hardy soups that we always find comforting in the cold, windy winter. Cauliflower and cashews are both mellow representatives of their genres, but they combine here to make a bold soup. And both have buttery undertones, adding an earthy richness. Cauliflower has become a star in the modern nutritional hit parade, standing in for potatoes in a mash or by itself, roasting until its curly white edges turn deep gold. The florets soften entirely in this soup but keep their creamy white color. We like to puree about a quarter of the soup and pour it back into the pot with the chunky remainder. This gives the soup a thick texture without the addition of too much heavy cream. We've added a little cream to finish the soup, but if you choose to leave it out, the soup will still taste unctuous.

PREPARATION TIME: *20 minutes*
COOKING TIME: *35 minutes*
MAKES: *12 cups*

2 tablespoons olive oil

1 large onion, chopped

2 ribs celery, chopped

2 medium carrots, peeled and chopped

1 all-purpose potato, peeled and chopped

3 cloves garlic, finely chopped

2 teaspoons kosher salt

1½ cups (7½ ounces) coarsely chopped roasted cashews

4 cups (14 ounces) cauliflower florets (from 1 small head)

3 sprigs thyme

8 cups vegetable stock

½ cup heavy cream

½ teaspoon freshly ground black pepper

1. Heat the oil in a large saucepan over medium heat. Add the onion, celery, carrots, potato, and garlic. Season with ½ teaspoon salt and cook, stirring occasionally, until the vegetables begin to soften, about 5 minutes.

2. Add the cashews, cauliflower, thyme, and stock. Bring to a boil over high heat, stirring occasionally. Lower the heat until the soup is simmering and cook for about 30 minutes, or until the vegetables are soft. Remove the sprigs of thyme, but don't be concerned if the leaves have fallen off the stems.

3. Ladle 3 cups soup into a medium bowl. Using a handheld blender (see box page 146), puree until completely smooth. Return the puree to the pot. Add the heavy cream, stir well, and season with the remaining 1½ teaspoons salt and the pepper or to taste. Serve immediately. Store any cooled leftovers in a covered airtight container in the refrigerator for up to 3 days. Reheat any quantity of soup over low heat.

## Go for a Spin

Whether your greens are delicate—baby spinach, Boston lettuce, mache—or sturdier, like frisée and watercress, they will benefit from careful handling. First fill a large bowl with cool water. Next, trim the greens by removing thick stems, cores, and large ribs that run along the center of each leaf. Swish the greens gently in the bowlful of water and let them rest for a minute so that any grit or dirt sinks to the bottom. Lift the greens from the water—a large metal skimmer works well for this—and let them drain for a few seconds before transferring them to a salad spinner. Spin well and then put the greens into a serving or mixing bowl. Most greens can be cleaned up to several hours or even a day in advance. Wrap them loosely in paper towels, put them in a plastic bag, and store in the vegetable drawer of the refrigerator until needed.

# Classic Spinach Salad with Poppy Dressing

Poppy-seed dressings date back to Colonial American times but became the rage on spinach salad in the 1960s. This traditional combination of ingredients and flavors holds up beautifully for the modern palate. Sprinkling salt and sugar on the minced onion gives the dressing a bit of extra flavor from the extracted juices while softening the onion.

PREPARATION TIME: *20 minutes*
MAKES: *6 servings*

8 cups baby spinach, washed and spun dry (see box page 158)

6 slices (¼ pound) bacon, cooked until crisp and crumbled

3 large hard-boiled eggs, cut into ¼-inch slices

½ pint grape tomatoes

1 small red onion, thinly sliced

FOR THE POPPY DRESSING

½ small onion, finely chopped

2 tablespoons sugar

1 teaspoon kosher salt

2 teaspoons dijon mustard

¼ cup distilled white vinegar

½ cup extra-virgin olive oil

¼ teaspoon freshly ground black pepper

2 tablespoons (½ ounce) poppy seeds

1. Place the spinach in a large salad bowl. Add the crumbled bacon, sliced eggs, tomatoes, and red onion. Toss gently.
2. Make the poppy dressing: Stir the onion, sugar, and salt together in a small bowl. Let stand for 10 minutes. Stir in the mustard and vinegar, then whisk in the olive oil in a slow, steady stream. Stir in the black pepper and poppy seeds.
3. Pour the dressing over the salad, toss gently to coat all ingredients, and serve.

# Lentil and Walnut Salad

Given their ancient history and protein-filled nature, it seems logical to team lentils and walnuts. Many varieties of lentils are available, and any of them can be used in this recipe. We generally prepare this with the run-of-the-mill supermarket variety, but the choice is yours. Lentils cook quickly compared to other legumes, so be mindful when they are on the stove. We roast the vegetables to evoke as much sweetness as we can and then toss them together in a vinaigrette. Lentils have a bit of a peppery undertone, and that flavor, along with their healthy and balanced nutritional profile, makes them a suitable companion for the hard-working walnuts.

PREPARATION TIME: *20 minutes*
COOKING AND ROASTING TIME: *30 minutes*
MAKES: *8 to 10 servings*

2¼ cups (1 pound) lentils

1 small onion, cut into quarters

1 bay leaf

1 sprig thyme

1 cup quick-cooking couscous

3 medium carrots, peeled and cut into ½-inch dice

2 red bell peppers, cored, seeded, and cut into ½-inch dice

2 tablespoons freshly chopped thyme

1½ teaspoons kosher salt

2 tablespoons extra-virgin olive oil

2 cups (7 ounces) coarsely chopped walnuts, toasted

½ teaspoon freshly ground black pepper

FOR THE WALNUT VINAIGRETTE

3 tablespoons balsamic vinegar

¼ cup finely chopped shallots

1 teaspoon Dijon mustard

3 tablespoons walnut oil

3 tablespoons extra-virgin olive oil

½ teaspoon kosher salt

¼ teaspoon freshly ground black pepper

1. Preheat the oven to 400°F.
2. Place the lentils, onion, bay leaf, and thyme sprig in a large saucepan. Pour in enough cold water to cover by 4 inches. Bring to a boil over medium-high heat, stirring occasionally. Skim any foam that rises to the surface. Lower the heat until the liquid is simmering and cook until the lentils are soft but still intact, about 30 minutes. Be careful not to overcook; lentils will lose their shape and become mushy.
3. Drain the lentils in a colander and rinse with cold water to stop the cooking. Discard the bay leaf, thyme, and onion. Place the lentils in a large bowl and set aside.
4. While the lentils are cooking, prepare the couscous, vegetables, and vinaigrette.

5. Place the couscous in a small bowl and pour in 1 cup water. Set aside for 30 minutes, or until the couscous is softened.

6. Place the carrots and peppers on a roasting pan. Scatter the chopped thyme and 1 teaspoon salt over them. Drizzle the olive oil over the vegetables and toss. Bake for 20 to 30 minutes, or until the vegetables begin to brown around their edges. Remove from the oven and set aside to cool.

7. Make the vinaigrette: Whisk the balsamic vinegar, shallots, and mustard together in a small bowl until smooth. In a slow, steady stream, whisk in the olive oil and walnut or canola oil. Add the remaining ½ teaspoon salt and the pepper or to taste. Toss the dressing with the lentils.

8. Add the cooled vegetables, couscous, and chopped walnuts to the lentils. Mix well and taste for seasoning, adding the remaining ½ teaspoon salt and the pepper. Serve immediately. Store leftovers in the refrigerator in an airtight container for up to 3 days.

# Wild Rice and Cashew Salad with Sesame-Ginger Vinaigrette

We have produced thousands of pounds of this salad over many years of catering. Its nutty flavor, chewy-crunchy texture, and zippy dressing make it a favorite with many of our customers. The fact that it can be made one to two days ahead and keep its integrity makes it a favorite with us. A native American plant, wild rice is really the seeds of an aquatic grass, not a grain. In the mid-1980s, when we kicked off our catering business, wild rice was a luxury. We used to purchase ours directly from a Native American tribe in Minnesota. Although it is now more readily available, it is still gathered by hand in the upper Midwest.

PREPARATION TIME: *15 minutes*
COOKING TIME: *45 to 55 minutes*
MAKES: *8 to 10 servings*

1 pound wild rice

3 teaspoons kosher salt

FOR THE VINAIGRETTE

3 tablespoons rice wine vinegar

4 teaspoons honey

1 tablespoon freshly grated ginger

2 tablespoons soy sauce

5 tablespoons extra-virgin olive oil

2 tablespoons roasted sesame oil

———————

1½ cups (7½ ounces) coarsely chopped roasted cashews

2 red bell peppers, cored, seeded, and cut into ⅓-inch dice

1 bunch scallions, white and green parts, thinly sliced

½ teaspoon freshly ground black pepper

1. Place the wild rice in a strainer and rinse under cold water until the water runs clear, about 1 minute. Fill a medium saucepan three-quarters full with cold water. Add the rice and 2 teaspoons of the salt and bring to a boil over medium heat. Lower the heat until the liquid is simmering, cover, and cook for 45 minutes, or until the rice is tender and the grains are splitting open. Drain the rice in a colander and rinse with cold water to stop it from cooking.

2. While the rice is cooking, prepare the vinaigrette: Place the vinegar, honey, ginger, and soy sauce in the work bowl of a food processor. Process to mix, about 10 seconds. With the motor running, add the olive and sesame oils to the vinegar mixture in a slow stream. Set aside until the rice is ready.

3. Toss the cooled rice with the cashews, peppers, and scallions in a large bowl. Pour on the vinaigrette and add the remaining 1 teaspoon salt and the pepper. Toss to coat. Taste for seasoning and add more salt and pepper if needed. Serve immediately. Store leftovers in the refrigerator in an airtight container for up to 3 days.

# Pine Nut Tabbouleh

Cara first encountered this simple method for preparing tabbouleh in the *New York Times Natural Foods Cookbook* (1971) when she was in college. This unusual technique yields one of the easiest greens-and-grain salads to make ahead and serve to a crowd. The bulgur does not need to be cooked; instead it soaks overnight in the salad's dressing, absorbing its flavors and expanding as it would if cooked. The layered vegetables stay crisp, and the pine nuts add an intermittent rich contrast to the profusion of parsley.

PREPARATION TIME: *40 minutes, plus overnight to chill*
MAKES: *8 to 10 servings*

1 cup medium-grain bulgur

¾ cup freshly squeezed lemon juice

½ cup extra-virgin olive oil

10 plum tomatoes, cored, seeded, and cut into ½-inch dice

2 English cucumbers, peeled and cut into ½-inch dice

1 bunch scallions, white and green parts, thinly sliced

3 cups loosely packed freshly chopped flat-leaf parsley, stems removed

1½ cups (7½ ounces) pine nuts, toasted

1½ teaspoons kosher salt

½ teaspoon freshly ground black pepper

1. Place the bulgur in a large nonreactive serving bowl. Pour in the lemon juice, olive oil, and ¼ cup water. Mix well.
2. Layer the tomatoes, cucumbers, scallions, parsley, and pine nuts on top of the bulgur. Cover tightly and refrigerate overnight.
3. When ready to serve, remove the tabbouleh from the refrigerator, season with the salt and pepper, and toss well. Serve cold or at room temperature. Store leftovers in the refrigerator in an airtight container for up to 3 days.

## Culture and Cuisine

Nuts are the original locavore food, scooped from the fields and forests of our globe and eaten by regional peoples. As such, they played a worldwide role in the evolution of cuisine. Our study of nuts has become in part a study of the adaptive use of local resources, and we learned that as civilizations developed, nuts, like spices, followed trade routes, and accompanied travelers across vast expanses. So many people have used these local resources for thousands of years, and created sauces and dishes which we enjoy today.

# Mixed Greens with Mango, Coconut, and Macadamia Nuts

While in Hawaii, Andrea enjoyed a salad with a combination of exotic flavors like this. The fresh greens are just a backdrop for the tropical ingredients and can be varied according to what is available in the market. Mango nectar, easily found in supermarkets, helps thin the mango puree in the dressing without diluting its flavor. Make sure to seek out unsweetened coconut flakes that are as large as possible. Specialty and health-food stores sell large-flake coconut; finer coconut will give this salad a sandy texture.

PREPARATION TIME: *20 minutes*
MAKES: *6 to 8 servings*

### FOR THE MANGO DRESSING

½ large ripe mango, peeled and sliced

¼ cup mango nectar

1 tablespoon honey

2 tablespoons freshly squeezed lime juice

1 tablespoon freshly grated ginger

1 shallot, finely chopped

¼ cup extra-virgin olive oil

½ teaspoon kosher salt

### FOR THE SALAD

1 small head green leaf lettuce, cored, trimmed, torn into bite-sized pieces, and washed and spun dry (see box page 158)

1 small head frisée, trimmed, torn into bite-sized pieces, and washed and spun dry

1½ large ripe mangos, peeled and sliced

1 cup (3 ounces) unsweetened large coconut flakes (see headnote), lightly toasted

1 cup (5 ounces) coarsely chopped macadamia nuts, toasted

1. Make the dressing: Place the ½ mango, nectar, honey, lime juice, and ginger in a blender or food processor and puree until smooth. Using a fine-mesh sieve, strain into a small bowl. Discard the solids. Stir the shallot into the liquid. In a slow, steady stream, whisk in the oil until blended, then add the salt.

2. Place the lettuce and frisée in a large salad bowl. Pour half the dressing over the greens and toss. Add as much or as little of the remaining dressing as you like and toss again. If there is any left over, place it in an airtight container and store in the refrigerator for up to 3 days.

3. Scatter the mango pieces, coconut flakes, and macadamia nuts over the salad, and toss again before serving.

# Thai-Style Cucumber Salad with Roasted Peanuts

Cucumbers and jicama are crisp, cooling vegetables that combine well with classic Thai flavors. The jicama, like the peanut, is a native American plant that is now cultivated throughout Asia. While it looks like a pale, overgrown radish, it tastes like a sweet water chestnut. Peanuts have been part of Thai cuisine for only 150 years; we cannot imagine these flavors without the salty, robust crunch that the peanuts add to the mix. Seeding the seedless English cucumbers may seem unnecessary, but even the seedless variety has small white seeds that contain lots of extra fluid, which can make the salad too wet. Split the cucumber in half lengthwise and remove the central portion with a small spoon or melon-ball scoop. For a more complete meal we often serve this salad alongside our Hanger Steak (page 260).

PREPARATION TIME: *20 minutes, plus 20 minutes standing*
MAKES: *6 to 8 servings*

3 English cucumbers, peeled, seeded, and thinly sliced

1 tablespoon kosher salt

1 medium jicama, peeled and cut into matchsticks (see Note)

1 large carrot, peeled and grated

1 red onion, cut in half and thinly sliced

1 red bell pepper, cored, seeded, and cut into small dice

½ cup freshly chopped mint

½ cup freshly chopped basil

¾ cup (3¾ ounces) chopped roasted salted peanuts

Freshly ground black pepper

FOR THE LIME DRESSING

¼ cup freshly squeezed lime juice

2 tablespoons nam pla (Thai fish sauce)

1 tablespoon packed light brown sugar

1. Toss the cucumbers and 1 tablespoon salt together in a colander in the sink. Let stand for 20 minutes. Squeeze the cucumbers to release as much water as possible and pat dry.

2. Transfer the cucumbers to a large serving bowl and add the jicama, carrot, onion, red pepper, mint, basil, and peanuts. Stir to combine. Season with salt and pepper to taste.

3. Make the dressing: Whisk the lime juice, nam pla, and brown sugar together in a small bowl. The vegetables and dressing can be prepared a day in advance, as long as they are kept separately and stored in the refrigerator.

4. To serve, pour the dressing over the salad, toss, and serve immediately.

**NOTE:** To peel a jicama, slice off the top and bottom. Using a paring knife, carefully follow the curve of the vegetable to remove the skin and leave the flesh intact. (A large jicama may be easier to peel if cut in half.)

*Farro-Chickpea Salad with Sunflower Seeds (page 167)*

# Farro-Chickpea Salad with Sunflower Seeds

The Umbrian countryside is filled with sunflowers turning to face the arc of the sun over the course of the day. Although in Italy the seeds from these sunflowers are usually pressed for their oil, it seemed logical to us to pair them with farro, a nutritious hearty grain seen throughout that country. It can be found in most Italian grocery stores. The colors of the Italian flag are tossed into the mix—bright green asparagus, rosy red grape tomatoes, and creamy white ricotta salata.

PREPARATION TIME: *20 minutes, plus 1 hour standing*
COOKING TIME: *20 to 25 minutes*
MAKES: *8 to 10 servings*

2 cups farro

1 teaspoon kosher salt

1 pound asparagus, trimmed and cut into 1-inch pieces

1½ cups cooked chickpeas (see box page 76) or one 15-ounce can, drained and rinsed

1 pint grape tomatoes, cut in half lengthwise

1 small red onion, cut into small dice

1 cup (5 ounces) sunflower seeds, toasted

½ cup chopped Kalamata olives

2 cups (8 ounces) crumbled or chopped ricotta salata

¼ cup red wine vinegar

½ cup sunflower oil

½ cup chiffonade of fresh basil (see box page 115)

Freshly ground black pepper

1. Place the farro and 1 teaspoon salt in a large saucepan and add enough cold water to cover by 4 inches. Bring to a simmer over medium heat and cook until tender, about 20 minutes. Drain in a colander and rinse with cold water. Transfer to a serving bowl large enough to hold the remaining ingredients.

2. While the farro is simmering, cook the asparagus in a pot of boiling water with 1 tablespoon salt for 2 minutes. Drain well, rinse in cold water, and add to the cooled farro.

3. Add the remaining ingredients and toss. Season with salt and pepper to taste.

4. Keep the salad at a cool room temperature for 1 hour or cover and refrigerate for up to 2 days. Bring to room temperature at least 1 hour before serving.

# Bitter Greens with Roasted Pears and Spiced Hazelnuts

In the fall, when pears are at their peak, this salad enters our repertoire. We like to use them before they are perfectly ripe—maybe just the day before. Their fragrant flesh will yield just a tiny bit when pushed lightly with the side of your thumb. There are many available varieties, but we choose the most common, Bartlett or Anjou. They are easy to find in the markets, and they exude the perfume of the season. The delicate bitterness of the greens balances beautifully with the pears. But their connective tissue, as it were, is the hazelnuts. They are the bridge between the other ingredients; their spice and crunch are a foil for both.

PREPARATION TIME: *10 minutes*
ROASTING AND COOKING TIME: *20 minutes, for the pears and spiced hazelnuts*
MAKES: *6 servings*
EQUIPMENT: *1 rimmed baking sheet lined with parchment paper*

### FOR THE ROASTED PEARS

2 nearly ripe Anjou or Bartlett pears, peeled, stemmed, cored, and cut into ¼-inch slices

1 tablespoon extra-virgin olive oil

### FOR THE SPICED HAZELNUTS

1 tablespoon extra-virgin olive oil

1 cup (5 ounces) coarsely chopped blanched hazelnuts

½ to 1 teaspoon cayenne pepper

2 teaspoons kosher salt

### FOR THE DRESSING

3 tablespoons sherry vinegar

1 large shallot, finely chopped

1 teaspoon Dijon mustard

¼ cup extra-virgin olive oil

2 tablespoons hazelnut oil

1 teaspoon kosher salt, or to taste

½ teaspoon freshly ground black pepper, or to taste

### FOR THE GREENS

2 cups (3 ounces) frisée, washed, trimmed, and torn into bite-sized pieces

2 cups (3 ounces) young dandelion greens, washed and torn into bite-sized pieces

3 Belgian endives, washed, cut in half, cored, and sliced

1 teaspoon kosher salt, or to taste

½ teaspoon freshly ground black pepper, or to taste

1. Make the roasted pears: Preheat the oven to 425°F. Place the pears on the prepared baking sheet and drizzle the olive oil over them. Toss lightly and roast for 15 to 20 minutes, until the edges of the pears begin to color slightly. Set aside to cool.

2. Meanwhile, make the spiced nuts: Heat the olive oil in a medium skillet over medium heat. When the oil begins to shimmer lightly, add the hazelnuts, cayenne, and salt. Cook, stirring continuously, until the aroma fills the air, about 5 minutes. Set aside to cool.

3. Make the dressing: Whisk the vinegar, shallot, and mustard together in a small bowl until smooth. In a slow stream, whisk in the olive and hazelnut oils. Season with the salt and pepper.

4. Toss the greens together in a large salad bowl. Just before serving, add the pears, hazelnuts, and half the dressing. Toss gently until the greens and pears are coated with dressing. Taste and add more dressing if you like. Serve immediately.

# Arugula Salad with Manchego and Lacquered Almonds

This simple salad is a delicate balance of sweet, sour, salty, and spicy flavors. Preparation of the lacquered almonds is inspired by a Chinese technique—first they are boiled in sweetened syrup and then they are baked until glossy. The sweet almonds are the yin to the yang of the sour lemon vinaigrette. Manchego provides a salty richness, while the arugula adds a peppery base to round out this salad.

PREPARATION TIME: *10 minutes*
COOKING AND BAKING TIME: *50 minutes, for the laquered almonds*
MAKES: *6 servings*
EQUIPMENT: *1 rimmed baking sheet lined with parchment paper*

### FOR THE LACQUERED ALMONDS

¼ cup honey

¼ cup light corn syrup

½ teaspoon kosher salt

2 star anise

1 cup (4½ ounces) slivered almonds

### FOR THE LEMON VINAIGRETTE

2 tablespoons freshly squeezed lemon juice

1 shallot, finely chopped

½ cup extra-virgin olive oil

½ teaspoon kosher salt

¼ teaspoon freshly ground black pepper

### FOR THE SALAD

6 cups baby arugula, washed and spun dry (see box page 158)

One 4-ounce piece Manchego cheese

1. Make the almonds: Preheat the oven to 350°F. Bring the honey, corn syrup, ¼ cup water, salt, and star anise to a boil in a medium saucepan over medium heat. Slip the almonds into the syrup and cook for 20 minutes, or until the syrup begins to stick and the almonds are well coated. Using a fine-mesh sieve, strain the syrup. Discard the star anise. Pour the almonds onto the prepared baking sheet. Bake for 25 to 30 minutes, or until the almonds glisten. Cool completely. The almonds can be stored in an airtight container for up to 1 week.

2. Make the vinaigrette: Whisk the lemon juice and shallot together in a small bowl. In a slow, steady stream, whisk in the olive oil. Add the salt and pepper.

3. Place the baby arugula in a large salad bowl. Set aside.

4. When ready to serve, pour the vinaigrette over the arugula and toss. Using a vegetable peeler, shave the cheese into strips, placing them over the greens. Scatter lacquered almonds on the salad and serve.

# Roasted Beet Salad with Toasted Walnuts, Goat Cheese, and White Balsamic Vinaigrette

This refreshing salad is perfect for summer or fall, when beets are at their best. The tartness of the vinaigrette, the richness of the goat cheese, and the sweetness of the toasted walnuts combine beautifully with the earthiness of the beets.

PREPARATION TIME: *20 minutes*
ROASTING TIME: *1 hour, plus 30 minutes to cool*
MAKES: *4 servings*

2 pounds (about 6) medium beets

5 tablespoons extra-virgin olive oil

1 clove garlic, finely chopped

2 tablespoons white balsamic vinegar

½ teaspoon kosher salt

¼ teaspoon freshly ground black pepper

2 tablespoons freshly chopped thyme

½ cup (1¾ ounces) chopped walnuts, toasted

3 ounces mild goat cheese (such as Montrachet), crumbled

2 scallions, white and green parts, thinly sliced

1. Place a rack in the lower third of the oven and preheat to 350°F.
2. Remove the leaves and stems from the beets, leaving about 1 inch of stem above the beet. Discard the greens or reserve for another use. Scrub the beets clean. In a small bowl, toss the beets with 2 tablespoons olive oil. Place them in a roasting pan and bake in the preheated oven until tender, about 45 minutes. Pierce with a paring knife to test for doneness: the knife should slide easily into the beet. Set the beets aside to cool.
3. When the beets are cool, peel them with a paring knife. Cut into ½-inch slices perpendicular to the stem and place in a medium bowl. Set aside.
4. In a small bowl, mix the garlic, balsamic vinegar, salt, pepper, and thyme. Whisk in the remaining 3 tablespoons olive oil. Pour the dressing over the cooked beets and toss gently.
5. Arrange the beets on a round or oval serving dish. Scatter the walnuts, goat cheese, and scallions over them. Season with salt and pepper to taste. Serve immediately.

**TIP:** Both the beets and the dressing can be made in advance, and tossing the beets with the dressing and then letting them sit may actually improve the flavor, as the beets absorb the dressing more fully. Dressed beets can be covered with plastic wrap and refrigerated for up to 2 days, but bring them to room temperature before serving. You can also refrigerate roasted beets for a day or so before slicing them and tossing them with the dressing, which is especially convenient if you are using the oven for another purpose. Don't forget to wear gloves when peeling and handling beets, to prevent your hands from staining a deep crimson.

*Fresh almonds and nectarine*

CHAPTER 6

# Greens, Beans, and Grains

# Nuts and Bolts of Greens, Beans, and Grains

**The United States has seen a renaissance, maybe even a revolution, in** the way we perceive, purchase, and cook vegetables in the past few years. More different kinds are available than ever before, and their quality continues to improve, in part because our access to farm-fresh produce has increased.

Fresh vegetables are the key ingredients in these recipes, and while the phrases "buy seasonally" and "buy locally" have almost become clichés in the twenty-first century, that doesn't make the message any less important. It takes some skill and concentration to tailor your menu to local and seasonal availability, but you will notice the difference in vibrant flavors and colors that can't be obtained in any other way.

In general, freshness and flavor go hand in hand. Look for firm, unbruised, and unwrinkled specimens and buy what you will use. Tempting as they may be, extra vegetables will age in your refrigerator, and their flavor and nutrients will wilt with them over time. We are realists, however, and we certainly understand that everyone can't use only what is seasonal and available all the time. That is a good philosophy to use as a guideline, but it won't stop us from purchasing celery in December. It does, however, make us more mindful of where our produce comes from and what freshness really means.

When we were growing up, most American households saw more or less the same dinner every night: a piece of meat, a vegetable, and a starch. These days there is much talk about the "new center of the plate," which basically means changing the proportions of our meals to include a healthy serving of starch (preferably a whole grain), a large amount of vegetables, and less meat. Nuts and seeds are a particularly welcome addition to the grains and other starches that are taking center stage, lending a little crunch to these soft-textured dishes. It doesn't hurt that nuts and seeds also pump up their nutritional value.

It is not only the proportions of what's on the plate that have changed; the components of the plate have changed too. So many interesting grains and other side dishes are available today that it would be silly—not to mention sad—to limit yourself to mashed potatoes and white rice. Visit a supermarket and you will find a sea of rice varieties on the shelves: jasmine, basmati, sushi-style, and so forth. Then there are couscous (not a grain but a pasta) and quinoa, barley and bulgur. The choices are practically endless.

# Brown Buttered String Beans Amandine

String beans amandine is a dress-up dish from our childhood. Made in the simplest of ways back then, often from boxes of frozen French-style green beans, they were set on the table with a crown of toasted slivered almonds on holidays and at celebratory dinners, when company was coming. We loved them. This is a modern, everyday version. It is easy to make by blanching the string beans the day before you need them, and we like to use the small French haricots verts that are so readily available now. Even though the memories are age-old, the taste is up-to-date.

PREPARATION TIME: *20 minutes*
MAKES: *6 to 8 servings*

1½ pounds string beans, trimmed

½ stick (4 tablespoons) unsalted butter

¾ cup (3 ounces) slivered almonds

2 tablespoons finely chopped shallots

1 tablespoon freshly squeezed lemon juice

1 teaspoon kosher salt

½ teaspoon freshly ground black pepper

1. Bring a large pot of water with 1 tablespoon salt to a boil over high heat. Set a large bowl of ice water near the sink.

2. Blanch the string beans in the boiling water for 3 to 4 minutes, or until crisp-tender. Drain the beans in a colander in the sink and immediately submerge them in the ice water to stop them from cooking and keep them bright green and crisp. Drain the beans, pat them dry, and set them aside. The beans may be prepared a day in advance through this step. Be sure the beans are cold and dry and store them in a resealable plastic bag in the refrigerator overnight. If chilled, bring the string beans to room temperature before proceeding with this recipe.

3. Melt the butter in a large skillet over medium-low heat. Cook the butter slowly for 3 to 4 minutes; it will turn amber. When the butter is lightly browned, add the almonds and toss to coat. Cook until the almonds are lightly toasted, about 3 minutes. Add the chopped shallots and beans and cook, stirring, until the shallots are softened and translucent and the beans are heated through, about 2 minutes.

4. Transfer the beans to a serving bowl and add the lemon juice, salt, and pepper, adjusting to taste. Toss well and serve warm.

# Orange-Braised Winter Squash with Pumpkin Seeds

As fall rolls in, pumpkins and other winter squashes, such as acorn, Hubbard, butternut, and kabocha fill market shelves. We love their seasonal flavors and bright oranges and yellows, so similar to the colors of the leaves on the trees at the same time. Although peeling and seeding winter squash may seem like a chore, the results are well worth it. Prepared squash is sold in cellophane bags, but the quality is almost always disappointing. If convenience is an issue, this recipe, excluding the pumpkin seeds, can be cooked up to 2 days in advance and kept refrigerated.

PREPARATION TIME: *20 minutes*
COOKING TIME: *25 minutes*
MAKES: *4 servings*

2 tablespoons olive oil

1 large yellow onion, chopped

2 cloves garlic, finely chopped

2 medium winter squash (about 3 pounds total) of any variety, peeled, seeded, and cut into ¾-inch dice

1 teaspoon ground cumin

½ teaspoon ground cinnamon

½ teaspoon ground coriander

1 teaspoon kosher salt

Pinch cayenne pepper

½ cup freshly squeezed orange juice

½ cup vegetable stock

½ cup (2¾ ounces) pumpkin seeds, lightly toasted

2 tablespoons freshly chopped cilantro (optional)

Freshly ground black pepper

1. Heat the olive oil in a Dutch oven or stockpot over medium heat until glistening. Add the onion and garlic and cook, stirring, until wilted, about 5 minutes.
2. Stir the squash into the pan and season it with the cumin, cinnamon, and coriander. Stir in the salt and cayenne and mix well. Add the orange juice and stock and bring to a boil. Lower the heat until the liquid is simmering, stir well, and cover. Cook until the squash is tender, about 20 minutes; a knife will easily pierce the squash when it is done.
3. Transfer the squash to a serving dish, sprinkle it with the pumpkin seeds and the cilantro, and season with salt and pepper to taste. Serve warm.

**VARIATION:** If you prefer a slightly spicier and smokier version, add 1 tablespoon of chopped chipotle in adobo to the pan with the orange juice and stock. Chipotles in adobo are dried smoked jalapeños simmered in a simple tomato sauce and sold in small cans.

# Swiss Chard, Leeks, and Hazelnuts

Late in the summer, as days get shorter and the farmers' markets brim with produce, we search out Swiss chard, one of our favorite leafy greens. We always see three types of Swiss chard: Rainbow chard is multihued, with red, orange, and yellow stems; red chard has red stems; and the most commonly found chard has white stems. All three have broad, lustrous, deep green leaves. As vivid as the colored chard is, we prefer the white. Red and yellow chard tends to release its juices when cooked, and we don't like the way they muddy the colors around them. Whatever kind you choose, the leaves and stems need to be treated like two separate vegetables. After rinsing the chard, use a paring knife to remove the stems from the leaves, running parallel to the stems. The stems can be trimmed, sliced, and sautéed. The leaves can be chopped and sautéed as well, but they will cook more quickly than the stems. The combination with leeks just seems natural. Hazelnuts are the crunchy bridge between the leeks and the chard. To prepare the leeks, cut off the green tops and split the white bulbs down the middle. Rinse the cut bulbs and then soak them in cold water for 5 minutes. Rinse them again before slicing.

PREPARATION TIME: *25 minutes*
COOKING TIME: *10 minutes*
MAKES: *4 servings*

2 tablespoons olive oil

1 tablespoon hazelnut oil

3 medium leeks, cleaned and sliced (see headnote)

2 cloves garlic, finely chopped

2 pounds Swiss chard, trimmed (see headnote), rinsed, and cut into 1-inch pieces

1 teaspoon kosher salt

½ teaspoon freshly ground black pepper

¾ cup (3¾ ounces) coarsely chopped hazelnuts, toasted

1. Heat the olive oil and hazelnut oil in a large skillet over medium heat until glistening. Add the leeks and garlic. Reduce the heat to low and cook, stirring often, until the leeks are wilted and translucent, about 5 minutes.
2. Carefully add as much Swiss chard as will fit in the pan, making sure to separate and add the stems first; they will take a minute longer to cook. The water that clings to it from washing will be enough to wilt the chard. Cook, stirring constantly, until wilted, about 1 minute. Remove the Swiss chard with tongs to a colander set over a bowl to drain any excess liquid. Repeat with the remaining chard.

3. Remove the cooked Swiss chard from the colander and the pan so that most of the liquid is left behind. Put the Swiss chard in a serving dish and toss well to ensure that the garlic and leeks are dispersed. Season with the salt and pepper, adjusting to taste, and toss with the hazelnuts. Serve warm or at room temperature.

# Roasted Vegetables with Pecan-Balsamic Glaze

This recipe is great for serving a crowd, especially over the fall and winter holidays. It can easily be multiplied and is flexible: you can substitute any fall root vegetables for those listed, as long as you keep the quantities balanced. The natural juices of the earthy vegetables combine with the balsamic vinegar and coat the pecans, lending the dish a tangy sweetness. The vegetables can be prepared up to 2 days in advance. Cool them, then refrigerate them in a covered casserole dish. Reheat the vegetables in a 350°F oven for about 30 minutes, or until they are heated through, then toss in the sage and serve warm.

PREPARATION TIME: *20 minutes*
ROASTING TIME: *45 to 50 minutes*
MAKES: *4 servings*

1¾ cups (8 ounces) pearl onions, peeled (see Note)

2 medium parsnips, peeled and cut into ½-inch slices

1 large turnip or rutabaga, peeled and cut into 1-inch pieces

1 bulb fennel, trimmed, halved, cored, and cut into 1-inch pieces (see box page 144)

2 medium carrots, peeled and cut into ½-inch slices

¼ cup olive oil

¼ cup good balsamic vinegar

1½ teaspoons kosher salt

½ teaspoon freshly ground black pepper

2 bay leaves

½ cup (2 ounces) finely chopped pecans

2 tablespoons freshly chopped sage

1. Preheat the oven to 400°F.
2. Toss the vegetables with the olive oil in a mixing bowl. Add the vinegar, salt, pepper, and bay leaves and toss well. Transfer the seasoned vegetables to a roasting pan.
3. Bake, stirring occasionally, until the vegetables are barely tender, 35 to 40 minutes. Stir in the pecans and return to the oven for 10 minutes.
4. Remove and discard the bay leaves. Add the sage, toss the vegetables well, and season with salt and pepper to taste. Serve warm.

NOTE: To peel pearl onions, first blanch them in a large saucepan of boiling water for 2 minutes. Drain well and refresh under cold running water until cool enough to handle. Peel the onions, using a paring knife to help with the stem and core ends.

# Kohlrabi Slaw with Sesame-Ginger Vinaigrette

Kohlrabi, a member of the cabbage family, is a jewel of a vegetable, filled with flavor and nutrients. The name kohlrabi comes from the German *kohl*, or cabbage, and the Swiss-German *rabi*, for turnip. It has a moist, crisp texture and a mild, slightly sweet flavor, not dissimilar to that of broccoli stems. Often eaten raw in the West, kohlrabi is a mainstay in Kashmiri and Indian cuisines, where it is generally served cooked. We love it in place of cabbage in a coleslaw and use it on top of or alongside Red Lentil–Cashew Sliders (page 269). *(See photo page 266.)*

PREPARATION TIME: *20 minutes*
MAKES: *6 servings*

### FOR THE SLAW

- 1 bunch kohlrabi (about 1 pound), bulbs peeled and cut into ¼-by-¼-by-2-inch strips
- 1 medium red onion, thinly sliced
- 1 large carrot, peeled and grated
- 3 tablespoons freshly chopped flat-leaf parsley

### FOR THE VINAIGRETTE

- 2 tablespoons rice wine vinegar
- 1 tablespoon finely chopped ginger
- 1 tablespoon honey
- 1 tablespoon soy sauce
- ¼ cup canola oil
- 1 tablespoon roasted sesame oil
- ½ teaspoon kosher salt
- ½ teaspoon freshly ground black pepper
- ¼ cup (1¼ ounces) sesame seeds, toasted

1. Combine all the ingredients for the slaw in a medium nonreactive bowl.
2. Make the vinaigrette: Whisk the vinegar, ginger, honey, and soy sauce in a small bowl until blended. Whisk in the oils in a slow stream. Pour the dressing over the vegetables, season with the salt and pepper, adjusting to taste, and toss with the sesame seeds. Serve immediately or chill for up to 4 hours.

# Crunchy Walnut-Cauliflower Gratin

Cauliflower is another healthful member of the cabbage family. We prefer white cauliflower for this dish—it looks nicer—but green and purple cauliflower are also available. (As far as we can tell, they all taste the same.) When purchasing cauliflower, look for tight heads without any brown spots. Cauliflower is easy to find, inexpensive, and quick to cook. If it has a defect, it's that it can be a bit bland. Cooking it as a gratin with a touch of cream and some cheese and a crisp walnut and breadcrumb topping makes it shine.

PREPARATION TIME: *20 minutes*
COOKING TIME: *30 minutes*
MAKES: *6 servings*
EQUIPMENT: *One 10-inch gratin dish, well buttered*

1 head cauliflower (about 1½ pounds), cored and separated into florets (see Note)

2 tablespoons olive oil

½ cup finely chopped shallots

2 cups heavy cream

1 teaspoon kosher salt

½ teaspoon freshly ground black pepper

¼ teaspoon freshly grated nutmeg

1½ cups (5¼ ounces) walnut pieces, lightly toasted

2 tablespoons walnut oil or olive oil

½ cup (⅔ ounces) plain breadcrumbs

½ cup freshly grated Parmesan cheese

2 tablespoons freshly chopped flat-leaf parsley

1. Preheat the oven to 350°F. Bring a large pot of water with 1 tablespoon of salt to a boil over high heat and place a bowl of ice water near the sink.
2. Blanch the cauliflower in the boiling water until crisp-tender, about 3 minutes. Drain in a colander in the sink and then plunge the cauliflower into the ice water. Drain again, pat dry, and set aside.
3. Heat the olive oil in a medium saucepan over medium heat. Add the shallots and cook, stirring, until wilted, about 3 minutes. Add the heavy cream, bring to a boil, then lower the heat until the liquid is simmering. Simmer until slightly thickened, about 10 minutes. Season with the salt, pepper, and nutmeg.
4. Toss the cauliflower, cream, and ½ cup walnuts together in a large bowl until the cauliflower is coated. Pour the mixture into the prepared gratin dish.
5. Heat the walnut oil in a small skillet over low heat. Add the breadcrumbs and toss and stir until they are lightly toasted, about 5 minutes. Remove from the heat; add the remaining 1 cup walnuts, the Parmesan, and the parsley. Scatter the breadcrumb mixture over the cauliflower evenly and cover the gratin dish with aluminum foil.

6. Bake for 20 minutes. Remove the foil and cook until the gratin is bubbling and the breadcrumbs are golden brown, about 10 minutes. Serve hot.

NOTE: The easiest way to separate a head of cauliflower into florets is to start by cutting out the central core with a paring knife. Working with your hands, break the head into large pieces, then into florets, dividing them where they branch off naturally from the main stem. You will end up with florets of slightly different sizes, which will give the dish a natural look.

# Shredded Brussels Sprouts with Chestnuts

There are several ways to cook Brussels sprouts, and often we split them, toss them with a little olive oil, season them with salt and pepper, and just roast them on a baking sheet. When something a little more special is called for, shredded sprouts with chestnuts fill the bill. We love Brussels sprouts that are still attached to their stalks—they tend to be fresher than those that have been separated, and their Christmas-tree-like appearance just makes us smile. But we are almost as pleased with small containers of sprouts covered with cellophane and a rubber band. What's most important is that the little green orbs are firm, with intact leaves. It takes a little work to slice and shred them, but sautéed Brussels sprouts with chestnuts make an elegant side dish.

PREPARATION TIME: *20 minutes*
COOKING TIME: *5 minutes*
MAKES: *4 servings*

2 tablespoons unsalted butter

2 tablespoons olive oil

2 cloves garlic, finely chopped

1½ pounds Brussels sprouts, hard short stems removed, cut in half, and thinly sliced

2 tablespoons dry white wine

1 teaspoon kosher salt

½ teaspoon freshly ground black pepper

1 cup (6 ounces) crumbled chestnuts, toasted

1. Melt the butter in a large skillet over medium heat and add the olive oil. Add the garlic and stir. Cook until fragrant, about 2 minutes.
2. Quickly add the shredded sprouts and stir until coated. Add the wine and season with the salt and pepper, adjusting to taste. Cook until wilted, about 1 minute. Add the chestnuts and toss until well mixed. Serve warm.

# Pistachio-Almond Rice Pilaf

Many years ago, when Cara was in cooking school, she learned to make rice pilaf using a method that was foreign to her. Every package of rice had different cooking instructions, and most called for twice as much water as rice. At the end of the cooking time, Cara always found moisture at the bottom of the pot, or the rice was too sticky and moist. With professional instruction, she learned to use only one and a half times as much liquid as rice and to start with boiling liquid and a bay leaf, add the rice, stir once, cover, and cook without stirring for 17 minutes, always at a simmer. The simple long-grain rice was perfectly cooked this way, and any pilaf ingredients that were to be added—sautéed onions, celery, or nuts—were cooked first. This method has never failed. Start with long-grain white rice, and adhere to the 17-minute rule. It works.

PREPARATION TIME: *30 minutes*
COOKING TIME: *20 to 25 minutes*
MAKES: *6 to 8 servings*

2 tablespoons olive oil

1 large onion, cut into ½-inch pieces

4 ribs celery, cut into ½-inch pieces

2 cups long-grain white rice

3 cups chicken stock

1 bay leaf

1½ teaspoons kosher salt

¾ cup (3 ounces) sliced almonds, toasted

¾ cup (3¾ ounces) coarsely chopped pistachios

1 tablespoon unsalted butter

½ teaspoon freshly ground black pepper

1. Heat the oil in a medium saucepan over medium heat. Add the onion and celery and cook, stirring occasionally, until wilted, about 5 minutes. Add the rice and stir to coat.
2. Pour in the chicken stock and bring to a boil. Add the bay leaf and salt. Lower the heat until the stock is just simmering. Stir the rice once, put the lid on, and cook for 17 minutes (don't peek!). Turn off the heat and let the pilaf rest for 5 minutes, still covered.
3. Add the almonds, pistachios, butter, and pepper and fluff the rice. Season with salt to taste. Serve warm.

# Toasted Coconut Black Rice

Black rice is a showstopper, plain and simple. When cooked, it is a deep purplish black. Its intact husk is full of fiber, iron, and anthocyanin, a colorful pigment known for its ability to attract pollinators. Black rice is usually used in sweet rice dishes in its native Asia, but we like to use it in savory dishes. It does take longer to cook than white rice, so plan accordingly.

PREPARATION TIME: *5 minutes*
COOKING TIME: *40 minutes*
MAKES: *6 to 8 servings*

1 cup unsweetened coconut milk

2 cups chicken stock

2 cups black rice, rinsed

¾ cup (2¼ ounces) unsweetened coconut flakes, toasted

¼ cup thinly sliced scallions, white and green parts

1 teaspoon kosher salt

½ teaspoon freshly ground black pepper

1. Bring the coconut milk and stock to a boil in a medium saucepan over high heat. Add the rice and return to a boil. Lower the heat until the liquid is simmering, cover the pan, and cook until all the liquid is absorbed and the rice is cooked, about 30 minutes. The rice will be tender but still have a tiny core of firmness. Remove from the heat and let stand 5 minutes before fluffing or stirring.
2. Stir in the toasted coconut flakes and scallions. Add the salt and pepper, adjusting to taste. Serve warm.

# Warm Pumpkin Seed Quinoa

Quinoa is a high-protein seed that is cooked and eaten like rice. First domesticated in the Andean region of Peru, it became an important food source for the native peoples of the region before the Spanish conquest. It has found new popularity here in North America in the twenty-first century. Vegetarians love it for its balanced nutrition and adaptable flavor. Although we often prepare quinoa as a side dish, as we do here, cooked quinoa also makes a great breakfast, especially when tossed with toasted almonds and fresh berries.

PREPARATION TIME: *20 minutes*
COOKING TIME: *25 minutes*
MAKES: *6 to 8 servings*

2 tablespoons olive oil

1 large onion, chopped

3 cloves garlic, finely chopped

1 red bell pepper, cored, seeded, and chopped

1 teaspoon ground cumin

½ teaspoon ground cinnamon

2 cups quinoa

3½ cups vegetable stock or chicken stock

1 teaspoon kosher salt

½ teaspoon freshly ground black pepper

¾ cup (4 ounces) pumpkin seeds, toasted

2 tablespoons freshly chopped cilantro

1. Heat the olive oil in a medium saucepan over medium heat. Add the onion and garlic. Stir and cook until the onion is wilted, about 5 minutes. Add the red pepper, cumin, and cinnamon. Cook until the red pepper begins to soften, 3 or 4 minutes.
2. Stir in the quinoa. Add the stock, salt, and pepper and bring to a boil. Lower the heat until the liquid is simmering, cover, and cook until all the liquid is absorbed, 15 to 20 minutes. Remove from the heat and let stand, still covered, for 5 minutes.
3. Stir in the pumpkin seeds and cilantro. Season with salt and pepper to taste and serve warm.

# Maple-Pecan Mashed Sweet Potatoes

Some of Cara's relatives used to object to being served anything but traditional mashed white potatoes on holidays. But she has weakened their stubborn resolve with this dish, which is fast becoming a holiday favorite in her family. (These are a big hit in Andrea's family too.) Grade B maple syrup is darker than grade A, and we like its slightly stronger, robust flavor.

PREPARATION TIME: *45 minutes*
BAKING TIME: *15 to 20 minutes*
MAKES: *6 to 8 servings*
EQUIPMENT: *One 10-inch gratin dish, lightly buttered*

**2 pounds (4 large potatoes) sweet potatoes, skins on**

**½ stick (4 tablespoons) unsalted butter, melted**

**½ cup grade B maple syrup**

**2 to 4 tablespoons heavy cream**

**1 tablespoon freshly grated ginger**

**2 teaspoons kosher salt**

**½ teaspoon freshly ground black pepper**

**¾ cup (3 ounces) coarsely chopped toasted pecans**

1. Place the sweet potatoes in a pot large enough to hold them comfortably and pour in enough cold water to cover them. Bring to a boil over high heat, then lower the heat until the water is simmering. Cook until the potatoes can be easily pierced with a fork, about 30 minutes, depending on their size. Drain in a colander.

2. Preheat the oven to 350°F.

3. When the potatoes are cool enough to handle, peel away the skin, cut them into 3 or 4 pieces each, and place them in the work bowl of a food processor. Process until the potatoes are smooth, 1 to 2 minutes. With the machine running, pour in the butter and process until incorporated.

4. Add the maple syrup, cream, ginger, salt, and pepper and process to mix, about 30 seconds. You may see fibrous strands from the potatoes; that is fine. Scrape the potatoes into the gratin dish and fold in the pecans or, if you prefer, garnish the top with the pecans. The dish can be made up to this point and refrigerated for up to 2 days.

5. Cover the dish with aluminum foil and bake for 10 to 15 minutes. Uncover and bake for an additional 10 to 12 minutes. Serve warm. If it has been prepared in advance and refrigerated, increase the total baking time to 45 minutes.

# Summer Squash and Corn Mélange with Almonds

This dish is our simple version of a ratatouille, with some subtractions and some additions. We love the combination of squash and corn; they always seem to marry seamlessly, maybe because they are two of the foods that were domesticated in the Americas before the era of Columbus. Although almonds had a long way to travel to join these two vegetables, we find that the three go very well together.

PREPARATION TIME: *15 minutes*
COOKING TIME: *15 minutes*
MAKES: *4 servings*

4 tablespoons olive oil

1 large onion, cut in half and sliced

3 cloves garlic, chopped

2 yellow squash, stems and blossoms removed, cut into ¾-inch slices

2 green squash, stems and blossoms removed, cut into ¾-inch slices

1½ teaspoons kosher salt

6 plum tomatoes, seeded and chopped

1½ cups fresh corn kernels, cut from 3 small ears

2 tablespoons freshly chopped marjoram

¾ cup (3½ ounces) coarsely chopped slivered almonds, toasted

½ teaspoon freshly ground black pepper

1. Heat the olive oil in a large skillet or a Dutch oven over medium heat. Add the onion and garlic and cook until wilted, about 5 minutes. Add the squash, sprinkle with ½ teaspoon salt, and stir. Cook for 3 or 4 minutes, until the squash begins to give off its liquid and soften.

2. Add the tomatoes and corn and stir. Simmer for 5 minutes. Remove the pan from the heat, toss in the marjoram and the almonds, and season with the remaining 1 teaspoon salt and the pepper or to taste. Transfer the mélange to a serving dish and serve hot. This recipe can be prepared up to 2 days in advance and stored well wrapped in the refrigerator. It can be reheated or served cold.

# White Beans with Sun-Dried Tomatoes and Roasted Walnuts

Cannellini beans are often known as a poor man's meat in Italy. This Tuscan dish offers lots of protein from the beans as well as the nuts. It's best to toss the beans with the vinaigrette while they are still warm so they can fully absorb the flavors. We have been known to take leftovers and mash them coarsely, then spread the mash on toasted Italian bread. With a light drizzle of walnut or olive oil and a few shards of shaved Parmesan, it makes a great hors d' oeuvres.

PREPARATION TIME: *45 minutes*
MAKES: *4 servings*

3 cups cooked cannellini beans (see box page 76) or two 15-ounce cans, drained and rinsed

1 bulb garlic

1 tablespoon olive oil

¾ cup (4½ ounces) drained oil-packed sun-dried tomatoes

1 large red onion, chopped

1 cup (3½ ounces) coarsely chopped toasted walnuts

5 ribs celery, trimmed and thinly sliced

2 tablespoons chopped sage

Kosher salt and freshly ground black pepper

FOR THE RED WINE VINAIGRETTE

2 tablespoons red wine vinegar

¼ cup finely chopped shallots

1 teaspoon Dijon mustard

¼ cup extra-virgin olive oil

2 tablespoons walnut oil

½ teaspoon kosher salt

¼ teaspoon freshly ground black pepper

1. Preheat the oven to 350°F.
2. Place the beans in a large bowl and set aside.
3. Cut off the top of the garlic bulb, drizzle the olive oil over the cut surface, and wrap the garlic loosely in aluminum foil. Place it on the bottom rack of the oven and bake for 45 minutes, or until the garlic is golden, soft, and tender. Unwrap the garlic and cool.
4. Place the sun-dried tomatoes in a small saucepan with cold water to cover. Bring to a boil over medium-high heat. Remove the pan from the heat and let it stand for 15 minutes. When cooled, drain the tomatoes and roughly chop them into ¼-inch pieces. Add them to the warm beans.

5. Separate the cooled garlic into cloves and squeeze the soft pulp from each. Coarsely chop the pulp and add it to the beans along with the onion, walnuts, celery, and sage.

6. Make the vinaigrette: Whisk the red wine vinegar, shallots, and mustard together in a small bowl. In a slow, steady stream whisk in the olive oil and walnut oil to combine. Whisk in salt and pepper to taste.

7. Pour the dressing over the bean mixture and toss well. Taste for seasoning, adding salt and pepper if needed. Cover the bowl with plastic wrap and chill for at least 1 hour or overnight before serving.

# Barbecued Baked Beans with Pecans

Nothing says baked beans more than the first summertime barbecue. Adding pecans to these baked beans is something that we have done forever. The nuts blend perfectly with the sauce and add richness to this homey dish. Don't be scared away by the long preparation time—the oven does almost all the work. Baked beans need to cook slowly to build layers of the perfect flavor, and this recipe does just that. If you are pressed for time, you can use canned beans to replace freshly cooked beans; some of the depth of flavor may be lost, but you can't go wrong with baked beans with simply grilled meats, burgers, or hot dogs at a barbecue.

PREPARATION TIME: *40 minutes*
BAKING TIME: *1 hour 10 minutes*
MAKES: *6 to 8 servings*

5 cups cooked navy beans (see box page 76) or three 15-ounce cans, drained and rinsed

¼ pound salt pork or bacon, thinly sliced

2 large onions, chopped

2 teaspoons kosher salt

½ teaspoon freshly ground black pepper

1 cup tomato puree

½ cup packed dark brown sugar

1 tablespoon Dijon mustard

1 tablespoon Worcestershire sauce

1 cup (4 ounces) coarsely chopped pecans

1. Preheat the oven to 350°F.
2. Pour the beans into a large Dutch oven; add enough water to cover them.
3. In a large skillet over medium heat, partially cook the pork or bacon to release some of the fat. Remove the meat from the pan with a slotted spoon and sprinkle it over the beans.
4. Add the onions to the skillet and cook in the fat over medium heat, until softened, about 5 minutes. Pour the onions and fat over the beans, add the salt and pepper, and stir.
5. In a small bowl, whisk together the tomato puree, brown sugar, mustard, and Worcestershire sauce. Stir in the pecans. Mix the tomato mixture into the beans. Cover and bake until the beans are completely tender, 1 to 1½ hours. Check once or twice to make sure there is enough liquid; if the level of the liquid dips below the beans, add a little more water,
6. Remove the dish from the oven and serve the beans hot. The leftover beans can be stored in an airtight container for up to 3 days in the refrigerator. To reheat, bake them in a 350°F oven, covered, for 30 to 45 minutes, until bubbly and heated through.

# Black Bean Feijoada with Brazil Nuts

Feijoada, a stew of black beans with sausage and smoked meats, is the national dish of Brazil. We substitute Brazil nuts for some of the meat, and they add an unmistakable flavor of their own. Traditional feijoada is served as a main course, but our less meaty version works best as a side dish that pairs with simply prepared fish or shellfish or roasted meats.

PREPARATION TIME: *30 minutes*
COOKING TIME: *25 to 30 minutes*
MAKES: *6 to 8 servings*

2 tablespoons olive oil

2 large onions, chopped

4 ribs celery, chopped

4 cloves garlic, finely chopped

2 bay leaves

½ pound sweet pork sausages with fennel

3 cups cooked black beans (see box page 76) or two 15-ounce cans, drained and rinsed

1 cup (5 ounces) chopped Brazil nuts

1½ teaspoons kosher salt

½ teaspoon freshly ground black pepper

1. Heat the olive oil in a large saucepan over medium heat. Add the onions, celery, garlic, and bay leaves and cook until the onions are wilted, about 5 minutes. Remove the sausages from their casings and crumble them into the saucepan. Cook, stirring, until the sausages are browned, about 10 minutes.

2. Add the beans to the saucepan and stir in the Brazil nuts, salt, and pepper. Add 1 cup of water and bring to a boil. Lower the heat to a simmer and cook, covered, 10 to 15 minutes. Check during the cooking process and add more water if the level of the liquid dips below the beans.

3. When the beans are done, remove the pan from the heat and remove and discard the bay leaves. Season with salt and pepper to taste. Pour the feijoada into a serving dish and serve warm.

*Keema Matar (page 205) wrapped in pita*

# Saucing It Up

# Nuts and Bolts of Nut-Thickened Sauces

**Sauces, liquids that are served as an enhancement to a primary food, are** often thickened, because thick sauces stick to food and moisten it more efficiently than thin ones. While reductions, starches, spices, proteins, and fats are all effective thickening agents, nuts are wonderful, because they both thicken and add flavor (as opposed to cornstarch, for example).

Nuts and seeds thicken liquid in two ways. First, their oils can be emulsified in a sauce, thickening in a straightforward way. Second, the dry particles in the nuts and seeds can absorb liquids, acting as minute sponges, and thicken the sauce that way as well.

Usually either a protein (such as meat) is cooked directly in a sauce or the sauce is served over a separately cooked protein. Nut sauces of the second kind can also be served as spreads or dips, as we do with our Romesco, Skordalia, and Tarator in Chapter 2—they are truly versatile.

Nut-thickened sauces cross cultural boundaries, and nuts have been used to thicken sauces and stews for as long as mankind has cooked. One of the beauties of these sauces is that they can be used interchangeably with almost any protein, so while we suggest a certain protein with each recipe, feel free to substitute your preference.

Here is a review of nut-thickened sauces from around the world:

**SPAIN**: The most common of Spain's nut-thickened sauces is romesco, which can be used as a dip or a sauce; it is made with dried chiles and almonds and/or hazelnuts. Picada, a paste made from almonds, saffron, garlic, and parsley, is often stirred into a thinner liquid. Pepitoria, a third Spanish sauce is created with almonds, fried garlic, and hard-boiled egg and is not quite as common.

**ITALY**: Italy's classic sauce is pesto. Traditionally it is made from pine nuts, basil, and cheese, but more contemporary versions have included walnuts, peanuts, and cashews along with an assortment of fresh herbs.

**GREECE**: Greece features a sauce called skordalia, a paste made from almonds or walnuts in combination with stale bread or cooked potatoes, garlic, extra-virgin olive oil, and lemon juice or vinegar. Some versions of this sauce have yogurt in them.

**TURKEY**: The Turkish sauce tarator is similar to skordalia and consists of almonds, walnuts, or hazelnuts with garlic, bread, water, lemon juice, and olive oil.

**MEXICO**: The seemingly infinite variety of moles and pipians from Mexico feature sesame seeds, pumpkin seeds, peanuts, and almonds. There are sauces in every conceivable color, made from chiles, vegetables, spices, starches, and sometimes chocolate.

**INDIA**: India's korma dishes, mild curries that feature different meats and vegetables, are often thickened with almonds, cashews, coconut, or white poppy seeds.

**SOUTHEAST ASIA**: In general, the countries of Southeast Asia have a long history of coconut-milk curries, although they cannot be categorized under a single name.

# Pipian Rojo

Pipian, a traditional Mexican sauce, can be either red or green. (See Pipan Verde, page 199.) It is quite flavorful, and piquant without being overwhelmingly spicy. This is a simple red pipian made with both pumpkin seeds and sesame seeds. It really livens up a plain piece of chicken but goes equally well with pork, fish, or shrimp. The sauce can be made ahead, cooled, and kept for 3 days in the refrigerator, well covered.

PREPARATION TIME: *30 minutes, plus 30 minutes standing time for chiles*
COOKING TIME: *30 minutes*
MAKES: *3½ cups*

3 pasillo chiles, stems and seeds removed and discarded

3 ancho chiles, stems and seeds removed and discarded

4 tablespoons canola oil

1 large white onion, chopped

½ cup (2½ ounces) sesame seeds, toasted

½ cup (2¾ ounces) pumpkin seeds, toasted

2 teaspoons ground cumin

½ teaspoon ground cinnamon

1 teaspoon kosher salt

2 cups chicken stock

1. Place the chiles in a heatproof bowl and cover them with boiling water. Allow them to sit for 15 to 30 minutes, until they appear softened and are cool enough to touch. Drain them, place them in the food processor, and puree them well, about 45 seconds.

2. Heat the oil over medium-high heat in a large skillet. Add the onion and cook until it begins to brown, about 15 minutes. Add the pureed chiles. There will be some sizzling; do not worry. Grind the sesame seeds and the pumpkin seeds in a blender and add to the chiles in the skillet. (If the seeds do not grind easily, add 1 cup of the stock.) Season the mixture with the cumin, cinnamon, and salt, stirring well with a wooden spoon or heatproof spatula. Add the chicken stock and continue to cook until the sauce thickens, about 15 minutes. Serve immediately or refrigerate the sauce for up to 3 days in an airtight container.

3. Pipian Rojo can be served in a variety of ways. For example, season 2 pounds skinless bone-in chicken thighs with salt and pepper and brown them in 2 tablespoons of oil. Then cook them in the pipian for about 40 minutes, until tender and pulling away from the bone a tiny bit. Two pounds of cubed boneless pork shoulder also works well. If you chose to serve the pipian with fish or shrimp, cook the seafood separately in a simple manner and toss with the pipian before serving.

# Pipian Verde

Pipian verde is pipian rojo's cousin (see page 198); they have pumpkin seeds in common, but this is a sauce of a different color. Sprung from the same culinary roots, the verde version has a perkier tale to tell. It is made with lettuces and herbs to impart its green color, and it has green chiles to help with the heat.

PREPARATION TIME: *15 minutes*
COOKING TIME: *35 minutes*
MAKES: *5 cups*

4 tablespoons canola oil

1 large onion, chopped

4 green poblano chiles, roasted, peeled, stemmed, and seeded (see page 74)

1½ cups (8¼ ounces) pumpkin seeds, toasted

2 cloves garlic

1½ cups fresh cilantro leaves

8 leaves romaine lettuce, ribs removed, chopped

1 bunch watercress, tough stems removed

2 teaspoons crushed anise seeds

2 cups chicken stock

1½ teaspoons kosher salt

2 teaspoons sugar

1. Heat the oil in a large skillet over medium-high heat, add the onion, and cook until the onion begins to brown, about 15 minutes.

2. Process the chiles, pumpkin seeds, garlic, ¾ cup cilantro, the romaine lettuce, and the watercress in the work bowl of a food processor until pureed, about 1 minute. Add to the cooked onion and stir. Mix in the anise and chicken stock, stir until blended, and cook over medium heat for about 20 minutes, until the sauce thickens. Return the thickened sauce to the food processor and add the remaining ¾ cup cilantro. Puree for 1 minute, until smooth, then season with the salt and sugar.

3. Like pipian rojo, this sauce can be used in a variety of ways. To maintain its bright green color, do not cook it for a great length of time after the last bit of cilantro is added. In this case, it is best to cook a roast, such as duck, pork, or fish, separately and then add the sauce to the meat and heat them together.

# Mole Negro

The preparation of mole negro, from the Oaxaca and Puebla areas of Mexico, is a family affair, and a public ritual as well. The ingredients are assembled at home but traditionally taken to the community's *molidor*, where a professional grinds them together. Every family has its own recipe, but all include roasted chiles and some type of nut or seed, usually peanuts, almonds, sesame seeds, or pumpkin seeds. We developed this recipe based on information from a long list of sources, including writers Rick Bayless, Diana Kennedy, Susana Trilling, and Roberto Santibañez, but our greatest help came from Reina, the Pueblan dishwasher at Cara's restaurant, Quarropas, in White Plains, New York. On Mondays, when the restaurant was closed, Reina would often create a fabulous mole that was served with turkey for the staff meal. People sometimes assume that the deep brown color of mole negro comes from chocolate, which is frequently included, but the appealing color derives mostly from toasted chiles. Toasting those chiles is an art in itself, because they have to be cooked to just the right point—undercooked chiles will not pack enough of a roasted punch, and overcooked chiles will taste burned. We have tried to streamline this recipe to make the complex mole-making process as simple as possible without sacrificing the integrity of the results.

PREPARATION TIME: *45 minutes, plus 30 minutes standing time for chiles*
COOKING TIME: *1 hour 15 minutes*
MAKES: *5 cups*

3 ancho chiles, stems removed and discarded, seeds removed and saved

3 guajillo chiles, stems removed and discarded, seeds removed and saved

2 pasilla chiles, stems removed and discarded, seeds removed and saved

2 ripe medium tomatoes

4 tomatillos, husked

1 stale or day-old corn tortilla

1 slice day-old bread

4 tablespoons canola oil

¼ cup raisins

½ cup (2½ ounces) sesame seeds

½ cup (2½ ounces) almonds

½ cup (2½ ounces) roasted peanuts

3 cups chicken stock

6 cloves garlic

1 sprig thyme

1 sprig oregano

1½ ounces Abuelita brand Mexican drinking chocolate

1 teaspoon kosher salt

1. Place the three types of dried chiles in a medium heatproof bowl. Cover them with boiling water and set them aside until they are softened, about 30 minutes. While the chiles are soaking, heat a cast iron or very heavy skillet over medium-high heat, until it is nearly smoking hot. Place the reserved chile seeds into the hot skillet and toast them, stirring frequently, until they are golden brown, about 2 minutes. Pour them out of the skillet and set them aside.

2. Place the skillet back on medium-high heat, and add the tomatoes and tomatillos. Allow the heat to char the outside of the vegetables and, using a pair of tongs, rotate them until all sides are blackened. Be careful not to burn them, their blistered exteriors will add a smoky note to the sauce, but if they are burned they will taste acrid. Remove them, place them in another bowl, and set them aside.

3. While the skillet is back on medium-high heat, place the stale tortilla and the slice of bread into the pan. Toast them quickly, turning them over with the tongs to prevent burning, until they are both golden, about 2 minutes. Remove them from the skillet and set them aside with the tomatoes and tomatillos .

4. Carefully wipe the skillet with a clean towel, return it to the medium-high heat, and add 2 tablespoons of the oil. Add the raisins when the oil is hot—they will immediately plump up, in about 1 minute. Add the reserved chile seeds and the sesame seeds, almonds, and peanuts. Stir continuously with a kitchen spoon until all the nuts are toasted and golden, 3 to 5 minutes. Add 2 cups of the chicken stock and turn off the heat.

5. When the contents of the skillet are cool enough to handle, pour them into a blender. Drain the chiles from their soaking water, and add them to the blender. Add the cooled tomatoes and tomatillos. Tear up the toasted tortilla and bread and place them, along with the garlic cloves, in the blender.

6. Puree until smooth, 2 to 3 minutes. Add additional chicken stock, 1/4 cup at a time, to make sure the mixture becomes a thick liquid, blending another minute.

7. Heat the remaining 2 tablespoons of oil over medium heat in a large skillet until it is shimmering, and carefully add the puree from the blender. Add the thyme and oregano. Bring the sauce to a simmer; it will thicken as it cooks. After 15 minutes, break up the chocolate and whisk it into the simmering sauce. Continue to cook until the sauce has the thickness of a milkshake, about another 10 minutes. Remove the sprigs of thyme and oregano, and season with the salt. Serve hot, over roasted turkey or chicken, as it often is in Puebla and Oaxaca. The sauce can be made in advance, cooled, and refrigerated in an airtight container for up to 3 days.

# Mole Rojo

This is the red version of the mole sauce on page 200. The quantities of ingredients are different, as is the combination of chiles. Mole rojo is a little complicated, but its intense flavor is worth the required attention to detail. Again, this recipe was created from a compilation of sources such as Diana Kennedy, Rick Bayless, Susana Trilling, and Roberto Santibañez. Unfortunately, Reina did not make moles rojos, because they were not traditional in her family or her village. This is good with poultry, but its color and flavor are a perfect match for pork loin.

PREPARATION TIME: *45 minutes, plus 30 minutes standing time for chiles*
COOKING TIME: *1 hour 15 minutes*
MAKES: *5 cups*

12 ancho chiles, stems and seeds removed and discarded

12 red pasilla chiles, stems and seeds removed and discarded

2 ripe tomatoes, cored

1 medium onion, cut into quarters

8 cloves garlic

1 teaspoon kosher salt

½ teaspoon freshly ground black pepper

½ teaspoon ground cloves

½ teaspoon ground allspice

3 cups chicken stock

4 tablespoons canola oil

¼ cup (1¼ ounces) sesame seeds

½ cup (2½ ounces) blanched almonds

1. Heat a griddle or a cast iron skillet over medium-high heat and toast the chiles until slightly darkened on all sides, rotating them with tongs, 5 to 10 minutes. Remove them to a heatproof bowl. Pour boiling water over the chiles and let stand until cool, about 30 minutes. While they are cooling, char the tomatoes, onion, and garlic, using the same griddle or skillet. Place them in a blender; add the salt, pepper, cloves, and allspice and puree until smooth, about 2 minutes. If the mixture is too dry to puree successfully, add a little chicken stock. Set the mixture aside. Drain the cooled chiles and place them in the blender, in batches if necessary, and puree to liquefy, about 1 minute. Pass this mixture through a food mill or fine-mesh strainer to remove any seeds or skin. Set aside.

2. Wipe out the skillet or use a new one. Heat 2 tablespoons canola oil over medium-high heat until it is shimmering. Toast the sesame seeds over medium heat, stirring often, until they start to turn golden, about 3 minutes. Remove from the pan and set aside. Add the almonds to the skillet and stir. Cook until they are golden, about 5 minutes. Remove them from the pan and set aside. When they have cooled, grind them in a blender, adding ½ cup stock if necessary, and set aside.

3. Heat the remaining 2 tablespoons canola oil in the skillet over medium-high heat until it is shimmering. Cook the tomato mixture until it dries slightly, about 10 minutes. Add the chile mixture, stir well to combine, and cook for another 10 minutes. Add the nut mixture and whisk to ensure that it is well blended in. Whisk in the remaining stock and cook until the sauce has thickened, about 20 minutes. Serve the sauce with roasted pork loin or tenderloin. It can be made in advance, cooled, and refrigerated in an airtight container for up to 3 days.

*Keema Matar (page 205) served with pita bread and Coconut Chutney (page 97)*

# Keema Matar

Julie Sahni, the great Indian chef, has taught us plenty about the subcontinent's use of nuts. In this recipe, based loosely on Sahni's original from *Classic Indian Cooking*, the sauce is thickened with cashew butter. Sahni warns against using too much cashew butter, and we have found her recommendation of 3 tablespoons to be just right. It yields a sauce that has the texture of heavy cream and is just enough to bind the sauce and ground beef together. You can find cashew butter in most supermarkets these days; just make sure it is made from roasted and unsalted cashews. Sahni compares this dish to Texas chili, and like many slow-simmered dishes, it can be made up to 2 days ahead and reheated. Garnish the finished dish with some roughly chopped roasted cashews. *(See additional photo page 194.)*

PREPARATION TIME: *15 minutes*
COOKING TIME: *1 hour to 1 hour 15 minutes*
MAKES: *6 generous servings*

2 tablespoons canola oil

2 large onions, finely chopped

2 cloves garlic, finely chopped

1 tablespoon finely chopped ginger

1 tablespoon ground cumin

2 teaspoons ground coriander

1 teaspoon turmeric

½ teaspoon crushed red pepper flakes

1 teaspoon ground ginger

1 teaspoon ground fennel seeds

2 bay leaves

2 pounds lean ground beef

1½ teaspoons kosher salt

1 red bell pepper, seeded and chopped into 1-inch pieces

2 cups seeded chopped tomatoes

1½ cups cooked chickpeas (see page 76) or one 15-ounce can, drained and rinsed

1 bottle (12 ounces) pale Indian Beer, such as King Fisher

3 tablespoons cashew butter

½ cup (2½ ounces) chopped roasted cashews

1. Heat the oil in a large skillet over medium heat and add the onions. Cook until the onions are a deep golden and caramelized, stirring occasionally, about 15 minutes. Add the garlic and ginger and stir to combine, making sure nothing sticks to the bottom of the pan. Lower the heat and add the cumin, coriander, turmeric, red pepper flakes, ginger, fennel, and bay leaves. Cook the mixture on low heat for 5 more minutes, until the fragrance of the spices fills the air.

*continued*

2. Add the ground beef to the skillet and break it up with a spoon, mixing the meat with the onions and cooking it at the same time. Increase the heat to medium and continue cooking, stirring occasionally, until the meat is no longer pink, about 10 minutes. Season with the salt.

3. Add the bell pepper, tomatoes, chickpeas, beer, and cashew butter and mix well. Turn the heat to low and let the dish simmer for about 30 minutes. Stir 2 or 3 times during cooking to make sure nothing is sticking to the bottom of the skillet.

4. Stir in the chopped cashews and season with salt to taste. Serve in pita bread, in a bowl with the Pistachio Raita (page 86) or with the Coconut Chutney (page 97). Leftovers should be wrapped airtight and refrigerated for up to 3 days.

## Nut Oils and Nut Butters

The luscious fats in nuts make flavorful oils and butters that we happily use in our cooking and baking. These same fats can be a little fragile, with short shelf lives, but with proper purchase and storage they are terrific nut additions to your pantry. They deepen flavors, thicken sauces, moisturize baked goods, and add a smooth finish to salad dressings.

Oils that are cold pressed in small batches are the most flavorful ones. Walnuts, almonds, hazelnuts, pecans, macadamias, and pine nuts are used for this purpose. Before they are pressed, the nuts are lightly toasted. Our best advice for purchasing nut oils is think small, and only buy a quantity that you can use in 3 months. Once opened, rancidity becomes a problem. Keep them away from sunlight, and use them rapidly. Refrigeration will keep them tasty a little longer, but some oils become cloudy as a result. These oils contain Vitamin E and Omega 3 fatty acids. They do not hold up to heat, and are best used for finishing sauces or adding to a vinaigrette.

Peanut butter may be the great American favorite, but almond butter, cashew butter, and sunflower seed butter are following close behind. Untarnished as spreads on toast, we have learned to use them in baking, adding moisture and flavor to cakes and cookies. We whisk them into sauces instead of a roux, believing we've chosen a healthier and tastier path. We prefer the natural versions, or our homemade varieties (page 88) with very little or no added sugars. Butters have a longer shelf life than oils, but still need to be treated with care. The oils in natural butters tend to separate to the top, and they should be stirred into the body of the butter before using. We refrigerate them for up to six months, but often eat them straight from the jar with a spoon, and then they don't last that long!

# Korma Sauce with White Poppy Seeds

Korma is a versatile, mild curry sauce that is often thickened with nuts and white poppy seeds. In northern India, where korma originated, cashews and coconut are frequently used along with the poppy seeds. We always jump at any chance to use white poppy seeds, which are relatively unknown in the United States. (If you have trouble finding them, see Sources, page 365.) Korma is not just a sauce but also a braising liquid—it is meant to have food cooked in it rather than to be poured over cooked food. In step 2, after the onion and spice paste are cooked, add any fish, poultry, or meat that responds well to a quick braise. Or cook the protein separately and add it to the cooking sauce. One of our favorites is boneless chicken thighs. For added flavor, season them with salt and pepper and brown them in a separate skillet in 2 tablespoons canola oil before adding them to the cooked sauce.

PREPARATION TIME: *15 minutes*
COOKING TIME: *12 to 15 minutes*
MAKES: *3 cups*

2 large onions, chopped

4 cloves garlic, chopped

One 2-inch piece ginger, chopped

½ cup (2½ ounces) white poppy seeds

4 teaspoons ground cumin

4 teaspoons ground coriander

2 teaspoons turmeric

1 teaspoon ground cinnamon

1 teaspoon ground cardamom

½ teaspoon ground cloves

Small pinch saffron threads soaked in ¼ cup boiling water

4 tablespoons canola oil

2 cups plain yogurt

1 teaspoon kosher salt

1 teaspoon freshly ground black pepper

4 tablespoons freshly chopped cilantro

1. Puree the onions, garlic, and ginger in a blender. If the vegetables are too dry to puree, add water, 1 tablespoon at a time, until well blended. Add the poppy seeds and blend very well to crush them. Add all the ground spices and the saffron and blend well.

2. Heat the canola oil in a large skillet over medium heat until shimmering, about 2 minutes. Lower the heat, add the onion-spice mixture and cook over medium-low heat until it dries out and becomes fragrant, about 10 minutes. Stir the sauce to prevent sticking.

3. Whisk in the yogurt, salt, and pepper. Sprinkle the sauce with the chopped cilantro before serving. Serve hot.

# Basil–Pine Nut Pesto

This is the classic pesto, the one by which all others are defined. While *pesto* just means "paste," or a combination of ingredients that are mashed together, the world's most famous pesto is this combination of basil, garlic, cheese, pine nuts, and olive oil native to the Liguria region of Italy. This will seem like a very large amount of basil, but you will be amazed at how it breaks down and shrinks when processed.

PREPARATION TIME: *10 to 15 minutes*
MAKES: *1½ cups*

2 cloves garlic

½ cup (2½ ounces) pine nuts, toasted

4 cups (about 4 ounces) fresh basil leaves, loosely packed

1 cup extra-virgin olive oil

⅔ cup (¾ ounces) freshly grated Parmesan cheese

1 teaspoon kosher salt, or to taste

½ teaspoon freshly ground black pepper, or to taste

1. Pulse the garlic in the work bowl of a food processor 6 to 8 times, until finely chopped. Add the pine nuts and basil and process to a thick, finely ground paste, about 1 minute. With the machine running, pour in the olive oil in a slow, steady stream.

2. Scrape the pesto into a mixing bowl and stir in the Parmesan cheese and the salt and pepper. Pesto can be refrigerated for up to 1 week in an air tight container. To prevent it from discoloring, press a piece of plastic wrap directly on the surface before sealing the container.

3. To serve with pasta, cook 1 pound pasta until al dente (see box page 214). Before draining the pasta, ladle 1 cup of the pasta cooking water into a large saucepan, add the pesto, and stir over low heat until smooth and warm. Drain the pasta and add it to the pesto, tossing to coat. Serve immediately.

VARIATION: *Sage-Walnut Pesto*
Substitute 2 cups loosely packed sage, stems removed, for the basil and 1 cup (3½ ounces) toasted walnuts for the pine nuts.

VARIATION: *Parsley Pesto*
Substitute 4 cups loosely packed flat-leaf parsley, stems removed, for the basil. Also substitute either 1½ cups (5 ounces) toasted walnuts or 1 cup (5 ounces) toasted blanched hazelnuts for the pine nuts. Add ¼ cup walnut or hazelnut oil in addition to the 1 cup of extra-virgin olive oil.

VARIATION: *Sun-Dried Tomato and Hazelnut Pesto*

Substitute 2 cups (12 ounces) drained oil-packed sun-dried tomatoes for the basil and ¾ cup (3¾ ounces) toasted hazelnuts for the pine nuts.

VARIATION: *Three-Herb Pesto*

Substitute 1½ cups loosely packed basil, 1½ cups loosely packed flat-leaf parsley, and 1 cup fresh mint leaves, all stems removed, for the basil. Increase the toasted pine nuts to 1 cup (5 ounces). Increase the extra-virgin olive oil to 1¼ cups.

VARIATION: *Thai Peanut Pesto*

Add a 1-inch piece of fresh ginger, peeled and roughly chopped, to the food processor with the garlic. Replace the basil with 2 cups loosely packed cilantro and 2 cups loosely packed mint, both with stems removed. Substitute 1½ cups (7½ ounces) roasted peanuts for the pine nuts and peanut oil for the olive oil. Use 1 cup desiccated coconut flakes instead of Parmesan cheese. While the pasta is cooking, warm 1 cup unsweetened coconut milk in a large saucepan over low heat. Add 1 teaspoon sriracha sauce and 4 teaspoons fish sauce, then add the pesto and whisk until smooth and warm.

VARIATION: *Cashew Curry Pesto*

Add 3 roasted, peeled, and seeded red bell peppers (see box page 74) to the food processor with the garlic. Omit the basil and replace the pine nuts with 1½ cups (7½ ounces) roasted cashews. Add 1 tablespoon curry powder, 1 teaspoon ground cumin, and ¼ teaspoon cayenne pepper. Omit the black pepper. Mix with one cup of pasta cooking water and toss with 4 ounces mild goat cheese broken into ¼-inch pieces before serving.

VARIATION: *Pesto Cream Sauce*

Prepare half a recipe of Basil–Pine Nut Pesto and set aside. Heat 1 tablespoon olive oil in a saucepan over medium heat. Add 2 finely chopped shallots, season with 1 teaspoon salt, and cook, stirring, until the shallots are translucent, about 5 minutes. Pour in 2 cups heavy cream and simmer until lightly thickened, about 10 minutes. This replaces the pasta cooking water. Immediately before serving, stir the pesto into the cream sauce and whisk to blend. Serve immediately.

*Chilled Spicy Peanut Noodles (page 215), topped with scallions, peanuts, and black sesame seeds*

CHAPTER 8

# Noodles and Nuts

# Nuts and Bolts of Noodles

**Combining nuts and pasta is as natural as adding salt to pasta cooking** water (a must in our opinion). Many types of pasta are recommended in these recipes; soba noodles, rice vermicelli, fresh egg pasta, and dried semolina pasta. They are all different. Soba noodles are made from buckwheat flour and taste hardy and earthy. Rice vermicelli is threadlike and delicate. Fresh egg pasta is tender and soft and typically should be used immediately. Dried pasta is another thing altogether. Made from semolina flour and water, it keeps almost indefinitely and makes a quick base for a satisfying meal.

The sauce we toss our pasta with is as varied as our noodles. Pesto may be the most recognized nutty sauce for pasta and we've given many variations in Saucing It Up (see page 208). Here we have chosen to emphasize some of our other favorites, from Chilled Spicy Peanut Noodles (page 215) to Hungarian Poppy Noodles (page 220).

Dried pasta has a more substantial, chewier texture than fresh pasta and holds up to longer cooking times. Often you boil it in salted water, drain it in a colander, and then combine it with sauce on the stovetop for a few minutes, tossing it over low or medium heat so that it absorbs the sauce thoroughly. If the pasta is to be served at room temperature or is stuffed, a quick rinse with cold water while in the colander will stop the pasta from cooking and prepare it for a toss in a cold sauce or enable it to be handled for stuffing. (See box page 214 for more on cooking pasta.)

Dried pasta comes in an almost infinite variety of shapes—penne, fusilli, spaghetti, and so forth. Ironically, there are almost as many categories of pasta as there are types, including tubes, strands, micro pastas, and many more. Italians, who are, after all, the experts when it comes to pasta, will tell you that certain shapes should be paired with certain sauces; usually long pasta is matched with thin sauces and thick-cut pasta with chunky sauces. We're not quite so rigid. While we've chosen a preferred pasta shape for each recipe, in most cases you can substitute your favorite.

We tend to pair noodles and nuts with sauces of similar ethnic origins, although we believe there are no boundaries. Mixing and matching pasta varieties with world-ranging sauces may be an enlightening way to rearrange expected flavors.

One pound of pasta typically makes 4 large servings or 6 smaller servings. In Italy, pasta is served as a *primo*, or first course, followed by an entrée and vegetable side dishes, but for many Americans it is the ideal one-dish meal.

## Cooking Pasta

To cook 1 pound of fresh or dried pasta, bring 6 quarts water to a boil in a covered large pot over high heat. When the water is boiling, add 2 tablespoons kosher salt. Add the pasta. If you are cooking long dried pasta, such as spaghetti, wait a few seconds for the portion of the pasta in the water to soften, then use a wooden spoon to bend the pasta so its entire length is submerged. No matter what kind of pasta you are cooking, stir it immediately after you add it to the pot, reduce the heat to medium, return it to a boil, and then continue to stir occasionally throughout the process.

Dried pasta will take longer to cook than fresh pasta, and cooking times will vary according to the shape. Dried pasta can take anywhere from 6 minutes (for little shapes such as orzo and ditalini) to 15 minutes (for larger, thick shapes such as bucatini). Fresh pasta usually cooks much more quickly, in 3 to 5 minutes (provided it is not a filled ravioli, which may take a little longer). For dried pasta, start checking for doneness at 6 minutes by tasting a piece. When it is done, it should have a firm yet tender texture, with no hard white interior. Start checking fresh pasta at 3 minutes, also by tasting a piece. Fresh pasta will absorb less water than dried when cooking and will tend to float to the surface of the water when done. It too should have a firm yet tender texture. Be careful not to overcook either type—overcooked pasta is mushy and unappealing.

# Chilled Spicy Peanut Noodles

This is an upscale (and, dare we say, much tastier) version of the cold sesame noodles that used to come free with every Chinese takeout order in New York City. The black tea lends an astringent quality to the sauce that cuts the richness of the peanuts and really brings it all together. If you like the noodles fiery hot, increase the amount of chili oil; if you prefer them milder, cut the chili oil in half. *(See photo page 210.)*

PREPARATION TIME: *15 minutes*
COOKING TIME: *10 to 15 minutes*
MAKES: *4 to 6 servings*

### FOR THE NOODLES

1 pound soba noodles, Chinese-style egg noodles, or thick spaghetti

1½ teaspoons toasted sesame oil

### FOR THE PEANUT SAUCE

One 1-inch piece ginger, finely chopped

2 cloves garlic

½ cup smooth natural peanut butter

¼ cup soy sauce

2 tablespoons toasted sesame oil

2 tablespoons freshly squeezed lime juice

1 tablespoon rice wine vinegar

2 tablespoons honey

1½ teaspoons hot chili oil

1 tablespoon tahini

¼ to ½ cup brewed black tea, cooled

### FOR FINISHING

3 scallions, white and green parts, thinly sliced

½ cup (2½ ounces) coarsely chopped roasted peanuts

1 tablespoon (¼ ounce) black sesame seeds (optional)

1. Cook the noodles. (See box page 214.)
2. Drain in a colander and rinse under cold water. Drain well and transfer to a bowl. Toss with the sesame oil and refrigerate while preparing the sauce.
3. Make the sauce: Process the ginger and garlic in the work bowl of a food processor for 15 to 20 seconds, until finely chopped. Add the peanut butter, soy sauce, sesame oil, lime juice, vinegar, honey, chili oil, and tahini and process until the sauce is smooth, about 1 minute. With the machine running, drizzle in ¼ cup black tea to thin and flavor the sauce. If needed, add an additional ¼ cup of black tea if your sauce is still as thick as sour cream. Transfer the sauce to a bowl, cover, and chill until ready to use. The sauce will keep for 3 days.
4. To serve, toss the noodles with the sauce until they are evenly coated. Place on a serving platter and sprinkle the scallions, peanuts, and sesame seeds, if you like, over the top.

*Almond-Crusted Macaroni and Cheese (page 217)*

# Almond-Crusted Macaroni and Cheese

Macaroni and cheese is one of the most notable American comfort foods, with a long, gooey, and yummy history. It was already on the menu at the White House during Thomas Jefferson's administration; Jefferson even had the pasta imported from Italy. The addition of a crisp almond crust makes this warm, homey dish truly stupendous. This macaroni and cheese makes a great repository for bits of leftovers, such as ½ cup diced ham, a cup of steamed broccoli florets, or even a cup of sliced mushrooms, lightly sautéed in a little olive oil. Just mix any of them, or a combination of them, into the sauce when you are adding the pasta. If you like your mac and cheese with a little kick, add ½ teaspoon cayenne pepper with the salt.

PREPARATION TIME: *30 minutes*
BAKING TIME: *30 minutes*
MAKES: *8 large servings*
EQUIPMENT: *One 9-by-13-inch gratin or casserole dish, lightly buttered*

1 quart whole milk

2 bay leaves

½ stick (4 tablespoons) unsalted butter

½ cup all-purpose flour

1 teaspoon kosher salt

½ teaspoon freshly ground black pepper

Pinch freshly grated nutmeg

6 cups (24 ounces) shredded cheese of any kind, such as sharp cheddar, havarti, or a combination

1 pound short pasta, such as elbows, medium shells, or farfalle

1 cup (4½ ounces) finely chopped slivered almonds

¾ cup plain dry breadcrumbs

1 tablespoon freshly chopped thyme

1. Preheat the oven to 350°F.
2. Pour the milk into a medium saucepan. Add the bay leaves and set the pan over low heat. (If the milk starts to bubble around the edges, remove it from the heat.) Melt the butter in a medium saucepan over low heat. Gradually whisk in the flour and continue to cook, stirring occasionally, until smooth and bubbling, about 5 minutes. The butter-and-flour mixture will begin to stick to the bottom of the pan slightly; be careful not to let it scorch. Remove the bay leaves from the milk and gradually whisk the hot milk into the butter-flour mixture. Bring to a boil over medium heat, then lower the

*continued*

heat and cook, stirring frequently and paying special attention to the bottom edges of the pan, until the mixture thickens, about 10 minutes. Season with the salt, pepper, and nutmeg. Add the shredded cheese and stir until the cheese is melted and the sauce is smooth. Keep the sauce over low heat, stirring occasionally, until the pasta is ready.

3. Cook the pasta until al dente (see box page 214).

4. Drain the pasta in a colander and add it to the sauce. Toss until thoroughly coated. Transfer the pasta and sauce to the gratin dish. Stir the almonds, breadcrumbs, and thyme together in a small bowl. Strew the mixture evenly over the top of the pasta. Bake until bubbly and browned, about 30 minutes. Serve immediately.

# Cashew and Coconut Rice Vermicelli

Rice vermicelli, sometimes called rice sticks, are long, skinny noodles sold dried in cellophane packages. It takes very little time to cook them, if you can really call their preparation cooking. All it takes is a pot of boiling water with 2 tablespoons of kosher salt. Drop the noodles in and turn off the heat—no boiling or simmering is necessary. Within minutes the noodles are soft. Drain them, and they are ready to be tossed with sauce and served. The sauce here is a coconut concoction infused with ginger and lemongrass and thickened with ground cashews. Great in its unadorned state, the dish can be enlivened with julienned snow peas and red peppers for a little added color and crunch. The noodles' chewy, sticky texture has a comforting appeal.

PREPARATION TIME: *10 minutes*
COOKING TIME: *25 minutes*
MAKES: *4 to 6 servings*

2 tablespoons olive oil

½ cup finely chopped shallots

One 1-inch piece ginger, finely grated

2 stalks lemongrass (bottom 3 inches only), trimmed and chopped

2 cups unsweetened coconut milk

½ cup (2½ ounces) finely ground roasted cashews

2 tablespoons honey

¼ cup freshly squeezed lime juice

1 pound rice vermicelli

¼ cup (¾ ounce) unsweetened coconut flakes, toasted

1 teaspoon kosher salt

½ teaspoon freshly ground black pepper

½ bunch chives, finely chopped

1. Heat the oil in a large saucepan over medium heat. Add the shallots, ginger, and lemongrass. Cook, stirring occasionally, until softened and fragrant, about 5 minutes.

2. Pour the coconut milk into the pan and bring to a boil. Lower the heat until the liquid is simmering and cook for 5 minutes. Remove from the heat, cover, and let sit for 15 minutes.

3. Using a fine-mesh sieve, strain the coconut milk mixture into a bowl. Discard the solids and return the coconut milk to the pan over medium heat. Whisk in the ground cashews, honey, and lime juice and cook until the milk begins to thicken, about 5 minutes.

4. Meanwhile, prepare the rice vermicelli (see headnote).

5. Drain the vermicelli in a colander and add them to the sauce. Toss to coat well and add the toasted coconut. Season with the salt and pepper, sprinkle with chives, and serve immediately.

# Hungarian Poppy Noodles

Eastern Europeans use nuts and seeds in many parts of their meals, not just desserts. Our friend Kathy Offner suggested this recipe, which we based on a recipe of her mother's, a Hungarian Holocaust survivor. We think the homey combination of golden brown onions and deep blue poppy seeds is just right. The noodles are soft and the poppy seeds are hard, and the textural contrast makes this an interesting side dish. We love mixing in some cottage cheese or fresh ricotta with leftovers.

PREPARATION TIME: *5 minutes*
COOKING TIME: *20 to 25 minutes*
MAKES: *4 to 6 servings*

1 stick (8 tablespoons) unsalted butter

4 onions, cut into ½-inch dice

½ teaspoon kosher salt

¼ cup (1¼ ounces) poppy seeds

1 pound wide egg noodles

Freshly ground black pepper

1. Melt the butter in a medium saucepan over medium heat. Add the onions, season with the salt, and cook, stirring, until the onions begin to turn golden, 10 to 15 minutes. Add the poppy seeds and stir to mix.
2. Cook the noodles until al dente (see box page 214).
3. Remove 1 cup water from the cooking noodles and stir it into the onion-poppy mixture. Drain the noodles in a colander and add them to the poppy-onion sauce. Toss to coat the noodles well. Transfer to a serving dish, season with salt and pepper to taste, and serve immediately

# Linguine with Tuna-Walnut Sauce

Our friend Ron Ciavolino was a gentleman, a master sommelier, and an amazing cook. His predilection was for Italian food, and he was quite talented at teaching his students how to appreciate the simple marvels of authentic Italian cuisine. This Sicilian-style recipe comes from his repertoire. He always used Italian tuna packed in oil, believing that the American water-packed version just had no punch. He was an instructor who taught wine classes in a suit, with a well-folded pocket square. His recipes are just as elegant as he was.

PREPARATION TIME: *10 minutes*
COOKING TIME: *20 to 25 minutes*
MAKES: *4 servings*

1¾ cups (15 ounces) Italian tuna packed in oil, strained and oil reserved

½ cup (3 ounces) Italian sun-dried tomatoes packed in oil, strained and oil reserved

1 large ripe tomato

½ cup extra-virgin olive oil

2 cloves garlic, chopped

¾ cup (2½ ounces) coarsely chopped walnut pieces

½ cup dry white wine

½ cup quartered Gaeta olives packed in oil

1 teaspoon kosher salt

1 teaspoon freshly ground black pepper

1 pound linguini

¼ cup finely chopped flat-leaf parsley

¼ teaspoon crushed red pepper flakes (optional)

1. Place the tuna and 2 tablespoons of its oil in a small bowl. Break the tuna into small pieces and set aside. Coarsely chop the sun-dried tomatoes and add them, with 2 tablespoons of their oil, to the tuna. Coarsely chop the fresh tomato and add it with all of its juices to the tuna and sun-dried tomatoes.

2. Heat the olive oil in a large skillet over medium heat. Add the garlic and cook briefly, about 30 seconds. Add the tuna mixture and the walnuts to the oil, bring to a simmer, and cook, uncovered, for 5 minutes. The sauce will thicken slightly.

3. Add 1 cup water, the wine, olives, salt, and pepper to the sauce. Cover and simmer gently for 10 minutes. If mixture begins to look too dry, add more water and olive oil, but no more than ¼ cup of each.

4. While the sauce is simmering, cook the linguini until al dente (see box page 214).

5. Drain the linguini in a colander and add it to the sauce. Toss to coat well. Transfer to a serving dish and sprinkle with parsley and the red pepper flakes if you like. Season with salt and black pepper to taste and serve immediately.

# Southern Italian Spaghetti with Pine Nuts

This pasta has its roots in Sicily but is perfectly at home on the American dinner table. We use it as a main course because the inclusion of broccoli rabe and cauliflower makes it a well-rounded dish. Anchovies, raisins, and pine nuts provide the salty, sweet, and savory elements so typically combined in Sicily. We see pine nuts as precious nuggets of goodness for their rich, smooth flavor, and they are well represented in this dish, tossed with a heavy hand. What a trio of flavors, and what a glorious pasta!

PREPARATION TIME: *10 minutes*
COOKING TIME: *30 minutes*
MAKES: *4 to 6 servings*

1 bunch broccoli rabe (½ pound), roughly chopped into 1½-inch pieces, tough bottoms of stems removed

½ cup olive oil

3 anchovy fillets, mashed

2½ cups (½ head, 10 ounces) cauliflower, cored and chopped into bite-sized pieces

2 cloves garlic, finely chopped

¾ cup dry white wine

1 teaspoon kosher salt

½ teaspoon freshly ground black pepper

½ cup (2½ ounces) pine nuts, toasted

¼ cup raisins

2 tablespoon freshly squeezed lemon juice

½ cup panko breadcrumbs

1 pound spaghetti

2 tablespoons freshly chopped flat-leaf parsley

Freshly grated Parmesan cheese

1. Preheat the oven to 350°F.
2. Bring a large saucepan of water to a boil over high heat. Set a bowl of ice water near the sink. Add the broccoli rabe to the boiling water and cook for 1 to 2 minutes, until it is slightly softened and bright green. Drain in a colander in the sink and then submerge the broccoli rabe in the bowl of ice water. Drain thoroughly and set aside.
3. Heat 4 tablespoons (¼ cup) oil in a large skillet over medium heat. Add the anchovies and cook until they begin to sizzle, about 30 seconds. Add the cauliflower and the garlic and cook for 1 minute; be careful not to burn the garlic.
4. Add the wine and season with the salt and pepper. Cook, covered, until the cauliflower is tender, about 4 minutes. Uncover and continue to cook until the wine is evaporated and the edges of the cauliflower begin to brown, about 5 minutes.
5. Stir in the broccoli rabe, pine nuts, and raisins and cook until warmed through, about 2 minutes. Remove from the heat and stir in the lemon juice. Set aside.

6. Toss the panko with 2 tablespoons of the remaining olive oil until the panko is evenly moistened. Spread into a thin layer on a rimmed baking sheet. Bake until the breadcrumbs are golden and crunchy, about 8 minutes.

7. Cook the spaghetti until al dente (see box page 214). Reserve 1 cup of pasta water.

8. Drain the spaghetti in a colander and transfer to a serving bowl. Drizzle with the remaining 2 tablespoons olive oil, add the cauliflower and broccoli rabe mixture and the pasta water, and toss. Sprinkle with the breadcrumbs and parsley. Serve warm, with the Parmesan cheese and freshly ground black pepper.

# Fettuccine with Leeks, Shrimp, and Toasted Almonds

In her first job after cooking school, Cara worked the hot line in a very busy Italian restaurant in New York City. One of the things she cooked every evening was a dish of tagliatelle, a wide, flat pasta, tossed with a huge pile of leeks. The leeks were packed with dirt when they arrived at the restaurant, and buckets of them had to be prepped during the day. Their green tops were lopped off and the remaining white bulbs were split down the middle, then rinsed, soaked, and rinsed again before they were sliced. Here we use plenty of leeks, and we advise you to make sure they are fully cleaned before you cook them. Mixed with shrimp and almonds, they remind us of the earth they came from, brightened by the brine of the sea.

PREPARATION TIME: *20 minutes*
COOKING TIME: *10 to 15 minutes*
MAKES: *4 to 6 servings*

3 tablespoons olive oil

4 large leeks, white parts only, split lengthwise, cleaned, and thinly sliced

2 cloves garlic, finely chopped

1 pound (about 24) large shrimp, peeled and deveined

1 cup dry white wine

1 cup chicken stock

1½ teaspoons kosher salt

1 teaspoon freshly ground black pepper

1½ cups (6 ounces) sliced almonds, toasted

¼ cup freshly chopped flat-leaf parsley

¼ cup freshly chopped basil

3 tablespoons unsalted butter

2 tablespoons freshly squeezed lemon juice

1 pound fresh or dried fettuccine

1. Heat the oil in a large skillet over medium heat. Add the leeks and garlic and cook, stirring occasionally, until softened, about 5 minutes.

2. Add the shrimp and toss until they turn pink, about 2 minutes. Gradually pour in the wine and chicken stock. Add the salt and pepper and continue to cook, stirring occasionally, until the shrimp are cooked through, about 3 minutes. Stir in the almonds, parsley, basil, butter, and lemon juice.

3. Cook the fettuccine until al dente (see box page 214).

4. Drain the fettuccine in a colander and transfer to a serving bowl. Toss with the sauce, season with salt and pepper to taste, and serve immediately.

# Creamy Potato Ravioli with Walnuts

You won't find these ravioli on any menu in Italy. The word *ravioli* comes from an Italian dialect word for garbage, because in the most frugal, creative recycling of leftovers, ravioli makers used any odd bits of cooked food to create fillings. These are an American comfort-food spin on the Italian classic. We use mashed potatoes and add nuts and cheese for the filling. We prefer to use high-quality wonton wrappers for the pasta. This makes creating the delicious morsels easy.

PREPARATION TIME: *30 minutes, plus 1 hour to cool the filling*
COOKING TIME: *45 minutes*
MAKES: *4 to 6 servings*

### FOR THE RAVIOLI

2 medium Yukon Gold potatoes (9 ounces), peeled and cut into 1-inch dice

1½ teaspoons kosher salt

1 tablespoon olive oil

1 small onion, cut into ¼-inch dice

1 clove garlic, chopped

½ cup (2 ounces) coarsely grated sharp cheddar cheese

¼ cup (1 ounce) finely chopped walnuts, toasted

½ teaspoon freshly ground black pepper

1 tablespoon freshly chopped sage

1 package wonton wrappers (see box page 226)

### FOR FINISHING

1 stick (8 tablespoons) unsalted butter

1 cup (3½ ounces) chopped walnuts, lightly toasted

Kosher salt and freshly ground black pepper

1. Place the potatoes in a medium saucepan and cover with cold water. Add 1 teaspoon salt and bring to a boil over medium-high heat. Reduce the heat to medium and simmer until the potatoes are soft, about 20 minutes. Drain in a colander. Place the potatoes in a bowl and mash them with a potato masher, or put them through a ricer. Set aside.

2. Heat the olive oil in a medium skillet over medium heat. Add the onion and garlic and cook until the onion is translucent, about 5 minutes. Add the onion and garlic to the potatoes. Stir them in, along with the cheddar and walnuts. Season with the remaining ½ teaspoon salt, the pepper, and the sage. The filling can be made up to 2 days ahead and kept in the refrigerator, wrapped airtight.

3. When ready to fill the ravioli, place 6 wonton wrappers on a lightly floured surface. Drop 1 tablespoon (about ½ ounce) filling onto the center of each wrapper.

*continued*

4. Using a pastry brush dipped lightly in water, paint the perimeter of one wrapper. Place another wrapper on top and gently press around the filling to push out any air and seal the ravioli. Repeat using the remaining wrappers and filling. The ravioli can be stacked between sheets of parchment paper, wrapped in plastic wrap, and refrigerated in an airtight container for up to 2 days.

5. When ready to serve, melt the butter in a large skillet over low heat and add the walnuts. Cook the ravioli in the boiling water (see box page 214) in batches of 6; when they float to the surface and are cooked through, about 5 minutes, remove them with a slotted spoon and add them to the skillet. Keep the skillet on low heat until all the ravioli are cooked and have been tossed in the butter. Season with salt and pepper to taste and serve warm.

### Wonton Wrappers

Nothing beats homemade egg pasta dough when it comes to making ravioli and other kinds of stuffed pasta. But life is complicated, and sometimes we don't have the time to roll out and cut our own dough. That's when we reach for packaged wonton wrappers, the type used to make Chinese pot stickers. You can find them in Asian markets and more and more often in the ethnic foods sections of mainstream grocery stores. Look for the ones that are thick white rounds; we find that these hold up best during cooking.

# Spinach, Pine Nut, and Ricotta–Stuffed Manicotti

Manicotti are wide sleeves of pasta that are usually cooked, filled with a stuffing, then layered in a baking dish and baked. We've always loved the classic filling of ricotta and spinach but have found that it can be a little mushy. A cup of toasted chopped pine nuts tossed into the mix solves that problem and elevates this Italian-American classic to new status.

PREPARATION TIME: *35 to 40 minutes*
BAKING TIME: *45 minutes, plus 10 minutes standing time*
MAKES: *6 generous portions*
EQUIPMENT: *One 9-by-13-inch baking dish*

### FOR THE SAUCE

2 pounds plum tomatoes, blanched, skins removed, and chopped, or one 28-ounce can whole tomatoes or crushed tomatoes.

6 tablespoons olive oil

1 onion, chopped

½ cup freshly chopped basil

½ cup full-bodied red wine, such as Merlot or Cabernet Sauvignon

Kosher salt and freshly ground black pepper

### FOR THE PASTA

1 pound (14 pieces) dried manicotti

### FOR THE FILLING

1 tablespoon olive oil

1 large clove garlic, finely chopped

1 pound baby spinach rinsed

Kosher salt and freshly ground black pepper

½ pound fresh ricotta cheese (see box page 229)

½ cup (2½ ounces) finely chopped toasted pine nuts

¼ cup (⅓ ounce) freshly grated Parmesan cheese

1 tablespoon finely chopped flat-leaf parsley

Freshly grated nutmeg

### FOR FINISHING

1 cup (8 ounces) shredded mozzarella cheese

Freshly grated Parmesan cheese

Freshly ground black pepper

*continued*

1. Preheat the oven to 350°F.

2. Make the sauce: In a blender or the work bowl of a food processor, puree the tomatoes until smooth, about 1 minute. Heat the oil in a medium saucepan over medium heat and add the onion. Cook until the onion is translucent, about 5 minutes. Gently add the tomato sauce. Stir in the basil and red wine and season with salt and pepper to taste. Bring the sauce to a simmer, reduce the heat to low, and continue cooking while you are preparing the filling.

3. For the pasta: Cook the manicotti (see box page 214) until tender but firm, 8 to 9 minutes. Drain carefully so the manicotti do not break, then rinse under cold water. Drain again and set aside.

4. Make the filling: Heat the olive oil in a large skillet over medium heat. Add the garlic and stir until fragrant, about 2 minutes. Be careful not to let the garlic brown. Add the spinach, season lightly with salt and pepper, and stir just until the spinach is wilted. Be careful not to overcook the spinach, or it will be bitter. Immediately remove the skillet from the heat, scrape the spinach into a colander to drain, and let it cool.

5. When the spinach is cool, chop it coarsely and put it in a medium bowl. Stir in the ricotta, pine nuts, Parmesan, and parsley. Season with salt, pepper, and nutmeg to taste. Using a spoon, fill the manicotti shells with the spinach filling.

6. Spread half the tomato sauce over the bottom of the baking dish. Place the filled manicotti in the dish (they should fit snugly) and top with the remaining sauce. Scatter the mozzarella over the top and cover the dish with aluminum foil. Bake for 30 minutes. Uncover and bake until bubbly, about 15 minutes more. Let stand for 10 minutes before serving. Serve with freshly grated Parmesan and season with pepper to taste.

## Fresh Ricotta

Fresh ricotta is not actually a cheese but a byproduct of cheesemaking. It can easily be made at home, but it is commercially available at Italian specialty stores year round and is especially plentiful during the holiday seasons. It is scooped from its pot when made and then strained. The resulting product is far superior to standard supermarket brands. It is very light in texture, smooth in flavor, and quite perishable. It will spoil about 4 days after it is purchased, so plan ahead to use it all.

*Roasted Halibut with Pistachio Crust and Herb Vinaigrette (page 234)*

CHAPTER 9

# Family Style

# Nuts and Bolts of Family Style

**Lots of very different dishes are included in this chapter, and all the** recipes focus on a protein in the center of the plate: fish, seafood, poultry, or meat. They utilize a long list of cooking methods, such as roasting, braising, sautéing, and poaching. As we experimented and developed these recipes, we discovered something amazing: any main dish is open to the inclusion of nuts. They play a wide variety of roles here, and they play them all well. They form crusts and fill stuffings, garnish sauces and shine through stews. We have chosen recipes that are simple to prepare but are chock-full of flavor, and are based on ingredients that are easy to purchase.

Our first group of recipes focuses on fish, and we utilize three cuts of them: thin fillets, thick fillets, and steaks. For example, flounder is a thin fillet, and halibut is a thick fillet. Salmon is cut into thick fillets or steaks. As long as you use fish from the same category, they are generally interchangeable. And since freshness is paramount with fish, you're better off substituting something that looks good for the fish called for in the recipe rather than buying something subpar simply because that's the variety of fish we've indicated on the page. Selecting the freshest is straightforward, but when shopping for fish that has already been removed from the bone, some freshness indicators are already out of sight. Start with a reputable fishmonger, and choose fish that looks and smells fresh: shiny skin, smooth and moist flesh, and the faint hint of the sea.

Seafood also makes an appearance in this chapter. We use shrimp like a convenience food, keeping it in the freezer and using it when a culinary whim takes hold. Soft-shell crabs are a favorite but seasonal indulgence that had to be included, being on our short list of all-time favorite foods.

Chicken is the go-to dinner for many folks. With its categorical cousin duck, chicken takes a worldwide tour here and lands in the center of our plate for many reasons. It is low in fat, has a mild flavor, is appealing to almost everyone, and like a culinary chameleon, can change styles and flavors to fit any mood. We find it quick and easy to prepare and delicious to eat.

We don't eat as much meat as we used to, but nuts complement the flavor of meat beautifully, and help round out gaps in nutritional needs. Many of our meat recipes feature a long, slow braise, coaxing the richest flavors and most tender textures from the protein. Quick sautés and pan sears also have their place, and as for all our meat dishes, nuts and seeds elevate them to a beautiful central role in family-style cooking.

# Roasted Halibut with Pistachio Crust and Herb Vinaigrette

Halibut has become a bit of a luxury, but we splurge on it every now and then. Thick and substantial, the pistachio topping and herb vinaigrette stand out like stars with it. The crust on the fish acts like a shield, keeping the moisture in. We pile on enough to build a good green layer and roast it until the fish just begins to firm up. The pistachios get a little crumbly and golden around the edges, and we like that. The vinaigrette is best made shortly before you use it, so it keeps its fresh herbal vibrancy. *(See photo page 230.)*

PREPARATION TIME: *25 minutes*
ROASTING TIME: *10 minutes*
MAKES: *4 servings*

Four 6 to 8-ounce halibut fillets

½ cup whole milk

1 cup (5 ounces) pistachios

¼ cup breadcrumbs

¼ cup plus 2 tablespoons olive oil

2 tablespoons freshly chopped basil

1 tablespoon chopped thyme

1 shallot, finely chopped

1 teaspoon kosher salt

½ teaspoon freshly ground black pepper

FOR THE VINAIGRETTE

¼ cup white wine vinegar

1 clove garlic, finely chopped

1 shallot, finely chopped

¾ cup olive oil

½ cup freshly chopped basil

1 teaspoon kosher salt

½ teaspoon freshly ground black pepper

1. Preheat the oven to 400°F.
2. Place the fish in a shallow nonreactive pan and pour the milk over it. Set it aside.
3. Process the pistachios in the work bowl of a food processor, until roughly chopped, about 10 seconds. Add the breadcrumbs, ¼ cup oil, basil, thyme, and shallot. Pulse until the mixture forms a bright green paste, about 1 minute. Little chunks of pistachio will dot the mixture, and that adds a little crunch to the crust.
4. Remove the fish from the milk and lightly pat it dry. Drizzle 1 tablespoon oil onto a shallow baking pan and place the fish on top. Season the fish with the salt and pepper. Divide the pistachio mixture equally among the fillets and pat it down to help it stick. Pour the remaining 1 tablespoon oil on top.
5. Roast the fish for 10 minutes, until it is just firm and the green crust becomes a little browned around the edges.

6. Make the vinaigrette: Place the vinegar in small mixing bowl and add the garlic and shallot. Slowly whisk in the olive oil. Add the basil, salt, and pepper and stir well. (If you make the vinaigrette a day in advance, leave the basil out and add it at the last minute, so it does not lose its color.)

7. Spoon half the sauce onto a serving platter and place the halibut on top. Serve the remaining sauce in a bowl with a spoon on the side.

# Grilled Salmon Steaks with Pistachio-Lime Butter

Compound butters are a good something-up-your-sleeve way to make a simple weeknight main course a little special. Compound butters are simply butter amalgamated with all kinds of ingredients, and they can be made weeks ahead and frozen or days ahead and refrigerated. Countless combinations of herbs and nuts can beautifully top a perfectly grilled piece of fish; this is just one of our favorites.

PREPARATION TIME: *20 minutes, plus 1 hour for the butter to chill*
GRILLING TIME: *8 to 10 minutes per salmon steak*
MAKES: *4 generous servings*

### FOR THE COMPOUND BUTTER

1 stick (8 tablespoons) unsalted butter, softened

1 shallot, finely chopped

1 tablespoon freshly squeezed lime juice

½ cup (2½ ounces) coarsely chopped pistachios, toasted

1 tablespoon finely chopped chives

½ teaspoon kosher salt

¼ teaspoon freshly ground black pepper

### FOR THE SALMON

Four 6-ounce salmon steaks

2 tablespoons freshly squeezed lime juice

2 tablespoons olive oil

½ teaspoon kosher salt

½ teaspoon freshly ground black pepper

1. Make the compound butter: Pulse the softened butter in the work bowl of a food processor for 30 seconds, until smooth. Add the remaining ingredients and process for 10 to 15 seconds, until everything is well mixed. Scrape the mixture onto a piece of parchment paper and roll it up into a cylinder about 1½ inches in diameter. Twist both ends of the parchment, squeezing the butter to tighten. Place in the refrigerator for at least 1 hour, until the butter is firm, or up to 3 days. Alternatively, wrap the butter in plastic and freeze for up to 3 months.

2. Prepare the salmon: Heat an outdoor grill or a grill pan on the stovetop to medium-high heat. In a nonreactive plate or bowl, coat the salmon with the lime juice, olive oil, salt, and pepper. Grill the steaks about 4 minutes on each side, until they are just firm to the touch and slightly charred. As soon as they come off the grill, place a ½-inch slice of compound butter on top of each one; it will melt, coating the steak and leaving bites of pistachios on top. Serve warm.

VARIATION: *Sesame-Cardamom Butter*

Replace the pistachios with ¼ cup (1¼ ounces) toasted sesame seeds and the chives with ¼ teaspoon ground cardamom. Add 1 tablespoon roasted sesame oil while pulsing the butter.

VARIATION: *Walnut-Tarragon Butter*

Replace the pistachios with ½ cup (1¾ ounces) coarsely chopped toasted walnuts and the chives with 1 tablespoon finely chopped tarragon.

---

## Compound Butters

While traditional French cooking features compound butters with just shallots and herbs, we have found that nuts and seeds provide terrific variations from the expected. Here are some of our favorite combinations. We pop a thin slice of the butter onto almost any grilled fish, or on chicken. Be careful: a little goes a long way.

# Black and White Sesame–Crusted Trout with Chive Oil

We are happy to serve farm-raised rainbow trout, which are farmed in an ecologically sound way, without any negative impact to the environment. Nearly all the trout available in America is farm-raised, and the industry sets an example as a producer of environmentally friendly and healthy food. Trout is a delicate and tasty fish and can be prepared in a flash. Ask your fishmonger to remove the head if it doesn't please you on the plate. Both black and white sesame seeds are used to create the speckled crust. Because the fish is fried flat in a skillet, you can cook only one at a time in an average pan. If you are serving a group, cook the fish one by one and place them on a rack on a pan in a 250°F oven while the rest are cooking. We like to serve these drizzled with a little chive oil, which adds both color and a perky freshness. It can be made a day ahead and kept airtight in the refrigerator.

PREPARATION TIME: *10 minutes, plus 8 hours for the oil to chill*
COOKING TIME: *5 to 7 minutes per trout*
MAKES: *4 generous servings*

### FOR THE CHIVE OIL

1 bunch chives

½ cup olive oil

### FOR THE TROUT

4 freshwater trout, boned and trimmed

¾ cup whole milk

¼ cup (1¼ ounces) white sesame seeds

¼ cup (1¼ ounces) black sesame seeds

¼ cup all-purpose flour

1 teaspoon kosher salt

½ teaspoon freshly ground black pepper

2 tablespoons canola oil

1. Make the chive oil: Bring a small saucepan filled with water to a boil and drop in the chives. Immediately remove them and plunge them into a bowl of ice water to stop their cooking. Drain them well and pat them dry. Place them in a blender with the olive oil and puree until smooth, about 1 minute. Transfer to an airtight container and steep in the refrigerator overnight. Strain the oil well by pouring it through a double layer of moistened cheesecloth set inside a strainer. Refrigerate the oil in a sealed container until ready to use.

2. Preheat the oven to 250°F.

3. Prepare the fish: Place the trout in a medium bowl and pour the milk over it, ensuring that the fish are all covered. In another bowl, mix the white sesame seeds, black sesame seeds, flour, salt and pepper. Heat the canola oil in a large skillet over medium heat.

Remove the trout one by one from the milk, allowing any excess milk to drip off. Place the trout flesh side down into the seed mixture and press. Flip the fish over and dredge the skin side. One by one, place the trout flesh side down into the skillet and cook until it begins to whiten and firm up, about 3 minutes. Flip the trout and cook for 2 more minutes. Keep the cooked trout in the warm oven on a rimmed baking sheet until all of them have been cooked. To serve, drizzle some chive oil on a serving platter and place the fish on top. Serve warm.

# Sautéed Flounder with Pecan Succotash

Succotash is a mélange of vegetables, usually lima beans and corn. The word, referring to cooked corn, comes from the language of the Native American Narragansett tribe, who lived in what is now New England. The addition of pecans is our modern twist, but it is in keeping with the wholly American feel. Fillet of flounder is easy to cook and is ecologically sustainable, making it a responsible choice to pair with these vegetables. Simply sautéed in a skillet, this is a dish best served in the summer when beans, corn, and tomatoes are at their peak.

PREPARATION TIME: *15 minutes*
COOKING TIME: *10 minutes, plus 2 minutes per flounder fillet*
MAKES: *4 generous servings*

1 cup fresh shelled lima beans

1 cup fresh corn kernels, cut from 2 or 3 ears

4 plum tomatoes, seeded and chopped

¾ cup (3 ounces) pecan pieces, toasted

6 scallions, white and green parts, thinly sliced

1 tablespoon fresh thyme leaves

4 tablespoons olive oil

½ cup all-purpose flour

1½ pounds flounder fillets, four 6-ounce pieces

2 tablespoons freshly squeezed lemon juice

¼ cup dry white wine

1½ teaspoons kosher salt

½ teaspoon freshly ground black pepper

1. Preheat the oven to 250°F.
2. Blanch the lima beans in a small saucepan of boiling salted water for about 5 minutes. Drain. Place them in a large bowl, add the corn, tomatoes, pecans, scallions, and thyme, and gently mix. Set aside.
3. Heat 2 tablespoons olive oil over medium heat in a large skillet. Place the flour on a large plate and dredge the flounder in it. Shake off any excess and cook the flounder 2 pieces at a time in the oil for about 1 minute on each side, until golden brown and crispy. Be careful when you turn the flounder over, because it can easily flake and fall apart; your best bet is to use a broad fish spatula. Remove the flounder from the skillet, place it on a rimmed baking sheet, and keep it warm in the oven. Add the remaining 2 tablespoons oil to the skillet and cook the remaining fish. When all of the fish has been cooked and placed in the oven, add the lima bean mixture to the skillet and cook, stirring, until the lima beans are tender and the tomatoes are soft, about 5 minutes. Add the lemon juice and white wine, and cook for 2 minutes, until the liquid is slightly reduced. Season the vegetables with the salt and pepper and stir. Place the fish on a serving platter, pour the warm succotash over it, and serve.

# Vatapa

## BRAZILIAN FISH, SHRIMP, AND NUT STEW

Vatapa is a thick, protein-rich stew that hails from the Bahia region of Brazil. Traditionally vatapa features dende oil, a bright orange processed palm oil that is both difficult to get here and full of saturated fat. We have substituted olive oil. Ground nuts thicken the coconut-milk broth, just as peanut butter thickens the ground-nut soups of Africa. Indeed, that's one of many clues that led culinary historians to believe that vatapa has African origins and emerged during the sixteenth-century slave trade in Brazil.

PREPARATION TIME: *10 minutes, plus 1 hour for the fish to chill and marinate*
COOKING TIME: *30 minutes*
MAKES: *4 generous servings*

1 pound white fish fillets (such as snapper, mahi-mahi, or grouper), cut into 2-inch cubes

1 pound (about 16) jumbo shrimp, peeled and deveined

1 bunch cilantro, stems removed and roughly chopped

1 tablespoon grated ginger

4 tablespoons olive oil

2 jalapeño peppers, roughly chopped, seeds removed if you like a less spicy flavor

1 tablespoon mustard seeds

1 large onion, chopped

3 cloves garlic, chopped

2 ounces dried shrimp (see Note)

1 cup (5 ounces) roasted peanuts

1½ cups (7½ ounces) Brazil nuts, coarsely chopped

3 cups coconut milk

2 bay leaves

6 black peppercorns

1 teaspoon kosher salt

1 lime, cut into 8 wedges

1. Place the fish and shrimp in a large resealable plastic bag and add half the cilantro, the ginger, and 2 tablespoons olive oil. Mix well. Refrigerate for 1 hour.

2. Place the jalepeño peppers, mustard seeds, onion, garlic, dried shrimp, peanuts, and Brazil nuts in a blender. Add 1½ cups coconut milk and puree until smooth, about 1 minute. Heat a large skillet over medium heat and add the remaining 2 tablespoons olive oil. Pour the paste from the blender into the skillet and cook until fragrant, about 5 minutes. Add the remaining 1½ cups coconut milk, the bay leaves, and the peppercorns and whisk until the ingredients are well incorporated. Season with the salt, lower the heat, and simmer until you have a perfumed broth, about 15 minutes.

*continued*

3. Remove the fish and shrimp from the refrigerator and add them to the skillet. Cook for 5 to 7 minutes, until the shrimp turn pink and the fish is opaque. Remove and discard the bay leaves and peppercorns. Serve the vatapa hot, garnished with the lime wedges and the remaining cilantro, in a large bowl. White rice is a good accompaniment.

NOTE: Dried shrimp comes in small cellophane packages that are available at Asian and Spanish markets. They add a deep saltiness to a dish. Use them in their entirety—there is no need to remove the head or clean them.

### Cleaning a Soft-Shell Crab

Soft-shell crabs are purchased alive and whole, and must be cleaned before they are prepared. If not done by your fishmonger, it is easy to do in your kitchen. First, using a sharp knife or kitchen shears, remove the eyes of the crab by cutting across its body, removing a strip about ¼ inch below the top. Discard the strip. Next, turn the crab over and lift up one pointed edge so you can see the grayish white gills. Pull them off from the right and the left undersides of the crab and discard them. Finally, with the crab still on its back, pull off and discard the flap in its middle, known as the apron. Your crab is now clean. Just rinse it and pat it dry, and use it as soon as possible after cleaning. If there is any time between cleaning and cooking, keep cleaned soft-shell crabs in the coldest part of your refrigerator.

# Sautéed Soft-Shell Crabs with Hazelnuts and Orange Butter

We always look forward to the short soft-shell crab season, which generally lasts from Memorial Day until Labor Day. Soft-shell crabs are not a specific species but instead are crabs that have molted, or shed their shells, and have not grown new shells yet. With no shelling needed, they make a quick and easy meal, especially if your fishmonger cleans them for you. Delivered to restaurant kitchens in flat cardboard boxes, the live crabs are covered with seaweed and wet newspaper. A quick touch shows they are fresh, and alive, and freshness is paramount with soft-shell crabs.

PREPARATION TIME: *15 minutes*
COOKING TIME: *20 minutes*
MAKES: *4 generous servings*

8 large soft-shell crabs, cleaned (see box page 242)

1 cup whole milk

½ cup all-purpose flour

4 tablespoons canola oil

2 tablespoons finely chopped shallots

1 navel orange, cut into segments, with accumulated juice

¼ cup dry white wine

½ cup (2½ ounces) coarsely chopped hazelnuts, toasted

2 tablespoon freshly chopped thyme

1 teaspoon kosher salt

½ teaspoon freshly ground black pepper

2 tablespoons unsalted butter

1. Place the crabs in a bowl and pour the milk over them. Let them soak for a few minutes.
2. Preheat the oven to 250°F.
3. After they have soaked, remove the crabs from the milk and pat them dry. Place the flour in a shallow dish and dredge the crabs in it shaking off any excess. Heat 2 tablespoons canola oil in a large skillet over medium-high heat and place 4 of the crabs, back side down, in the oil. Cook for about 3 minutes, until the edges take on a rosy color. Flip the crabs over and continue to cook for 3 minutes. Remove them from the pan when they are cooked through and keep them warm in the oven on a rimmed baking sheet. Heat the 2 remaining tablespoons of oil and cook the remaining 4 crabs.
4. Lower the heat to medium, add the shallots, and stir. Add the orange segments with their juice, and the white wine and simmer for 2 minutes. Add the hazelnuts, thyme, salt, and pepper. Finish the sauce by swirling in the butter. Pour the warm sauce over the crabs and serve on a platter.

# Curried Shrimp with Toasted Coconut and Peanuts

A world of curries exists—they are eaten everywhere from Africa to Hawaii. Every country has its own variations, from preferred spices to different cooking methods. We have made this shrimp curry as simple as it can be, and it is a meal you can prepare in 15 minutes or so. The shrimp are poached in a spicy simmering coconut broth. Make sure the sauce doesn't come to a boil when the shrimp are cooking, as that would toughen their sweet flesh. This can be served with any simple rice dish, and we love it with Pistachio Raita (page 86) on the side.

PREPARATION TIME: *15 minutes*
COOKING TIME: *15 to 20 minutes*
MAKES: *4 generous servings*

½ cup (1½ ounces) unsweetened coconut flakes

One 2-inch piece ginger, chopped

4 cloves garlic, chopped

1 large onion, chopped

1 large green chile, such as jalapeño, stemmed, seeded, and chopped

2 cups coconut milk

2 tablespoons canola oil

2 teaspoons mild curry powder

1 teaspoon garam masala

1 teaspoon turmeric

1 teaspoon ground cumin

1½ pounds (about 24) jumbo shrimp, peeled and deveined

½ cup (2½ ounces) chopped roasted peanuts

1. Place the coconut flakes, ginger, garlic, onion, and chile in a blender. Add ½ cup coconut milk and puree until a paste is formed, about 2 minutes.

2. Heat the canola oil in a large skillet over medium-high heat. Add the curry powder and cook, stirring constantly, for about 1 minute. Add the coconut paste and continue cooking for 5 minutes, until the paste begins to dry and almost sticks to the bottom of the pan. Add the garam masala, turmeric, and cumin and stir well with a wooden spoon, ensuring that the paste does not dry out. Cook 2 more minutes. Add the remaining 1½ cups coconut milk and stir. Bring to a simmer, lower the heat, and add the shrimp. Cook for about 3 minutes, until the shrimp are pink and cooked through. Sprinkle with the peanuts and serve warm in a shallow bowl.

# Royal Palace Coconut Chicken

This recipe comes to us from our good friend and mentor Nick Malgieri. Thai palace cuisine is typified by foods cooked in coconut milk or coconut cream instead of fat or water. For this lush chicken salad, chicken breasts are slowly simmered in coconut cream, then combined with Thai seasonings—lemongrass, chiles, cilantro, mint, and lime juice. In Thailand, a salad like this is served over sliced banana blossoms or batter-fried morning glory stems. We use shredded Napa cabbage as a base instead. Its crunch contrasts nicely with the creamy chicken. If you don't have any lemongrass on hand, don't let that stop you, the salad is still delicious even without it.

PREPARATION TIME: *40 minutes, plus 1 hour to marinate*
COOKING TIME: *20 minutes*
MAKES: *4 generous servings*

### FOR THE CHICKEN

**2 cups Thai coconut cream**

**3 tablespoons nam pla (Thai fish sauce)**

**2 or 3 boneless chicken breast halves (about 1 pound)**

**1 tablespoon Thai palm sugar or packed light brown sugar**

### FOR THE SALAD

**4 serrano chiles, stemmed, cut in half, seeded, and cut crosswise into thin slices**

**2 teaspoons freshly grated lime zest**

**2 stalks lemongrass, trimmed to a 5-inch length, tough outer leaves removed, and thinly sliced (optional)**

**½ cup thinly sliced shallots**

**1 tablespoon freshly squeezed lime juice**

**½ small head (4 to 6 ounces) Napa cabbage, finely shredded (4 cups)**

**¼ cup freshly chopped cilantro**

**¼ cup finely chopped mint**

**¼ cup (1¼ ounces) finely chopped roasted peanuts**

1. At least 2 or 3 hours before serving the salad, combine the coconut cream with the fish sauce and sugar in a nonreactive skillet and bring to a simmer over medium heat. Slip in the chicken breasts, reduce the heat to low, and cook them at a gentle simmer for 15 minutes. Remove the pan from the heat and cool the chicken. Once it has cooled, shred it by hand and place it in a large mixing bowl; pour 1 cup of the cooked coconut cream mixture over it.

2. Add the chiles, lime zest, lemongrass, shallots, and lime juice to the bowl and use a rubber spatula to toss the ingredients together evenly. Cover the bowl with plastic wrap and leave it at cool room temperature for at least 1 hour. Do not refrigerate it, or the coconut cream will congeal in hard little lumps.

*continued*

3. Right before serving, taste the chicken salad and adjust the seasoning with more fish sauce and lime juice if necessary.

4. Mix cilantro, mint, and peanuts in a small bowl and stir well. Place the shredded cabbage on a platter and pour the chicken salad over it. Top with the cilantro, mint, and peanuts. Serve immediately.

# West African Mafa

Peanut soups and stews are often made in West Africa, where the legume took hold in the seventeenth century. While the ground nuts thicken the stew, it is chock-full of chicken, okra, and tomatoes. Many of the spices may have come from the Americas or through Northern Africa, but the stew has complex flavor and a little heat. A simple rice dish is perfect to serve on the side; you can use it to spoon up all the nutty sauce that's left behind.

PREPARATION TIME: *15 minutes*
COOKING TIME: *50 minutes to 1 hour*
MAKES: *4 generous servings*

2 tablespoons canola oil

One 2- to-3-pound chicken, cut into 8 pieces

2 teaspoons kosher salt

2 cloves garlic, finely chopped

2 tablespoons freshly grated ginger

1 large onion, chopped

2 fresh jalepeños, seeded and chopped

1 teaspoon cumin seeds, toasted and ground

1 teaspoon coriander seeds, toasted and ground

1 teaspoon turmeric

½ teaspoon ground cinnamon

½ teaspoon freshly ground black pepper

1 cup smooth or chunky natural peanut butter

6 plum tomatoes, seeded and chopped

8 ounces fresh okra, cut into 1-inch slices

½ cup (2½ ounces) chopped roasted peanuts

1. In a large, deep skillet, heat the canola oil over medium heat. Season the chicken with 1 teaspoon salt, place it skin side down in the skillet, and cook until browned, about 5 minutes. Turn the chicken over and brown it on the other side. Don't overcrowd the pan—if the chicken doesn't fit in 1 batch, brown it in 2 batches. When the chicken is browned, remove it from the pan and keep it covered in a pan to the side.

2. Lower the heat and add the garlic, ginger, and onion. Cook until the onion is translucent, about 5 minutes. Add the jalepeños, cumin, coriander, turmeric, cinnamon, and pepper and stir, picking up all the bits from the bottom of the pan, about 3 minutes.

3. In a small bowl, whisk the peanut butter with 3 cups water. Add this mixture to the skillet and stir well to combine. Place the chicken back in the sauce, with any accumulated juices, cover, and cook for 15 minutes. Carefully lift the lid and add the tomatoes and okra. Place the lid back on top and cook for another 15 minutes over medium heat, until the chicken is cooked through and the meat of the drumsticks is just starting to pull up from the bottom of the bone. Season with the remaining teaspoon of salt or to taste.

4. Place the chicken on a serving platter and pour the sauce over it. Sprinkle the chopped peanuts over the chicken and serve warm.

*Spicy Chicken Chili with Cashews (page 249), served with Greek yogurt*

# Spicy Chicken Chili with Cashews

There are many kinds of chili in our repertoires, but the most interesting may be this chicken chili with cashews, which both of us make frequently. Chicken thighs and spices, as well as dark beer and chocolate, pump up this chili's many layers of flavor, and we believe it is one of the healthiest versions of chili you can make, as the cashews and beans contribute impressive amounts of fiber. In that spirit, we like to serve it with low-fat or nonfat Greek yogurt on the side instead of sour cream.

PREPARATION TIME: *40 minutes*
COOKING TIME: *50 minutes, with just an occasional stir*
MAKES: *6 generous servings*

3 tablespoons olive oil

2 large onions, chopped

4 cloves garlic, finely chopped

3 red bell peppers, seeded and chopped

2 jalapeño peppers, stemmed, seeded, and finely chopped

2 tablespoons ancho chile powder

1 tablespoon ground cumin

2 teaspoons dried oregano

1 pound boneless, skinless chicken thighs, cut into 1½-inch cubes

3 cups cooked cannellini or navy beans (see box page 76), or two 15-ounce cans, drained and rinsed

1½ cups cooked black beans, or one 15-ounce can, drained and rinsed

1 large can (28 ounces) plum tomatoes, chopped

One 12-ounce bottle dark beer

2 ounces unsweetened chocolate, chopped

1 cup (5 ounces) roasted cashews

1 teaspoon kosher salt

1. Heat the olive oil over medium-high heat in a Dutch oven or large heavy-bottomed saucepan and add the onions, garlic, red peppers, and jalapeños. Cook until they are wilted, about 5 minutes. Add the chile powder, cumin, and oregano and stir. Add the chicken and cook until browned, about 5 more minutes.

2. Add the beans, tomatoes, and beer. Lower the heat to a simmer, cover, and cook for about 30 minutes, until the chicken is entirely cooked. Add the chocolate and the cashews and stir. Cook on low heat, stirring occasionally, for another 10 minutes, until the chocolate is entirely melted and mixed in and the liquid is well blended. Season with the salt and serve warm.

# Chicken Bisteeya with Almonds

This recipe is an adaptation of a Paula Wolfert Moroccan classic from her book *Couscous and Other Good Food from Morocco*. Bisteeya is a savory pie made by wrapping chicken or squab and almonds in phyllo. Though it is a savory dish, it has a slightly sweet edge to it. Crackly browned phyllo never fails to impress—this is a beautiful dish as well as a delicious one. We have modernized the traditional recipe by replacing the eggs used to thicken the chicken mixture with almond butter. It reinforces the nutty flavor and shortens the preparation time.

PREPARATION TIME: *40 minutes*
COOKING TIME: *1 hour 40 minutes*
ROASTING TIME: *45 minutes*
MAKES: *6 to 8 servings*
EQUIPMENT: *One 10-inch cake pan, buttered and lined with parchment paper; 1 rimmed baking sheet lined with parchment paper*

1 large whole chicken (about 3 pounds), cut into 8 pieces

4 cloves garlic, finely chopped

½ cup freshly chopped flat-leaf parsley

½ cup freshly chopped cilantro

1 large onion, finely chopped

3 teaspoons kosher salt

3 cinnamon sticks

1 teaspoon freshly ground black pepper

½ teaspoon turmeric

1 teaspoon ground ginger

2 tablespoons canola oil

3 cups (15 ounces) whole almonds

¼ cup plus 2 tablespoons confectioners' sugar

½ teaspoon ground cinnamon

¼ cup freshly squeezed lemon juice

3 tablespoons almond butter

½ pound (12 sheets) phyllo dough

1 stick (8 tablespoons) unsalted butter, melted

1. Place the chicken in a large Dutch oven or small stockpot and cover with cold water. Add the garlic, parsley, cilantro, onion, 2 teaspoons salt, cinnamon sticks, ½ teaspoon pepper, turmeric, and ginger. Cover the pot and bring the liquid to a boil over high heat. Reduce the heat to low, skim off any gray foam that surfaces, recover, and simmer for 1 hour.

2. While the chicken is cooking, heat the canola oil in a large skillet over medium-low heat and add the almonds. Cook until toasted, stirring, about 5 minutes. With a slotted spoon, transfer the nuts to a paper towel and let cool. Pulse the nuts in the work bowl of a food processor until coarsely ground, about 30 seconds. Add ¼ cup confectioners' sugar and the ground cinnamon and pulse briefly to mix.

3. Remove the chicken pot from the heat and, using a slotted spoon, transfer the chicken to a bowl. Return the pot with the liquid to the stove, bring to a boil over medium-high heat, and cook until only 2 cups remain, about 30 minutes. Reduce the heat to low and add the lemon juice to the reduced liquid. Whisk the almond butter into the simmering liquid and continue to cook, stirring occasionally, until the liquid has thickened slightly, about 10 minutes.

4. Clean the cooled chicken, removing all the skin and bones. Shred the chicken into 1- to 2-inch pieces and place it in a large bowl. Season with the remaining 1 teaspoon salt and the remaining ½ teaspoon pepper, or to taste, then pour in the thickened poaching liquid and mix carefully. Set aside.

5. Preheat the oven to 400°F.

6. Open the phyllo dough and cover it with a damp towel to prevent it from drying out as you work. Place a piece of phyllo in the bottom of the prepared cake pan and use a pastry brush to butter it. Repeat with 5 more phyllo sheets, overlapping each sheet and coming up the sides of the pan.

7. Next take 2 leaves of phyllo, fold each in half, drizzle them with melted butter, and place them on the prepared baking sheet. Bake until crisp, about 2 minutes. Remove from the oven and cool.

8. Place all of the shredded chicken on the bottom of the phyllo-lined cake pan. Place the baked individual sheets of phyllo on top and scatter the sweetened almond mixture on top of them. Fold the edges of the uncooked phyllo into the center, butter them lightly, and place the remaining 2 pieces of phyllo on top, buttering each as you go. Tuck any extending pieces neatly into the sides of the pan. Butter the top of the pie and bake until golden brown, about 45 minutes. Sprinkle it with the remaining 2 tablespoons confectioners' sugar and serve hot directly out of the pan.

*Duck Breast with Glazed Walnuts and Warm Sherry Vinaigrette (page 253)*

# Duck Breast with Glazed Walnuts and Warm Sherry Vinaigrette

The evolution of this recipe is a funny story. It was created as a dinner entrée in Cara's restaurant, Quarropas, in the mid-1980s. As we were searching for recipes to include in our photo shoot, this salad immediately came to mind, and we knew it would make a beautiful plate. What we didn't count on was a 100-degree heat wave and its impact on our leafy greens, even in an air-conditioned studio. For those of you unfamiliar with the photo shoot process, recipes are selected, ingredients are purchased, and studio time is limited. This means that once the greens had wilted, there was no opportunity for a do-over. Thanks to the inspiration of our brilliant editor, we easily transformed this salad into a dinner plate. Most people are not accustomed to medium-rare duck meat, but we promise that once you've had a single taste, you'll want to eat duck this way all the time. Better supermarkets and butchers stock boneless duck breasts.

PREPARATION TIME: *35 minutes*
COOKING TIME: *20 minutes*
MAKES: *4 generous servings*
EQUIPMENT: *1 rimmed baking sheet, lined with parchment paper and lightly sprayed with nonstick spray*

4 boneless duck breasts, fat on

1 teaspoon kosher salt

½ teaspoon freshly ground black pepper

3 tablespoons finely chopped shallots

4 tablespoons sherry vinegar

1 tablespoon Dijon mustard

½ cup chicken stock

FOR THE GLAZED WALNUTS

½ cup sugar

2 tablespoons light corn syrup

3 cups (10½ ounces) walnut halves, toasted

1 teaspoon kosher salt

1. Using a sharp knife, score the duck breasts through the fat 3 or 4 times in a diamond pattern. Salt and pepper the breasts and place them skin side down in a large skillet. Turn the heat to medium-low and cook the duck undisturbed for 10 minutes, until the fat is released. Continue cooking until nearly all the fat has been rendered, about 5 more minutes. Carefully remove the duck breasts from the pan and pour out and reserve the fat, leaving behind just 1 tablespoon.

2. Return the duck breasts crispy side up to the pan and cook over medium heat for 5 minutes, until the breasts are medium-rare. Remove from the pan and set aside.

*continued*

3. Pour 4 tablespoons of the rendered fat into the skillet. Add the shallots and cook over medium heat until wilted, about 3 minutes. Whisk in the sherry vinegar and the mustard. Add the chicken stock and simmer for 2 more minutes.

4. Prepare the walnuts: mix the sugar, ¼ cup water, and the corn syrup in a medium sauce-pan and cook over medium heat, stirring constantly with a spoon or heatproof spatula. Bring the mixture to a boil and continue to cook for 5 to 8 minutes, until the syrup thickens and the bubbles pop more slowly as most of the liquid evaporates. Remove from the heat and stir in the walnuts, tossing well to coat thoroughly. Transfer the nuts onto the prepared baking sheet. Poke them apart with a fork while still warm and then cool completely. Sprinkle with the salt. The candied walnuts can be made early in the day and kept wrapped airtight until you are ready to serve.

5. Cut the duck breast across the width in ⅓-inch slices. Place on a platter and scatter the candied walnuts on top. Drizzle the sauce over the duck and nuts, or serve it on the side. Season with salt and pepper to taste.

# Beef Brisket with Walnuts

This is the traditional brisket that Cara makes for the Jewish holidays and has been selling to her clients throughout Westchester for years. Every time she shares this recipe, without fail, the recipient is surprised at how easy it is to make: this brisket simply sits in the oven for hours, untouched, until perfectly tender. Cara recommends cooking it a day ahead. Not only do the flavors meld beautifully overnight, but the excess fat rises to the surface with chilling, so removing it is a snap.

PREPARATION TIME: *40 to 45 minutes, plus overnight to chill*
ROASTING TIME: *3 hours, turning once halfway through*
MAKES: *6 generous servings*

1 tablespoon olive oil

One 3-pound beef brisket

1 teaspoon kosher salt

½ teaspoon freshly ground black pepper

1 large onion, chopped

3 large carrots, peeled and cut into ¼-inch dice

2 cloves garlic, finely chopped

1 cup full-bodied red wine, such as Merlot or Cabernet Sauvignon

One 28-ounce can tomatoes in juice, chopped or whole

6 sprigs thyme

2 bay leaves

1½ cups (5¼ ounces) walnut pieces

1. Preheat the oven to 325°F.
2. Heat the oil in a large skillet over medium heat. Season both sides of the brisket with the salt and pepper and add the brisket to the skillet, fat side down. Cook until browned, about 5 minutes. Turn the brisket over and brown the second side, another 5 minutes.
3. Place the browned brisket in a casserole or roasting pan that can hold the entire piece of meat laying flat and set aside.
4. Lower the heat and add the onion, carrots, and garlic to the fat that remains in the skillet. Stir and cook until slightly browned, about 5 minutes. Add the red wine, stir, and cook for 5 minutes. Add the tomatoes (break them up a bit with a spoon if they are whole, before you add them to the pan), thyme, bay leaves, and walnuts and cook for 2 more minutes, stirring occasionally.
5. Pour the mixture over the brisket, ensuring that the liquid comes three-quarters of the way up the sides of the meat—add water if you need to. Cover the casserole or roasting pan with aluminum foil and place it in the oven. After 1½ hours, remove it and turn the brisket over. Return the pan to the oven and cook for another 1½ hours.

*continued*

6. The brisket is done when it just begins to fall apart when prodded with a fork. Remove from the oven, cool, and refrigerate, covered, overnight. When ready to serve, remove the brisket from the sauce, and remove and discard the thyme and bay leaves. If any fat has risen to the top of the chilled sauce, remove it by skimming it off the surface with a spoon. Cut the brisket across the grain in ¼-inch slices. Place the slices and the sauce in a large saucepan and reheat on the stovetop for 15 or 20 minutes. Season with salt and pepper to taste. Serve hot.

# Medallions of Beef in Hazelnut Sauce with Wild Mushrooms

We believe there is nothing as good as a sautéed filet of beef dish for ease and elegance. Some believe that a filet of beef doesn't have enough flavor because it doesn't have a bone and it doesn't have a lot of marbled fat. We are happy to trade off some beefiness for convenience when cooking time is limited. For those of us without a great deal of beef in our diets, this tastes plenty meaty. Wild mushrooms and hazelnuts are a great match. Together they are redolent of the forest—woodsy, earthy, and crunchy. Choose wild mushrooms that are hearty, not delicate, such as shiitakes or baby bellas. No longer exotic, these can easily be found in markets.

PREPARATION TIME: *10 minutes*
COOKING TIME: *30 to 35 minutes*
MAKES: *4 servings*

2 tablespoons unsalted butter

1 tablespoon olive oil

1½ teaspoons kosher salt

½ teaspoon freshly ground black pepper

4 pieces filet mignon, about 6 ounces each

¼ cup finely chopped shallots

2 cups packed wild mushrooms, such as portobello, hard stems removed, sliced

1 cup (5 ounces) chopped hazelnuts, toasted

¾ cup port

1 cup chicken stock or beef stock

2 tablespoons heavy cream

1. Preheat the oven to 250°F.
2. Melt the butter with the oil in a large skillet over medium heat. Sprinkle 1 teaspoon of the salt and the pepper on both sides of the filets, place the meat flat side down in the hot pan, and sear for 3 minutes. Turn the filets over and brown on the other side, 3 more minutes. Remove the filets from the pan and keep warm in the oven.
3. Add the shallots and mushrooms to the skillet and cook over medium heat until the mushrooms give up their liquid, about 5 minutes. Add the hazelnuts and port and cook for 3 minutes. Add the stock and reduce the liquid for 5 more minutes. Season with the remaining 1 teaspoon salt. Add the cream and cook until the sauce is a tiny bit thickened, another 2 minutes.
4. Take the beef out of the oven; it should be medium-rare. If you like your beef cooked more, increase the oven temperature to 350°F and cook for 5 additional minutes for medium, 10 for medium-well done. Place the filets on a platter, pour the sauce over them, and serve.

# Braised Short Ribs with Sweet Potatoes, Prunes, and Chestnuts

We are so glad short ribs are popular. On the bone, they can be purchased in two different cuts, either across the bone, flanken style, or along the bone, English style. We prefer the English style, for their higher meat-to-bone ratio. Some folks like to take the bones out before serving, for a more formal presentation, but we are happy to see the bones on our plates. No denying where this delicious meat comes from; the bones are just a reminder. A long, slow braise along with chestnuts and sweet potatoes highlights the tenderness this beef can achieve. We love it with polenta, a soft bed for all the meaty juices that accumulate during cooking.

PREPARATION TIME: *20 minutes*
COOKING TIME: *2 hours 45 minutes, turning once halfway through*
MAKES: *4 generous servings*

2 tablespoons olive oil

3 pounds short ribs

1½ teaspoons kosher salt

½ teaspoon freshly ground black pepper

1 large onion, chopped

3 cloves garlic, finely chopped

2 bay leaves

6 sprigs thyme

1 cup full-bodied red wine, such as Merlot or Cabernet Sauvignon

1 to 2 cups chicken stock or beef stock

1½ pounds sweet potatoes, cut into 2-inch cubes

½ cup chopped pitted prunes

2 cinnamon sticks

1 cup (6 ounces) whole peeled chestnuts (see box page 144)

1. Heat the oil over medium heat in large skillet or Dutch oven. Sprinkle the short ribs on all sides with the salt and pepper and place the ribs meat side down in the hot oil. Brown for about 5 minutes, turn, and brown each remaining side for 5 minutes.

2. Remove the ribs from the skillet and set aside. Add the onion, garlic, bay leaves, and thyme to the skillet, stir, and, cook until the onion softens slightly, about 5 minutes. Add the wine and 1 cup stock and stir. Return the meat to the pan, cover, and lower the heat. Simmer for about 1 hour, turning once and checking to ensure that the meat is nearly covered in liquid. If not, add the remaining 1 cup stock.

3. Add the sweet potatoes, prunes, cinnamon sticks, and chestnuts to the skillet and recover. Continue to simmer for another 1½ hours, until the meat is tender and the sweet potatoes are soft. It is fine if the meat starts to fall of the bone. Remove and discard the bay leaves and cinnamon sticks. Serve the ribs hot, or chill and reheat the next day.

*raised Short Ribs with Sweet Potatoes, Prunes,
nd Chestnuts (page 258)*

*Hanger Steak with Soy, Chile, and Peanut Sauce (page 261)*

# Hanger Steak with Soy, Chile, and Peanut Sauce

The hanger steak is so named because it hangs between a cow's rib and its loin. Technically it is part of the diaphragm. Hanger steak can be a tough cut of meat if not prepared correctly, but when done right it's terrific, with lots of beefy flavor. Doing it right means cooking it quickly. Hanger steak is best medium-rare, though we give instructions in this recipe for cooking it further if that's not to your taste.

PREPARATION TIME: *10 minutes*
COOKING TIME: *25 to 30 minutes*
MAKES: *6 servings*

2 tablespoons olive oil

Six 7-ounce hanger steaks

1 teaspoon kosher salt

½ teaspoon freshly ground black pepper

2 cloves garlic, finely chopped

2 dried red chiles, stemmed and seeded

¼ cup soy sauce

2 star anise

1 cup chicken stock or beef stock

¾ cup (3¾ ounces) chopped roasted peanuts

½ cup sliced scallions, white and green parts (about 6)

1. Heat 1 tablespoon oil in a large skillet over medium heat. Season the steaks on both sides with the salt and pepper. Brown the steaks in the oil in batches, so you do not overcrowd the pan. It may take a few batches to do them all; add the remaining olive oil as needed. After each batch is browned, about 3 minutes on each side, transfer the steaks to a plate and keep going. When all the steaks have been seared and removed from the skillet, add the garlic and stir. Add the chiles, soy sauce, star anise, and stock. Bring to a boil, reduce the heat, and simmer for 5 minutes.

2. Return the steaks to the pan, with all the liquid that has accumulated on the plate. Add the peanuts and scallions. Make sure all the meat is coated with sauce. Remove and discard the chiles and star anise. Place the steaks on a platter, pour the sauce over them, and serve warm. This will make rare to medium-rare steak. If you like it cooked more, place the seared steaks in a pan and keep them in a 350°F oven while you are preparing the sauce.

# Spanish Veal Stew with Marcona Almonds

Marcona almonds are indigenous to Spain, and they are scattered throughout this traditional stew. We like to use cubed boneless veal shoulder for this recipe. It is easy to find in the supermarket, and when braised, cooks to a buttery tenderness. Many chefs would thicken the liquid of this stew with a roux, but we prefer swirling in some almond butter. It may not be traditional, but it will enrich the sauce, giving it a bit of texture and depth.

PREPARATION TIME: *25 minutes*
COOKING TIME: *1 hour to 1 hour 15 minutes*
MAKES: *4 generous servings*

2 tablespoons olive oil

1¾ cups (8 ounces) pearl onions, peeled

3 cloves garlic, finely chopped

1½ pounds veal shoulder for stew, cut into 1½-inch cubes

½ cup finely chopped Serrano ham or prosciutto

2 large carrots, peeled and cut into ½-inch slices

2 red bell peppers, seeded and cut into ½-inch strips

1 bay leaf

¼ cup brandy

¼ cup dry sherry

2 cups chicken stock or beef stock

1 cup (4 ounces) Marcona almonds, toasted

1½ teaspoons kosher salt

½ teaspoon freshly ground black pepper

⅓ cup freshly chopped flat-leaf parsley

2 tablespoons almond butter

1. Heat the olive oil in a large saucepan or Dutch oven over medium-high heat. Add the onions and cook until they are beginning to brown, about 5 minutes. Add the garlic, veal, and ham. Stir and allow to brown, about 5 more minutes. Add the carrots, red peppers, and bay leaf. Pour in the brandy and sherry and cook until about a third of the liquid evaporates, 5 minutes. Add the stock, bring the stew up to a boil, and lower the heat. Cover and simmer for 30 minutes, keeping the liquid at a low boil.

2. Remove the lid and add the almonds, salt, pepper, and parsley. Stir in the almond butter. Cook for 10 more minutes. Make sure the veal is fork-tender. Remove and discard the bay leaf and serve the stew hot.

# Tagine of Lamb with Preserved Lemons, Olives, and Almonds

A Moroccan tagine, a slow-cooked stew, is usually made in a conical earthenware pot (also called a tagine), but we find a regular Dutch oven works just as well. This is an exceptionally flavorful tagine, because the lamb marinates overnight in a spice mixture. If you have preserved lemons, (either homemade or store-bought) in your refrigerator, feel free to use them, but if not, we give instructions for whipping up a viable substitute in an hour or two.

PREPARATION TIME: *30 minutes, plus 8 hours to marinate*
COOKING TIME: *2 hours 45 minutes*
MAKES: *4 generous servings*

### FOR THE QUICK PRESERVED LEMONS

2 lemons, washed and cut into quarters

2 tablespoons kosher salt

1 bay leaf

1 pinch crushed red pepper flakes

### FOR THE TAGINE

2 pounds boneless lamb shoulder, cut into 1½-inch cubes

4 tablespoons olive oil

1 teaspoon ground cumin

1 teaspoon ground cinnamon

½ teaspoon turmeric

½ teaspoon ground coriander

½ teaspoon ground ginger

½ teaspoon cayenne pepper

½ teaspoon dry mustard

½ teaspoon ground cardamom

½ teaspoon kosher salt

½ teaspoon freshly ground black pepper

1 tablespoon freshly grated ginger

1 large onion, finely chopped

2 cloves garlic, finely chopped

1½ cups chicken stock

½ cup halved Moroccan black olives

4 carrots, peeled and cut into ½-inch slices

¾ cup (3½ ounces) slivered almonds, toasted

2 tablespoons chopped preserved lemons

1. Make the quick preserved lemons: Place the lemons in a small saucepan. Add the salt and 1 cup water and bring to a boil over high heat. Add the bay leaf and pepper flakes and lower the heat. Simmer for about 30 minutes, until the lemons are tender. Remove them from the liquid and cool. Chop what you need and refrigerate the remainder for future use.

*continued*

2. Place the lamb in a large, sturdy, resealable plastic bag. Whisk 2 tablespoons olive oil in a small bowl and add the cumin, cinnamon, turmeric. coriander, ground ginger, cayenne, dry mustard, cardamom, salt, and pepper. When well mixed, pour the spice mixture over the lamb in the bag and squeeze to distribute it evenly. Refrigerate overnight or for 8 hours.

3. To make the tagine, heat the remaining 2 tablespoons oil in a heavy skillet or Dutch oven over medium-high heat. Add the fresh ginger, onion, and garlic, stir, and cook until wilted, about 5 minutes. Add the seasoned lamb to the pan and cook for 5 minutes. Add the chicken stock, lower the heat, and simmer for about 1 hour, stirring occasionally. Add the olives, carrots, and almonds. Cook for 1 more hour, until the lamb is entirely tender. Garnish with the chopped preserved lemons and serve warm.

# Pork Loin Stuffed with Figs, Golden Raisins, and Chestnuts

This is special-occasion food to us. Whole roasts take longer to prepare, and they are often more expensive. This yields a dramatic presentation that is festive enough for a holiday.

PREPARATION TIME: *25 minutes*
COOKING TIME: *10 minutes*
ROASTING TIME: *45 minutes, plus 10 minutes to rest*
MAKES: *6 generous servings*

1 cup Calimyrna or Mission figs, stemmed and chopped

½ cup golden raisins

1½ cups quartered shallots

¾ cup freshly squeezed orange juice

2 tablespoons honey

1 cup (6 ounces) chestnuts, toasted

2 tablespoons freshly chopped rosemary

1 teaspoon kosher salt

One 2-pound boneless pork loin

1 tablespoon olive oil

½ teaspoon freshly ground black pepper

4 rosemary sprigs

1. Place the figs, raisins, and shallots in a small saucepan, cover with the orange juice and honey, and bring the liquid to a boil over medium-high heat. Lower the heat and allow the mixture to simmer for 5 minutes. Remove from the heat and cool, or make this combination up to a day ahead. When it is cooled or you are ready to cook, preheat the oven to 350°F and stir the chestnuts, chopped rosemary, and ½ teaspoon salt into the mix.
2. Cut the pork loin in half horizontally and open it like a book. Place the fruit-and-chestnut mixture in the center, lifting it from the liquid with a slotted spoon to strain. Fold the loin over to encase the filling. Don't worry if you have extra filling; it will go in the roasting pan.
3. Tie the loin together with butcher's twine and place it fat side up in a roasting pan. Drizzle the roast with the olive oil and season with the remaining ½ teaspoon salt and the pepper. Pour the rest of the fruit-and-chestnut mixture, with its liquid, into the bottom of the roasting pan. Place the sprigs of rosemary underneath the twine.
4. Roast for about 45 minutes, or until the meat is well browned and reaches 145°F on an instant-read thermometer. Remove from the oven and allow to rest for 10 minutes before slicing. Serve warm, with bits of fruit and chestnuts from the bottom of the pan.

*Red Lentil–Cashew Sliders (page 269) served with Kohlrabi Slaw with Sesame-Ginger Vinaigrette (page 181)*

CHAPTER 10

# Meatless Mains

## Nuts and Bolts of Meatless Mains

**As we've already discussed, nuts make a wonderful addition to many** different kinds of entrées, but they're especially useful in vegetarian dishes. The vegetarian eater faces two issues: protein and satiety. Nuts, with their copious amounts of both protein and fiber, handle both issues at once. These entrées are all excellent at the center of the plate (and though we're not vegetarians by any stretch, we try to eat meat-free meals at least a couple of nights per week), and they can also be served in smaller portions as side dishes.

# Red Lentil–Cashew Sliders

Vegetarian entrées were forever in demand at Cara's takeout shop, and as a result, she developed a repertoire of bean-and-nut burgers. Serve with Kohlrabi Slaw with Sesame-Ginger Vinaigrette (page 181) or Macadamia Mango Salsa (page 96), which gives these sliders a tropical feel. *(See photo page 266.)*

PREPARATION TIME: *30 minutes, plus 10 minutes to rest*
COOKING TIME: *15 to 20 minutes to cook lentils, 10 minutes per slider*
MAKES: *sixteen 3-ounce sliders*

1 cup (½ pound) small red lentils

1 bay leaf

2½ teaspoons kosher salt

1½ tablespoons olive oil

1 medium onion, finely chopped

1 clove garlic, finely chopped

¾ teaspoon ground cumin

⅛ teaspoon ground cinnamon

1 teaspoon turmeric

½ teaspoon freshly ground black pepper

½ cup (2½ ounces) chopped roasted cashews

1 small red bell pepper, seeded and chopped

1 large egg, lightly beaten

½ cup matzoh meal

3 tablespoons canola oil

1. Rinse the lentils under cold running water and drain. Place them in a medium saucepan, add the bay leaf and 1½ teaspoons salt, and cover by 2 inches with cold water. Bring to a boil over high heat, then lower the heat and simmer until the lentils are very soft and almost starting to lose their shape, 25 to 30 minutes. Slightly overcooked is preferred. Drain the lentils, pressing out all of the excess water. This step is important, since excess water will cause the burgers to fall apart. Transfer the lentils to a large mixing bowl, and coarsely mash them using the back of a fork or a potato masher.

2. Place the olive oil in a small skillet over medium-high heat, add the onion and garlic, and cook until translucent and soft, about 5 minutes. Stir them into the cooked lentils.

3. Add the cumin, cinnamon, turmeric, the remaining 1 teaspoon salt, the black pepper, the cashews, the red pepper, the egg, and the matzoh meal and mix well. Taste and adjust the seasoning if needed. Allow the mixture to rest for 10 minutes, or refrigerate it, well wrapped, as long as overnight, until ready to cook.

4. Heat the canola oil in a large skillet. Using a ¼-cup dry measuring cup, form 16 sliders, about 2 inches in diameter and 1 inch thick. Sauté the sliders in batches over medium heat until well browned and a crust forms, about 5 minutes per side. Serve warm.

# Black Bean and Pumpkin Seed Burgers

This dish is loosely based on a recipe that Jeremiah Tower includes in several of his books. It was always on the menu at his San Francisco restaurant, Stars. These savory bean cakes make a flavorful and satisfying vegetarian main course. Don't be surprised by their purplish hue. Topped with the tomato salsa, the color is terrific. The beans can be cooked a day before the burgers are prepared, spreading out the preparation time in what can be viewed as a lengthy recipe. Broken down into steps, it's a snap. This is as all-American as can be. Thousands of years ago, beans, pumpkins, and tomatoes were first grown in the Americas, and they meld together perfectly in this modern main.

PREPARATION TIME: *55 minutes*
COOKING TIME: *2 hours to cook the beans*
FRYING AND ROASTING TIME: *45 minutes*
MAKES: *8 burgers*
EQUIPMENT: *1 rimmed baking sheet lined with parchment paper*

### FOR THE BEANS

2½ cups (1 pound) dried black beans

1 bulb garlic, cut in half

1 small leek, cleaned, trimmed, and split in half

2 ribs celery

1 large or 2 medium carrots

3 springs flat-leaf parsley

3 sprigs thyme

2 large bay leaves

1 teaspoon kosher salt

### FOR THE BEAN BURGERS

½ cup freshly chopped cilantro

½ cup (2¾ ounces) chopped pumpkin seeds, toasted

1 tablespoon ground cumin

1 teaspoon ancho chile powder

2 tablespoons freshly squeezed lime juice

½ cup panko breadcrumbs

¾ teaspoon kosher salt

### FOR THE TOMATO SALSA

1 medium ripe tomato (6 ounces), cut in half, seeded, and cut into ½-inch pieces

2 tablespoons finely chopped white onion

2 tablespoons freshly chopped cilantro

1½ tablespoons finely chopped serrano chile

1 tablespoon freshly squeezed lime juice

¼ teaspoon kosher salt

### FOR FINISHING AND SERVING

¼ cup canola oil for frying

½ cup sour cream

2 tablespoons (½ ounce) pumpkin seeds, toasted

1. Rinse the beans, cover them with clean water, and soak overnight.
2. Place the beans in a large pot with 3 quarts water. Add the garlic, leek, celery, carrots, and herbs. Place the pot over medium heat and bring to a simmer. Lower the heat and cook the beans at a very gentle simmer, stirring often and adding more water as necessary to keep them covered by a couple of inches, until they are tender but still firm, 2 or 3 hours for dried beans, or 30 minutes for canned beans. When the beans are tender, add the salt and taste, adding a little more if necessary.
3. Cool the beans in the cooking liquid, then drain them in a colander, discarding the cooking liquid and all the vegetables and herbs. Let the beans drain as long as you can; several hours is fine.
4. Make the burgers: Transfer the beans to a bowl and use a potato masher to break them into a coarse paste. Do not puree them, or they will not have enough density to form the burgers. Add the cilantro, pumpkin seeds, cumin, chile powder, lime juice, breadcrumbs, and salt and mix thoroughly. Using a ½-cup dry measuring cup, form the mixture into 4-inch-diameter burgers. Wrap and refrigerate them until you are ready to cook them.
5. Prepare the salsa by combining all the ingredients in a bowl.
6. To finish the burgers, set a rack in the middle of the oven and preheat to 350°F. Place the oil in a skillet over medium heat. Once the oil is hot, sauté the burgers 2 or 3 at a time. Cook for 2 minutes on each side. Remove from the oil and place on the prepared baking pan. Repeat with the remaining burgers. When all the burgers have been fried, bake them until they are thoroughly heated through, about 15 minutes. You can keep them warm for 30 minutes, loosely covered with foil, in the oven at 250°F.
7. To serve, arrange each burger on a warm plate and top it with a spoonful of sour cream, some salsa, and a sprinkling of pumpkin seeds.

VARIATION: Substitute four 15-ounce cans (6 cups) black beans, rinsed and drained, for the dried beans. Omit the garlic, leek, celery, carrots, and herbs. Continue the recipe from step 4.

# Meatless Cassoulet with Walnut Dumplings

A traditional cassoulet is a laborious affair filled with a variety of meats, beans, and vegetables and requiring long, slow cooking. Our meat-free version is just as tasty, and more healthful too. The topping on a traditional cassoulet is garlic breadcrumbs, but we crown ours with a ring of puffy walnut dumplings. We love the contrast between the filling and the topping—a dense interior crowned with airy puffs. The dumplings obscure the deep flavors within; leaving the contrast to surprise.

PREPARATION TIME: *35 minutes*
COOKING TIME: *55 minutes to 1 hour*
MAKES: *6 generous servings*

### FOR THE CASSOULET

2 tablespoons olive oil

2 medium leeks, cleaned, split in half, and sliced

3 medium carrots, peeled, split in half, and cut into ½-inch slices

2 ribs celery, cut into ½-inch slices

3 cloves garlic

4 sprigs thyme

4 sprigs flat-leaf parsley

1 bay leaf

6 cups cooked white beans (see box page 76), liquid reserved, or four 15-ounce cans, drained, rinsed, and liquid reserved (see Note)

2 cups diced fresh tomatoes, or two-thirds of a 28-ounce can diced tomatoes in juice

½ cup (1¾ ounces) finely chopped walnuts, toasted

3 tablespoons tomato paste

2 cups vegetable stock

1 tablespoon sherry vinegar

1½ teaspoons kosher salt

½ teaspoon freshly ground black pepper

### FOR THE DUMPLINGS

1 cup all-purpose flour

¾ teaspoon baking powder

½ teaspoon baking soda

½ teaspoon kosher salt

¼ teaspoon freshly ground black pepper

¾ cup (2½ ounces) finely chopped walnuts, toasted

1 tablespoon unsalted butter, chilled

½ cup plus 2 tablespoons buttermilk

1. Make the cassoulet: Heat the olive oil in a Dutch oven over medium-high heat. Add the leeks, carrots, celery, garlic, thyme, parsley, and bay leaf and cook for about 15 minutes, until the vegetables are tender. Add the beans, tomatoes, walnuts, tomato paste, stock, and 2 cups reserved bean cooking liquid, and and bring to a simmer. Cook until the flavors are melded and the carrots are cooked all the way through, 15 to 20 minutes. Add the vinegar, salt, and pepper.

2. While the cassoulet is cooking, make the dumplings: Mix the flour, baking powder, baking soda, salt, and pepper in the work bowl of a food processor. Add the cold butter and process for about 10 seconds, until no visible pieces of butter remain. Transfer to a mixing bowl and stir in the walnuts and buttermilk until everything is moistened.

3. Dip a tablespoon into the cassoulet to heat it and then scoop the dumpling dough with it. Drop heaping tablespoons of dough into the simmering cassoulet. Repeat the process until all the dough is used. Cover the pot and cook on low heat for 20 to 25 minutes, until the dumplings are heated through. Remove and discard the bay leaf and herbs and serve the cassoulet hot. Wrap any leftovers in an airtight container and refrigerate for up to 3 days. Reheat gently over low heat and reseason with salt and pepper to taste.

NOTE: If you do not have 2 cups of liquid remaining from either cooked beans or drained canned beans, add water to reach 2 cups.

# Chiles Rellenos with Cheese and Pumpkin Seed Stuffing

Chiles rellenos is a dish native to Puebla, Mexico, that can now be found in other areas of that country as well as throughout the United States in Mexican restaurants large and small. The most traditional filling for chiles rellenos is a pork-based picadillo—a sweet-and-sour combination with capers, raisins, and almonds. Here we've given you a meatless option: a filling of cheese and pumpkin seeds that is deliciously gooey but also crunchy.

PREPARATION TIME: *1 hour*
FRYING TIME: *20 to 30 minutes*
MAKES: *4 generous servings*
EQUIPMENT: *Deep-fry thermometer; 1 rimmed baking sheet lined with paper towels*

8 large or 12 small poblano chiles, with stems on, roasted (see page 74)

FOR THE FILLING

1 tablespoon olive oil

1 medium onion, finely chopped

3 plum tomatoes, cut in half, seeded, and chopped

1 pound queso blanco or any white cheese that melts, cut into ¼-inch dice

1 cup (5½ ounces) finely chopped pumpkin seeds, lightly toasted

1 teaspoon kosher salt

½ teaspoon freshly ground black pepper

½ teaspoon ground cumin

————

¾ cup all-purpose flour

Pinch kosher salt

6 large eggs, separated

1 to 2 cups vegetable oil

1. To prepare the chiles for stuffing, clean the darkened outer skin, rinse, and pat dry. Cut a slit down the middle of one side. If you prefer your chiles less hot, remove the ribs and seeds from the inside. Set aside until the filling is prepared.

2. Make the filling: Heat the oil in a large skillet over medium heat, add the onion, and cook until wilted, about 5 minutes. Add the tomatoes and continue cooking until they soften, another 5 minutes. Pour the mixture into a medium bowl and cool. This can be done a day ahead. Mix the cheese, pumpkin seeds, salt, pepper, and cumin into the onion mixture and stir to combine.

3. Carefully place about ⅓ cup of filling through the slit and into the body of each pepper, taking care not to enlarge the slit. Repeat until all the chiles are filled. Make sure that the chiles are dry on the outside and lightly dust them with the flour and salt. In the bowl of a standing mixer fitted with the whip attachment or with a handheld beater, whip the

egg yolks to lighten, about 5 minutes. Transfer the yolks to a large bowl, clean the mixer bowl, and whip the egg whites until they are firm. Fold the yolks into the whites.

4. In a deep skillet, heat about ¾ inch oil until it reaches 375°F on the thermometer. Dip the floured chiles one by one into the egg batter and carefully place them in the hot oil. Fry them 3 or 4 at a time, turning occasionally with tongs until golden brown, about 10 minutes. Remove them from the oil and allow to rest on the prepared baking sheet in a warm spot. Serve them as is or with a tomato sauce. Season with salt and pepper to taste. These are best the day they are prepared, but reheat leftovers in a 325°F oven for 20 minutes.

*Vegan Black Bean and Pecan Tostada Stack (page 277), topped with*
*Pumpkin Seed Guacamole (page 80)*

# Vegan Black Bean and Pecan Tostada Stacks

This vegan entrée evolved from a lunch dish created for the hardworking kids of the Elm Street garden project in Yonkers, New York. With community help, the Elm Street garden has blossomed, and at the end of each growing season a hands-on cooking class incorporates what the students have grown. Cara made this filling and served it with soft tacos. Here we dress it up, stacking the tortillas and filling for a more formal entrée. Eat it with a knife and fork—the crunchy tortillas may shatter, but you can use the shards to scoop up the juicy filling.

PREPARATION TIME: *20 minutes*
COOKING TIME: *40 minutes*
MAKES: *4 servings*

2 tablespoons olive oil

1 medium onion, chopped

2 cloves garlic, finely chopped

2 sweet potatoes, peeled and cut into ½-inch pieces

2 ripe tomatoes, seeded and chopped

1 jalapeño pepper, seeded and chopped

1½ cups cooked black beans (see box page 76) or one 15-ounce can, drained and rinsed

½ cup fresh corn kernels, cut from 2 ears

1½ teaspoons ground cumin

1½ teaspoons kosher salt

½ teaspoon freshly ground black pepper

2 tablespoons freshly chopped cilantro

¾ cup (3 ounces) chopped toasted pecans

¼ cup canola oil

Twelve 4-inch corn tortillas

### FOR SERVING

Ripe avocado, freshly squeezed lime juice and sour cream, or Pumpkin Seed Guacamole (page 80)

1. Heat the olive oil in a medium skillet over medium heat. Add the onion and garlic and cook until softened, about 5 minutes. Add the sweet potatoes, tomatoes, jalapeño, and black beans. Mix in the fresh corn kernels and season with the cumin, salt, and pepper. Stir, and cook until the tomatoes have given up their juices and the sweet potatoes are fork-tender, about 10 minutes. Add the cilantro and pecans, stir, and set aside.

2. Heat the canola oil in a clean medium skillet over medium heat. When it comes to a shimmer, add a tortilla and cook for 1 minute, until it is crisp. Flip it and cook for another minute. Remove from the oil and place on a paper towel. Repeat with the remaining tortillas.

3. Place 4 tortillas on a serving platter. Put a small scoop of the bean-nut mixture on each one. Top each with a second tortilla. Put another small scoop of the bean-nut mixture on each stack, and top each again with the third and final tortilla. Divide the remaining mixture evenly for a final spoonful on the top. Serve with slices of perfectly ripe avocado, with a squeeze of fresh lime juice and a dollop of sour cream, or with a spoonful of pumpkin seed guacamole.

# Stuffed Kale with Almond, Quinoa, and Currant Filling

Kale and quinoa—sounds like fad food, but that is certainly not the intent. This recipe is based on a meat-filled cabbage made by Cara's grandmother, and it went through a few iterations before it landed here. When we first moved from a beef to a vegetarian filling, almonds and couscous fit the bill. As tastes and nutritional desires evolved, we kept the almonds and substituted quinoa for the couscous, as it has a similar texture but a healthier, protein-packed nutritional profile. Next came the change from cabbage to kale. Kale is easier to take apart and blanch for stuffing, eliminating the laborious coring and dissecting of a head of cabbage. Throughout these changes the sauce has not altered. It has the same sweet-and-sour tang that Cara loved in her childhood in her grandmother's traditional version. There is something to be said for evolution and modernization.

PREPARATION TIME: *30 minutes*
COOKING TIME: *45 minutes*
BAKING TIME: *35 to 40 minutes*
MAKES: *6 generous servings*

## FOR THE TOMATO SAUCE

2 tablespoons olive oil or canola oil

1 large onion, cut into ¼-inch dice

2 cloves garlic, finely chopped

One 28-ounce can crushed plum tomatoes

½ cup freshly squeezed lemon juice or distilled white vinegar

½ cup packed light brown sugar

½ teaspoon kosher salt

¼ teaspoon freshly ground black pepper

## FOR THE FILLING AND ASSEMBLY

1½ teaspoons kosher salt

1 cup quinoa

2 tablespoons olive oil or canola oil

1 medium onion, cut into ¼-inch dice

2 cloves garlic, finely chopped

½ cup currants

¾ cup (4 ounces) chopped toasted almonds

1 teaspoon ground cinnamon

¼ teaspoon freshly ground black pepper

2 large egg whites, lightly beaten

1 large bunch large-leaf (dinosaur) kale, stems removed

1. Make the tomato sauce: Place the oil in a medium saucepan over medium heat. Add the onion and garlic and cook until soft and translucent, about 5 minutes. Add the tomatoes and bring to a boil. Lower the heat and simmer, stirring occasionally, until the sauce is slightly thickened, about 15 minutes. Stir in the lemon juice, brown sugar, salt, and pepper. Cook for 10 more minutes, stirring occasionally. Remove from the heat, transfer to a bowl, and cool.

2. While the sauce is cooking, bring 1½ cups water with 1 teaspoon salt to a boil over high heat in a small saucepan. Add the quinoa and lower the heat. Simmer for 15 minutes, until the quinoa is soft and the seeds begin to open. Remove from the heat and set aside to cool.

3. Heat the oil in a medium skillet over medium heat. Add the onion and garlic and cook until soft and translucent, about 5 minutes. Add the quinoa, then add the currants, almonds, cinnamon, the remaining ½ teaspoon salt, and the pepper to the pan. Stir well to combine.

4. Add the egg whites to the quinoa mixture and stir with a spatula until the mixture holds together loosely. Scrape the filling into a bowl, cover, and refrigerate until ready to use, up to 24 hours.

5. Preheat the oven to 350°F.

6. Bring a large pot of water with 2 tablespoons of salt to a boil over medium-high heat. Drop leaves of kale into the boiling water. Using tongs, remove them in 2 or 3 minutes, when they are just wilted. Drop them into a colander in the sink and run cold water over them to stop them from cooking. This can be done in batches if the pot is not large enough to hold them all at once. You will need 12 leaves to stuff.

7. Pat the leaves dry with paper towels and lay them flat on the counter, smooth side up. Place about ⅓ cup filling in the center of each leaf, about 2 inches from the bottom. Fold the bottom up to cover the filling. Fold the right and left sides in toward the center, over the bottom, and roll until the filling is completely covered.

8. Spread ½ cup tomato sauce on the bottom of a 9-by-13-inch baking pan. Place the kale rolls seam side down in the pan. Pour the remaining tomato sauce over the rolls and cover the pan with aluminum foil. (Stuffed kale can be refrigerated at this point for up to 24 hours.) Bake until the kale looks translucent and all the rolls are heated through, 35 to 40 minutes. Serve warm, with sauce spooned over the top of the stuffed kale leaves.

# Chestnut and Apple Quiche

Chestnuts grow abundantly in the Cévennes, in southern France. First cultivated in the tenth century on the grounds of monasteries that dotted the region, they previously grew wild throughout Europe. When famine struck the area and other crops failed, chestnuts provided a nutritional lifeline to the people of Cévennes. From their utility grew culinary refinement, and this quiche is a nod to the flavors of the region. The sour cream dough is simple to prepare and easy to roll. It will be slightly flaky, and the sour cream keeps it tender. Not as eggy as a traditional quiche, this pie is filled with the chestnuts, tart apples, and goat cheese of the South of France, and eggs and cream are just used to bind their goodness together.

PREPARATION TIME: *1 hour, plus 2 hours to chill the dough*
BAKING TIME: *35 to 40 minutes*
MAKES: *6 generous servings*
EQUIPMENT: *One 10-inch tart pan with removable bottom*

### FOR THE SOUR CREAM DOUGH

2 cups all-purpose flour

½ teaspoon kosher salt

1 tablespoon sugar

1 stick (8 tablespoons) unsalted butter, chilled and cut into 8 pieces

¾ cup (6 ounces) sour cream

### FOR THE FILLING

2 tablespoons olive oil or canola oil

1 large onion, cut into ½-inch pieces

2 large tart, crisp apples such as Granny Smith, peeled and cut into ½-inch pieces

1½ cups (9 ounces) crumbled chestnuts

1 tablespoon freshly chopped thyme

1 tablespoon freshly chopped sage

1 teaspoon kosher salt

½ teaspoon freshly ground black pepper

3 large eggs

½ cup heavy cream

4 ounces goat cheese, crumbled

1. Make the dough: Place the flour, salt, and sugar in the work bowl of a food processor and process to combine, about 10 seconds. Add the butter and process until the mixture has a sandy texture, about 30 seconds. Whisk the sour cream to loosen it and add it to the food processor all at once. Pulse again at 1-second intervals, just until the dough is combined and begins to form a ball, about 30 seconds. Do not overprocess. You can use the dough right away, but for best results, wrap it in plastic wrap and chill it for 2 hours before rolling. It can be chilled for several days or frozen for up to 1 month. Bring the dough to cool room temperature before rolling.

2. Preheat the oven to 375°F.

3. On a clean, lightly floured surface, roll the dough into a 12-inch circle that is about ¼-inch thick (see box page 300). Fold it in half and then into quarters, lift it, and place the center of the wedge of dough in the center of the tart pan. Carefully unfold it and line the bottom of the pan. Lightly pat the dough in place, ensuring that it comes up the sides. Set aside in the refrigerator.

4. Make the filling: Heat the oil in a large skillet over medium heat, add the onion, and cook until golden, about 10 minutes. Add the apples and cook until soft, about 5 minutes. Pour the mixture into a medium bowl and stir in the chestnuts, herbs, salt, and pepper. Set aside to cool for 10 to 15 minutes.

5. When the mixture has cooled, place it in the chilled tart shell, spreading it evenly with a spatula and making sure it is flat. Break the eggs into a bowl, beat slightly, and add the cream and goat cheese. Mix thoroughly, then pour the custard over the filling in the quiche. Bake for 35 to 40 minutes, or until firm and golden brown. Serve warm. Wrap and refrigerate leftovers for up to 3 days. Reheat in a 350°F oven for 10 to 15 minutes.

# Vegetable Crumble with Crunchy Hazelnut Topping

This casserole was inspired by all the fruit crisps, cobblers, and crumbles with nut toppings that we have baked over the years. It can be made completely from scratch, or you can use any leftover vegetables that you have on hand. Either way, try to use seasonal vegetables whenever possible.

PREPARATION TIME: *40 minutes*
BAKING TIME: *30 minutes*
MAKES: *6 generous servings*
EQUIPMENT: *One 10-inch gratin dish, buttered*

### FOR THE VEGETABLES

2 tablespoons olive oil

2 leeks, split in half, cleaned, and sliced

2 carrots, peeled and cut into ¼-inch slices

1 large onion, cut into ¼-inch pieces

2 large portobello mushroom caps, gills removed, cut into ½-inch slices

1 cup heavy cream

2 cups (5 ounces) small broccoli florets, blanched

2 cups (8 ounces) asparagus, blanched, trimmed, peeled, and cut into 1-inch pieces

½ cup (⅔ ounce) freshly grated Parmesan cheese

½ cup (2½ ounces) chopped hazelnuts, toasted

1½ teaspoons kosher salt

¾ teaspoon freshly ground black pepper

2 teaspoons freshly chopped thyme

### FOR THE TOPPING

1 cup all-purpose flour

1 cup (3½ ounces) hazelnut flour

1 stick (8 tablespoons) unsalted butter, chilled and cut into small pieces

½ cup (2½ ounces) chopped hazelnuts, toasted

¾ teaspoon kosher salt

1 teaspoon freshly chopped thyme

Pinch cayenne pepper

Pinch freshly ground nutmeg

1. Preheat the oven to 350°F.
2. Cook the vegetables: Heat the oil in a large skillet over medium heat, add the leeks, carrots, onion, and mushrooms, and cook until crisp-tender, about 7 minutes. Add the cream and cook for 3 minutes, until the cream is just beginning to thicken. Transfer the mixture into a medium bowl and add the broccoli and asparagus. Stir in the Parmesan cheese, hazelnuts, salt, pepper, and thyme. Pour the mixture into the gratin dish and set aside.

3. For the topping: Mix the flours in a small bowl. Using your fingertips, add the butter, rubbing until only very small pieces remain, smaller than the size of a pea. Add the hazelnuts, salt, thyme, cayenne, and nutmeg and mix well. Crumble the topping over the vegetable filling. Bake for 30 minutes, until the topping is browned and the cream is bubbling. Serve warm. Wrap leftovers and refrigerate for up to 3 days. Reheat in a 325°F oven for 15 to 20 minutes.

*Pistachio Biryani (page 285)*

# Pistachio Biryani

Usually this traditional Indian dish is an elaborate preparation, but we have streamlined the recipe to make it easy for the home cook. It is a satisfying vegan main course and can be showcased with other Indian dishes. While we feature creamy white cauliflower and vibrant carrot with the pistachios, tossing any leftover cooked vegetables into this dish only helps to empty your refrigerator and add to its fragrant charm. Variations of biryani are plentiful, and all begin with basmati rice. Some have chicken and some showcase cashews, but we love pistachios. Their color just pops in contrast to the spiced rice, and their flavor is mellow and perfect.

PREPARATION TIME: *30 minutes*
COOKING TIME: *30 minutes*
MAKES: *6 to 8 generous servings*

1½ cups basmati rice

1 cinnamon stick, broken in half

1 bay leaf

4 teaspoons kosher salt

2 tablespoons canola oil

1 large onion, roughly chopped

2 cloves garlic, finely chopped

2 tablespoons freshly grated ginger

1 teaspoon ground cumin

1 teaspoon ground coriander

1 teaspoon turmeric

½ teaspoon freshly ground black pepper

1 small head (about 1 pound) cauliflower, separated into florets

2 large carrots, peeled and cut into ½-inch slices

1 cup (4 ounces) cut green beans, trimmed and chopped into 2-inch pieces

1 cup (5 ounces) chopped pistachios, toasted

2 tablespoons freshly chopped cilantro (optional)

2 tablespoons freshly chopped mint (optional)

1. Place the rice in a medium saucepan and cover with water to about 3 inches above the rice. Add the cinnamon stick, bay leaf, and 1½ teaspoons salt and cover. Bring to a boil over medium-high heat. Lower the heat and simmer for 12 to 15 minutes, until the rice is barely tender. Pour the rice out through a strainer and drain, but do not rinse. Place the rice back in the pot, cover it, and set it aside.

2. While the rice is cooking, heat the canola oil in a large skillet over medium heat. Add the onion, garlic, and ginger and cook until soft and fragrant, about 5 minutes. Add the cumin, coriander, turmeric, pepper, and the remaining 2½ teaspoons salt. Using a spoon or spatula that you don't mind staining (the turmeric may be difficult to rinse off), stir

*continued*

the spices into the onion mixture. Cook for 3 minutes, stirring once or twice to ensure that all the spices are well blended.

3. Add the cauliflower and carrots and pour 1 cup water over the vegetables. Cover and cook for 5 to 8 minutes, until the vegetables are still a little firm but a knife can pierce them. Add the green beans and cook another 2 minutes. Most of the water will evaporate, but a little saucy goodness should be left in the bottom of the skillet. The cauliflower may look orange, but it will remain white on the inside.

4. Pour the rice into a serving bowl and remove and discard the cinnamon and bay leaf. Add the vegetable mixture and the pistachios and mix thoroughly. Garnish with the chopped cilantro and mint, if you like. Store the leftovers in an airtight container in the refrigerator for up to 3 days.

# Savory Brown Rice–Walnut Loaf

The nut loaves of the budding vegetarian movement in the late 1960s were much maligned as leaden bricks, and often rightly so. But nut loaves don't have to be dense and joyless! We pack this nut-based loaf with lots of herbs and vegetables, and the result is a good deal lighter and fresher-tasting than those sad meatloaf wannabes of the past. Even a carnivore will be satisfied with a couple slices of this loaf and a green salad.

PREPARATION TIME: *30 minutes, plus 45 minutes to cook brown rice*
BAKING TIME: *1 hour*
MAKES: *6 generous servings*
EQUIPMENT: *One 9-by-5-inch loaf pan, buttered or oiled*

2 tablespoons olive oil

1 large onion, finely chopped

3 cloves garlic, finely chopped

1 cup chopped mushroom caps

1 cup shredded carrots

1 cup finely chopped celery

1 cup (3½ ounces) chopped walnuts, toasted

¼ cup (1¼ ounces) sesame seeds, toasted

2 cups cooked brown rice

4 large eggs, lightly beaten

½ cup (⅔ ounce) freshly grated Parmesan cheese

½ cup matzoh meal

1½ teaspoons kosher salt

¾ teaspoon freshly ground black pepper

2 tablespoons freshly chopped basil

1 tablespoon freshly chopped thyme

1. Preheat the oven to 350°F.
2. Heat the olive oil in a large skillet over medium heat. Add the onion, garlic, mushroom caps, carrots, and celery and cook until softened, about 10 minutes. Place the mixture in a medium bowl and add the walnuts, sesame seeds, rice, and eggs. Mix well. Add the Parmesan, matzoh meal, salt, pepper, basil, and thyme and combine. Pour into the loaf pan and bake for 1 hour, until firm. Cool for 10 minutes in the pan and unmold. Serve warm.

# Eggplant Lasagna with Hazelnut-Parsley Pesto

This is not a lasagna in the true sense of the word, but it is a layered dish whose composition mimics a traditional lasagna. Compatible with a gluten-free diet, layers of roasted eggplant stand in for the pasta. Crisp, green, fragrant parsley is a must, as it yields the brightest of pestos. This can be prepared a day ahead and baked on the day of serving. A bit of prep work is involved, so plan ahead. Make the pesto and roast the eggplant when you have the time and put the lasagna together at your leisure. It is a grand, warm, friendly dish.

PREPARATION TIME: *55 minutes, plus 30 minutes to rest and 10 to 15 minutes to prepare Parsley Pesto*
ROASTING TIME: *40 to 45 minutes*
MAKES: *8 servings*
EQUIPMENT: *2 rimmed baking sheets; one deep 9-by-13-inch baking dish*

3 medium eggplants, trimmed and cut lengthwise into ⅓-inch slices

2 tablespoons plus 1 teaspoon kosher salt

¼ cup olive oil

3 cups whole milk

1 bay leaf

1 stick (8 tablespoons) unsalted butter

1 cup all-purpose flour

½ teaspoon freshly ground black pepper

Parsley Pesto (page 208), made with hazelnuts

2 pounds fresh ricotta cheese (see box page 229)

2 large eggs

2 cups (8 ounces) freshly grated mozzarella cheese

1. Toss the eggplant with 2 tablespoons salt in a large bowl, making sure the salt coats the eggplant evenly. Transfer the eggplant to a colander, set the colander in the bowl, and set aside for 30 minutes.

2. Preheat the oven to 400°F.

3. Pat the eggplant slices dry with paper towels. Using a pastry brush, brush both sides of the slices with olive oil and place in a single layer on the baking sheets or in the roasting pans. Roast for 10 minutes. Flip the eggplant slices and roast until easily pierced with a fork, another 10 minutes. Remove from the oven and set aside to cool. The eggplant can be prepared ahead to this point. When the slices are cool, stack them gently in a resealable plastic bag and refrigerate for up to 24 hours.

4. Warm the milk and bay leaf in a small saucepan over medium heat until bubbles form around the edges, about 2 minutes, and remove from heat. Melt the butter in a medium saucepan over medium heat until foaming, about 2 minutes. Whisk in the flour and

cook until the mixture thickens and forms a smooth paste, about 5 minutes. Remove the bay leaf from the milk and ladle the warm milk into the butter-flour mixture, whisking constantly. Cook, stirring occasionally, until the sauce simmers and thickens, about 15 minutes. Make sure the sauce does not stick and burn on the bottom of the pot. Add 1 teaspoon salt and the pepper. Remove from the heat and place a piece of plastic wrap directly on the surface. Poke a few holes in the plastic with a paring knife to allow the steam to escape. Set aside.

5. Preheat the oven to 350°F.

6. Place the ricotta in a medium bowl and whisk in the eggs.

7. Spread one quarter (1 cup) of the sauce evenly over the bottom of the baking dish. Cover with a single layer of eggplant and spread with another one-quarter of the sauce. Stir the Parsley Walnut Pesto well, then whisk ½ cup warm water into it. Spread half the pesto over the sauce. In a medium bowl, stir the ricotta cheese with salt and pepper to taste. Spread half the ricotta over the pesto. Sprinkle with ⅔ cup grated mozzarella. Top with a layer of eggplant, then another one-quarter of the sauce, the remaining pesto, the remaining ricotta, and another ⅔ cup mozzarella. Finish with a layer of the remaining eggplant slices, the remaining sauce, and the remaining ⅔ cup mozzarella. Loosely cover the lasagna with aluminum foil and bake 40 to 45 minutes. Remove the foil and continue baking for 5 minutes so the cheese can brown slightly and bubble. Remove from the oven and let rest for 10 minutes before cutting and serving.

Clockwise from top: White Chocolate–Orange–Almond Bar (page 357); Chocolate-Covered Almonds (page 361); Lemon–Poppy Seed Cookies (page 339); Macadamia Crunch (page 360)

CHAPTER 11

# Sweet Grand Finale

# Nuts and Bolts of Sweet Grand Finale

**Desserts are a great way to begin a love affair with nuts and seeds. As** ambassadors for our chosen gems, we've convinced countless kids and adults alike to try a little something with nuts, a bite of crunchy cookie or a spoon of smooth pudding. Immediately, they are hooked. The treats in this chapter have a special place in the world of nuts and seeds, and every one of these recipes displays them in their most distinguished surroundings.

We start with nostalgic Toasted-Almond Ice Pops (page 294), which are easy to make, and can't be beat for a delightfully cool summer snack. They are followed by several of our favorite pies, cakes, cookies, and candies. In some cake and cookie recipes, such as Hazelnut Brownie Bottom Cheesecake (page 304), we use nut flour or ground nuts instead of wheat flour, making these desserts gluten-free. We feature a few fabulous ones like that, but we also love the crunch and pop of nuts mixed into a traditional cake batter.

We love to make our own "slice-and-bake" cookies—buttery centers surrounded by a nut or seed crust. They are the epitome of easy baking. Drop cookies and bar cookies are super simple too. We save the hand-rolled cookies, such as Classic Walnut Rugelach (page 340) and Pecan Nut Cups (page 348) for special occasions. They take a little more time, but reward us with shapes and textures that are unmatched.

A few confections crown our dessert chapter. We eat them after a dessert, as an extra, "we can't get enough" kind of treat. Excess? Maybe, but with nuts, we believe, there is no such thing!

# Toasted-Almond Ice Pops

In our childhood, whenever the Good Humor truck rang its bell and toured the streets of Long Island, neither of us could wait to get a toasted-almond ice pop. However, we owe the inspiration for these bars to our editor, Maria Guarnaschelli, who encouraged us to recall the best treats from our past, and these stood out. After fiddling with the recipe, we realized that we could create an outstanding nut-flavored ice pop based on the method used to make the Mexican ice pops known as *paletas*. They are creamy and smooth and created without eggs or the need for an ice cream churn. The result is terrific, a cross between the exotic-tasting ice cream bars of our childhood and the tropical treats we've had south of the border. They are unmistakably nutty, but if you want an even nuttier pop, stir ½ cup toasted chopped almonds into the milk base. If you over-mix the base, too much air will be incorporated, and you will lose the smooth texture. If this happens, let the base settle in the refrigerator; the air bubbles will rise to the surface, restoring the creamy texture to the mix. If you have more base than your molds can hold, keep it in the refrigerator and use it the next day when your molds are free.

PREPARATION TIME: *10 minutes, plus 8 to 12 hours to freeze*
MAKES: *eight 4-ounce bars*
EQUIPMENT: *1 set ice cream molds*

### FOR THE ICE POPS

1¾ cups (14 ounces) almond milk (see box page 295)

½ cup heavy cream

¼ cup whole milk

1 cup sweetened condensed milk

¼ teaspoon salt

1 teaspoon almond extract

2 tablespoons almond butter

### FOR FINISHING

Light corn syrup (optional)

1 cup (4 ounces) crushed toasted sliced almonds

1. Place all the ingredients for the ice pops in a blender and mix well, 30 to 45 seconds.
2. Pour the liquid into the ice cream molds and set them in the freezer to freeze overnight.
3. Working with a couple of bars at a time, remove them from the freezer and unmold according to the manufacturer's instructions.
4. Dip each bar in warm water to melt it slightly, or brush it with light corn syrup. Press the bar into the crushed almonds, covering it on all sides. Place on a parchment-lined pan and return it to the freezer until ready to serve. Repeat with the remaining bars. Store the bars well wrapped in plastic wrap for up to 1 week.

## ALMOND MILK

This milky drink made from ground almonds is lactose- and cholesterol-free and can be used as a substitute in many recipes that call for cow's milk. It is a godsend for the lactose-intolerant and those of us who love the slightly bitter taste of almonds.

Interestingly, almond milk is not a new invention; it has been used in the Islamic world for centuries. It was also a staple in medieval European kitchens. A recipe for almond milk appears in *Le Viandier* (de Taillevent), one of the world's earliest recipe collections, which dates back to the Middle Ages. Almond milk was useful in those days when refrigeration wasn't an option; unlike animal milk, it was not highly perishable. It was also permitted during Lent, when all animal products, including milk, were prohibited by the Catholic Church. Almond milk was used in sauces, nut flans, and as a natural thickener as well.

Commercial varieties of almond milk are increasingly available, often in shelf-stable packaging in health-food stores and grocery stores, where it sits next to soy milk, but it can be loaded with preservatives. Making almond milk is simple. Many recipes prepare it without any cooking. In our slightly sweet version (omit the agave if you prefer unsweetened), we bring the nuts to a boil before processing, then allow the liquid to cool to room temperature, which results in a very palate-pleasing almond milk.

PREPARATION TIME: *30 minutes, plus 30 minutes to cool*
MAKES: *2 ¼ cups*

**2 cups (10 ounces) natural almonds**

**3 tablespoons agave nectar or honey (optional)**

**Seeds of 1 vanilla bean**

1. Combine the almonds, 4 cups water, and the agave nectar or honey in a saucepan and bring to a boil over medium heat. Boil for 5 minutes (boiling for much longer will cause too much liquid to evaporate). Cool the almonds and liquid to room temperature, about 30 minutes.
2. Place the almonds and all the liquid in a blender and blend for 30 seconds to liquefy. The almond liquid will turn an off-white milky color. Working in small batches, using about ½ cup at a time, strain the mixture through a cheesecloth, twisting and squeezing to obtain as much liquid as possible. Whisk in the vanilla bean seeds. Store the almond milk in an airtight container in the refrigerator for up to 4 days. Save and refrigerate the leftover almond meal for another use. We stir it into oatmeal or use it as a topping for ice cream.

*Left to right: Toasted-Almond Ice Pop (page 294); Coconut Ice Pop (page 297)*

# Coconut Ice Pops

After such success with our Toasted-Almond Ice Pops (page 294), we thought, why stop there? We knew that coconut would be as good, and maybe even better.

PREPARATION TIME: *10 minutes, plus 8 to 12 hours to freeze*
MAKES: *Eight 4-ounce bars*
EQUIPMENT: *1 set ice cream molds*

FOR THE ICE POPS

1¾ cups (14 ounces) coconut milk

½ cup heavy cream

¼ cup whole milk

1 cup sweetened condensed milk

¼ teaspoon salt

1 teaspoon vanilla extract

½ cup (2 ounces) sweetened shredded coconut

FOR FINISHING

Light corn syrup (optional)

1 cup (4 ounces) sweetened shredded coconut, toasted

1. Place all the ingredients for the ice pops except the coconut in a blender and mix well, 30 to 45 seconds.
2. Transfer to a bowl and stir in the ½ cup coconut.
3. Pour the liquid into the ice cream molds and set in the freezer to freeze overnight.
4. Working with a couple of bars at a time, remove them from the freezer and unmold according to the manufacturer's instructions.
5. Dip each bar in warm water to melt it slightly, or brush with light corn syrup. Press the bar into the toasted coconut, covering it on all sides. Place on a parchment-lined pan and return it to the freezer. Repeat with the remaining bars. Serve immediately or store well wrapped in the freezer for up to 1 week.

# Traditional Pecan Pie

The classic southern pecan pie is nearly perfect in our eyes, but we've made some tiny adjustments to get it as close to ideal as we can. We've added a bit more bourbon for bite, a little heavy cream to make the filling smoother, and extra pecans, filling the shell to the brim. Pecan halves look beautiful in this pie, and we've been known to turn them all on their bellies and line them up for a picture-perfect pie. That's not necessary, but a sharp knife to cut the pie is, for that is what it takes to get through the surface. Pieces of pecans are less expensive and are easier to cut through but don't have the dramatic look of pecan halves. The body of the pie is really a custard; the eggs are the thickeners that bind all the nuts together.

PREPARATION TIME: *45 minutes, plus 2 hours to chill the dough*
BAKING TIME: *45 to 50 minutes*
MAKES: *One 9-inch pie, about 10 servings*
EQUIPMENT: *One 9-inch pie pan*

## FOR THE DOUGH

1¼ cups all-purpose flour

¼ cup (1¼ ounces) ground almonds or almond flour

½ teaspoon salt

¼ cup packed light brown sugar

½ stick (4 tablespoons) unsalted butter, chilled and cut into 8 pieces

1 egg, lightly beaten

1 egg yolk, lightly beaten

## FOR THE PECAN FILLING

¾ cup light corn syrup

1 cup packed light brown sugar

2 tablespoons unsalted butter

3 large eggs

2 large egg yolks

2 tablespoons heavy cream

3 tablespoons bourbon

¼ teaspoon salt

3½ cups (14 ounces) pecan halves

1. Make the dough: Place the flour, almonds or almond flour, salt, and sugar in the work bowl of a food processor and pulse to combine for 15 seconds. Add the butter and process continuusly for about 45 seconds, until the mixture has a sandy texture. Add the egg and egg yolk and process just until the dough is combined and begins to form a ball, 15 to 30 seconds. Do not overprocess. You can use the dough right away, but for best results, wrap it in plastic wrap and chill it for several hours before rolling. The dough can be chilled for several days or frozen for up to 1 month. Bring it to cool room temperature before rolling.

2. Preheat the oven to 350°F.

3. On a lightly floured work surface, roll the dough into a 12-inch circle (see box page 300). Carefully roll the dough onto the rolling pin, then unroll it over the pie pan. Trim the edges 1 inch beyond the lip of the pan and roll the dough under to make the rim of the crust slightly thicker. Using the tines of a fork lightly dipped in flour, press to indent the edge of the crust all the way around. Chill the pie crust, well wrapped, while preparing the filling. The crust can be prepared several days in advance and frozen before being filled and baked.

4. Make the pecan filling: Combine the corn syrup, brown sugar, and butter in a medium saucepan over medium heat. Bring to a boil and whisk to melt the sugar, about 5 minutes. Remove from the heat and cool for 30 minutes. In a medium bowl, whisk together the eggs, egg yolks, cream, bourbon, and salt. Whisk in the cooled syrup.

5. Arrange the pecan halves in the chilled or frozen crust. Pour the prepared filling over the nuts. Bake until the crust is golden and the filling is puffed and firm, 45 to 50 minutes. Cool the pie before serving. If the crust is darkening toward the end of the baking, cover it with aluminum foil to prevent it from burning.

---

## How Do You Know If the Dough Will Fit in the Pan?

All you need to figure out if you have the correct amount of dough is a scale and a ruler. Measure the diameter of your pie pan or tart pan. Take that measurement in inches and add 2. For example, if you have a 9-inch pie pan, your number should be 9 + 2 = 11. This magic number translates into the number of ounces of dough you need. In this case you would need 11 ounces. If you have a lot more dough than you need, your pie or tart crust will be too thick. When the crust is too thick, it does not cook properly and tends to be a bit raw. It's better to discard a little scrap of dough than to try to work with a crust that's too thick.

## Rolling Your Dough

Many people tell us that whenever they see a recipe that requires dough, they either skip right over it or try to substitute premade crusts, which inevitably leads to an inferior result. We are here to tell you that rolling dough is nothing to be afraid of. Follow these simple rules and we promise you success every time:

1. Make sure your work surface is clean.
2. Make sure you have the right amount of dough for the pan you are using (see box page 299).
3. Lightly flour your surface and rolling pin.
4. Always begin the way you need to end. In other words, if you are rolling dough into a circle, start with a circle: use your hands to shape the dough roughly into a circle. Do not knead the dough; simply shape it.
5. If the dough has been chilled and is very cold, allow it to warm briefly and pound it lightly with the rolling pin to soften it before you begin to roll. To do this, gently lift and press the rolling pin into the dough at 1-inch intervals. Then turn your dough and press into it again. As you do this, check and turn the dough often to make sure it is not sticking to the work surface. Reflour the work surface lightly as needed.
6. Once your dough has softened, begin rolling.
7. Roll on the dough, not over the dough. This means your rolling pin should never roll over the edge of the dough and touch the work surface.
8. Apply light, even pressure and roll from the center outward. Too much pressure can cause your dough to become misshapen. Rotate your dough one quarter to one-third of a circle each time.
9. Roll the dough onto the rolling pin to transfer it to the pan.

# Coconut Custard Tart

When we think of a coconut custard pie, we typically think heavenly, fluffy, creamy white, and golden. We changed the presentation from a traditional pie to a tart so we could double the coconutty flavors. The press-in crust was born of necessity when we needed a flour-free, leavening-free tart shell for a Passover dessert. It is easier to prepare than a rolled crust and takes no planning or chilling. Baking the filling—also made without flour, so the tart is gluten-free—in a tart pan instead of a pie shell dresses up the dessert just a little. The sides of the crust need to be a little thicker than a traditional dough would be. When you press the crust into the bottom and up the sides of the pan, make sure the mixture is about ½-inch thick. No chance that the crust will get soggy; it keeps its macaroon-like texture after the filling is set. Only the crust gets baked, not the coconut filling, and it can be prepared and kept, well wrapped, up to a day in advance.

PREPARATION TIME: *30 minutes*
BAKING TIME: *25 minutes, plus 4 hours to chill and set*
MAKES: *One 10-inch tart, about 10 servings*
EQUIPMENT: *One 10-inch removable-bottom tart pan lightly coated with nonstick spray*

### FOR THE CRUST

3 cups (12 ounces) sweetened shredded coconut

¼ cup sugar

2 teaspoons vanilla extract

3 egg whites, lightly beaten

### FOR THE FILLING

1 cup whole milk

1 envelope (¼ ounce) unflavored gelatin

5 large egg yolks

2 tablespoons cornstarch

1½ cups coconut milk

½ cup sugar

1¼ cups (5 ounces) sweetened shredded coconut, toasted

1 tablespoon unsalted butter

1. Preheat the oven to 350°F.
2. Make the crust: Mix all the ingredients together in a bowl to combine. Press the mixture into the bottom and up the sides of the prepared tart pan. Bake for 25 minutes, until the crust has golden brown edges and holds together. Remove from the oven and set aside to cool.

*continued*

3. Prepare the filling: Place ¼ cup milk in a small bowl. Sprinkle the gelatin over the milk and allow it to stand for 5 minutes. Pour the remaining ¾ cup milk into a medium bowl and whisk in the egg yolks and cornstarch. Place the coconut milk and sugar in a medium saucepan over medium heat and bring to a boil, stirring occasionally. Whisk about ¼ cup of the hot coconut milk into the cornstarch mixture to warm it. Return all of the cornstarch mixture to the saucepan with the simmering coconut milk. Stir in 1 cup toasted coconut and bring the mixture to a boil. Cook, stirring constantly, for 2 minutes. Remove from the heat and stir in the butter and the dissolved gelatin.

4. Transfer the filling to the cooled pie shell and spread it smooth with an offset spatula. Sprinkle the remaining ¼ cup toasted coconut on top. Chill until the filling is set, about 4 hours. Serve chilled or at a cool room temperature.

# Creamy Sesame "Riced" Pudding

Andrea's Syrian grandmother, Sitto, taught her to make this pudding when she was young. She called it "riced" pudding in her less than perfect English, and prepared it for nearly every Tutunjian family gathering. It's not a traditional custard like most rice puddings are, because it contains no eggs. The sweet liquid is thickened just with the starch of the rice, and that is enough. We've added tahini to Sitto's recipe, because it elevates the flavor of the sesame seeds. We suggest chilling the pudding overnight, but some of us cannot resist eating it while it is still warm. It is an exemplar of comfort food. In honor of their grandmother, the name "riced pudding" stuck with Andrea and her siblings.

PREPARATION TIME: *5 minutes*
COOKING TIME: *55 minutes to 1 hour, plus 4 hours to chill*
MAKES: *10 to 12 servings*
EQUIPMENT: *Ten to twelve 4-ounce serving dishes or one larger shallow serving dish*

| | |
|---|---|
| 1 quart whole milk | 2 teaspoons vanilla extract |
| Pinch salt | 2 tablespoons tahini |
| ⅔ cup long-grain white Carolina rice | ¼ cup (1¼ ounces) sesame seeds, toasted |
| ½ cup sugar | Ground cinnamon to taste |

1. Bring the milk, 2 cups water, and the salt to a boil in a heavy medium saucepan over medium heat. Watch it carefully so the milk does not overflow. Once it reaches a boil, add the rice and lower the heat to low. Stir well every 5 minutes and slowly bring the mixture back to a boil. Simmer for 45 minutes and continue to stir every 5 minutes.
2. The pudding should begin to thicken but it will still appear fairly loose. Add the sugar, turn up the heat to medium, and cook, stirring continuously, for 10 minutes more. The pudding will thicken but still look as though there is a little extra milk; the rice will absorb the remainder of the milk as it is cooling.
3. Remove the pan from the heat and stir in the vanilla and tahini. Transfer the pudding to a bowl to cool to room temperature. Cover and chill in the refrigerator for several hours or overnight.
4. When ready to serve, sprinkle with the toasted sesame seeds and cinnamon.

# Hazelnut Brownie Bottom Cheesecake

This gluten-free majestic showstopper has everything we crave in a special-occasion dessert. The bottom of the cake is a rich, moist brownie, and the hefty top is a creamy, hazelnut-studded cheesecake. Prepared at the same time, there is no sequential baking, saving lots of time. Our friend and remarkable recipe tester Susan Ryan baked her hazelnut brownie for us, and we were blown away by its flavor and texture. This dessert was created to feature that recipe. The cheesecake topping is a loose reference to Craig Claiborne's Hazelnut Cheesecake, first published in the *New York Times* in 1970. It was a favorite then, and remains so now; a perfect combination.

PREPARATION TIME: *55 minutes*
BAKING TIME: *1 hour to 1 hour 15 minues, plus overnight to chill and set*
SERVES: *10 to 12*
EQUIPMENT: *One 9-inch springform pan, buttered and bottom lined with parchment paper, outside of bottom wrapped in aluminum foil; one larger, flat pan*

## FOR THE BROWNIE BOTTOM

1 cup (3½ ounces) hazelnut flour

½ cup Dutch process cocoa (see box page 000)

½ teaspoon salt

2 sticks (½ pound) unsalted butter, cut into 8 pieces

6 ounces bittersweet chocolate, roughly chopped

3 large eggs

½ cup granulated sugar

¾ cup light brown sugar

1 teaspoon vanilla extract

## FOR THE CHEESECAKE TOP

1½ pounds cream cheese, room temperature (see Note)

⅓ cup heavy cream

1 cup sugar

3 large eggs

1 teaspoon vanilla

¾ cup (3¾ ounces) chopped hazelnuts, toasted

1. Preheat oven to 325°F.
2. For the brownie bottom: In a small bowl, mix the hazelnut flour, cocoa, and salt. Set aside.
3. Place 2 inches of water in a medium saucepan and bring to a simmer over medium heat. Place the butter and chocolate in a bowl that will fit snugly on top of the saucepan, and gently melt the butter and chocolate together, stirring occasionally. Remove the mixture from the heat and set aside.

4. In a medium bowl, whisk together the eggs, sugars, and vanilla. Pour the melted chocolate mixture into the egg mixture, and, using a rubber spatula, mix to combine. Add the hazelnut flour–cocoa mixture and stir until completely mixed. Turn the brownie batter into the prepared pan, and set aside.

5. For the cheesecake top: In the bowl of a standing mixer fitted with the paddle attachment, beat the softened cream cheese with the cream until smooth, about 2 minutes. Add the sugar and beat together until well blended but not airy, about 1 minute.

6. Add the eggs and vanilla and beat for 30 seconds. Stop the mixer and, using a rubber spatula, scrape down the sides of the bowl, then mix for another 30 seconds, until all ingredients are combined. Stir in the hazelnuts.

7. Pour the cheesecake mixture on top of the brownie bottom. Place the cake pan in a larger flat pan that can fully accommodate it, and pour an inch of hot water into that pan to surround the cheesecake.

8. Bake for 1 hour to 1 hour 15 minutes, until the cheesecake is almost fully set when jiggled, and it has a light golden brown rim and an ivory top. Remove it from its water bath and place on a rack to cool. Refrigerate the cooled cheesecake overnight. Bring to room temperature before serving.

NOTE: When preparing a cheesecake, always keep the ingredients at room temperature to mix as little as possible. Less mixing results in the creamiest cheesecake and prevents it from rising and collapsing. Overbaking cheesecake can cause the cake to crack down the middle and taste dry. It is best to remove the cheesecake when there is still a small ring, about 2 inches in diameter, in the center that appears undercooked. The residual heat will cook the cake the remainder of the way. Finally, prepare cheesecake a day in advance, allowing it to set firmly in the refrigerator overnight, and always bring it to room temperature before serving.

# Caramel Apple Peanut Upside-Down Cake

This recipe was conceived on a late-night phone call when we were tossing around recipe ideas. Our goal was to find a way to incorporate a frangipane into a caramel-flavored dessert, and we think we have landed a perfect 10. Frangipane is a ground nut–based filling for pastries, and can be made with many different nuts. The most commonly used are almonds, walnuts, and pecans. This presented our first challenge: how would peanuts do in such a treatment? Perfectly, it turns out, and we're delighted. Next we thought of ways to combine a caramel with the frangipane, and the classic tarte Tatin came to mind. Tarte Tatin is an apple-filled, caramel-coated upside-down tart, first made in France centuries ago. Our twenty-first-century version hints at the classic, with a nutty twist. The frangipane substitutes for the crust, and the apples fill the cake in a modernist way, chunked up and tossed with peanuts. This is best the day it is made, and eating it up will not present a challenge!

PREPARATION TIME: *1 hour*
BAKING TIME: *30 minutes*
MAKES: *One 10-inch cake, 10 to 12 servings*
EQUIPMENT: *One 10-inch cake pan, lined with parchment paper and coated with nonstick spray*

2 granny smith apples, peeled, cored, and cut into ½-inch pieces

1 tablespoon all-purpose flour

½ cup (2½ ounces) roasted peanuts

### FOR THE CARAMEL

½ cup sugar

1 tablespoon light corn syrup

¼ stick (2 tablespoons) unsalted butter

### FOR THE PEANUT FRANGIPANE

¾ stick (6 tablespoons) unsalted butter, softened

1/3 cup light brown sugar, firmly packed

2 tablespoons natural peanut butter

2 large eggs

2 teaspoons vanilla extract

½ cup (2½ ounces) finely ground roasted peanuts

½ cup all-purpose flour

½ teaspoon baking powder

1. In a large mixing bowl, toss the apples with the flour to coat evenly. Stir in the peanuts and place the apple mixture in the prepared cake pan. Set aside.

2. For the caramel: Mix together the sugar, corn syrup, and 1 tablespoon of water in a small saucepan over medium heat. Bring the syrup to a boil without stirring and allow it to cook until it is a golden caramel color, about 15 minutes. Remove it from the heat and stir in the butter. Pour the caramel over the apple mixture.

3. Preheat the oven to 350°F.

4. Make the frangipane: In the bowl of a standing mixer fitted with the paddle attachment, beat the butter and sugar until light, about 5 minutes. Add the peanut butter and beat for an additional 2 minutes. In a small bowl, whisk the eggs and vanilla together. In another small bowl, stir the ground peanuts, flour, and baking powder together, until well mixed. Add half the flour-nut mixture to the butter and beat to incorporate. Add all of the egg mixture, just until it is mixed in. Finally, add in the remaining flour-nut mixture only until absorbed. Spread the batter evenly over the apples and caramel, and bake until the cake is set and feels firm when lightly pressed, 40 to 45 minutes. Remove from the oven and cool for 15 minutes.

5. While the cake is still warm, place a rimmed plate on top, and carefully invert the cake onto the plate. Allow it to sit for 2 to 3 minutes before lifting the cake pan off. Serve immediately.

VARIATION: *Chocolate Caramel Banana Peanut Upside-Down Cake*
Substitute 3 ripe bananas, sliced ½-inch thick diagonally, for the apples and omit the tablespoon of flour. For the frangipane, reduce the all-purpose flour to ¼ cup and add ¼ cup sifted Dutch process cocoa powder (see box page 90). Fill and bake as instructed above.

# Poppy Seed Ring with Lemon Cream Glaze

Lemon poppy seed cake is a home-baking staple, but our way of preparing it features a twist. Most are made like a pound cake and have no leavening, but we lighten ours by folding in whipped egg whites. This gives the cake a lift, creating a dessert with an unexpectedly delicate texture. We cover the cake with a drippy lemon cream glaze, a tribute to Andrea's grandmother, Antoinette Bianco, who baked them and left them temptingly on the kitchen counter. They never lasted more than a day in her family, but you can wrap it well and store it in the refrigerator for at least 3 days. Make sure to butter and flour the Bundt pan, even if it is labeled nonstick. A well-prepared pan will prevent the cake from sticking, and with this one an unblemished surface is paramount, for any flaw can be seen through the glaze.

PREPARATION TIME: *45 minutes*
BAKING TIME: *1 hour*
MAKES: *1 Bundt cake, 10 to 12 servings*
EQUIPMENT: *One 12-cup Bundt pan, buttered and floured*

### FOR THE CAKE

3 cups cake flour

2 teaspoons baking powder

¼ teaspoon ground mace

¼ teaspoon salt

2 sticks (16 tablespoons) unsalted butter, softened

2 cups sugar

4 large eggs, separated

1 tablespoon freshly grated lemon zest

1 tablespoon freshly squeezed lemon juice

1 cup whole milk

½ cup (2½ ounces) poppy seeds

### FOR THE LEMON CREAM GLAZE

¼ cup honey

2 tablespoons unsalted butter

1 tablespoon freshly squeezed lemon juice

2 cups sifted confectioners' sugar

¼ cup heavy cream

Pinch salt

1.  Preheat the oven to 350°F.
2.  Make the cake: Mix the flour, baking powder, mace, and salt together in a bowl. Set aside. In the bowl of a standing mixer fitted with the paddle attachment, cream the butter with 1 cup sugar on medium speed until light and fluffy, about 5 minutes. Add the egg yolks, lemon zest, and lemon juice and beat until combined. Scrape the sides of the mixing bowl with a rubber spatula. Stir in half the dry ingredients, then all the milk, and then the remaining half of the dry ingredients. Mix each addition just until

incorporated, and scrape the sides of the mixing bowl before adding the next ingredient. Stir in the poppy seeds. Scrape the batter into a large bowl and wash and dry the mixer bowl thoroughly.

3. Using the whip attachment, whisk the egg whites in the clean bowl on medium speed until frothy, 2 to 3 minutes. With the mixer running, gradually add the remaining 1 cup sugar in a slow, steady stream. Whip the egg whites until they hold stiff peaks, about 7 minutes. The whites will be glossy and will hold their shape when the whip is gently pulled from the bowl. Stir one-third of the whipped egg whites into the batter to lighten it and then fold in the remaining whites. Transfer the batter to the prepared pan. Bake until the cake is well risen, firm to the touch, and a deep golden brown, about 1 hour. (A toothpick or thin knife inserted into the center of the cake will come out clean.) Cool the cake in the pan on a rack for 20 minutes and then invert the pan to release the cake onto the rack. Allow the cake to cool completely.

4. When ready to serve, prepare the glaze: Melt the honey, butter, and lemon juice together in a small saucepan over low heat. Place the confectioners' sugar in a bowl and stir in the butter-honey mixture, followed by the cream and salt. While still warm and pourable, drizzle the glaze over the entire cake. If the icing cools and thickens too much to be pourable, reheat gently over very low heat. The icing will not coat the cake completely, it will just drizzle over the top and down the sides. Serve the cake at room temperature.

# Pumpkin Seed Spice Cake

This is a family-style cake, beloved and straightforward. The pureed pumpkin adds requisite moisture and the cake stays tender for days. Andrea bakes this for her husband's fire department, where it is a favorite. At first it was made for holidays, then it was requested year-round, and now she sends it along as a matter of course. If you prefer to make this into a layer cake, double the cake and icing recipe. Bake the cake in a 12-by-18-inch rimmed baking sheet. Cut the layer in half when it has cooled, and sandwich it together with the icing.

PREPARATION TIME: *25 minutes*
BAKING TIME: *25 to 30 minutes, plus 15 to 20 minutes to cool*
MAKES: *Thirty-five 2-inch cake squares*
EQUIPMENT: *One 10-by-15-inch baking pan, buttered and lined with parchment paper*

FOR THE CAKE

4 eggs

1⅔ cups granulated sugar

1 cup canola oil

One 15-ounce can pumpkin puree

2 cups all-purpose flour

2 teaspoons baking powder

2 teaspoons ground cinnamon

¼ teaspoon freshly grated nutmeg

½ teaspoon ground ginger

¼ teaspoon ground cloves

1 teaspoon salt

1 teaspoon baking soda

½ cup (2¾ ounces) coarsely chopped pumpkin seeds, toasted

FOR THE ICING

4 ounces cream cheese, softened

1 stick (8 tablespoons) butter, softened

1 teaspoon vanilla extract

2 cups sifted confectioners' sugar

1. Preheat the oven to 350°F.
2. Make the cake: In the bowl of a standing mixer fitted with the whip attachment, whisk the eggs, granulated sugar, oil, and pumpkin puree until light and fluffy, about 3 minutes. In a medium bowl, combine the flour, baking powder, cinnamon, nutmeg, ginger, cloves, salt, and baking soda and mix well. Add the dry ingredients to the pumpkin mixture in three batches, mixing thoroughly after each addition. Fold in the pumpkin seeds and spread the batter in the prepared pan. Wash and dry the mixer bowl. Bake for 25 to 30 minutes, or until a thin knife or toothpick inserted in the center comes out clean.

3. While the cake is baking, prepare the icing: In the clean bowl of the standing mixer fitter with the paddle attachment, beat the cream cheese and butter together on medium speed until light and fluffy, about 5 minutes. Stir in the vanilla. Slowly add the confectioners' sugar, beating until smooth after each addition. Set aside until the cake has cooled.

4. Cool the cake in the pan on a rack for 15 minutes and then unmold. When it has fully cooled, place it on a cutting board or flat plate and ice the top only. Cut into 2-inch squares and serve.

# Triple-Ginger Pecan Loaf

Ginger may be our favorite go-to flavor. We love it in dishes both sweet and savory, but this triple-dose cake is on the list of all-time greatest hits. Its first appearance was at Cara's restaurant, Quarropas, and it has been with us in one form or another ever since. Ground, fresh, and candied ginger are incorporated here for a piquancy that is remarkable. Ginger is believed to have soothing properties, and considering how happy this cake makes us, we think it does. Each form of ginger has a slightly different flavor, and they certainly have differing textures. Dry or powdered ginger, so often found in baked goods, is warm and deep. Freshly grated ginger is bright and brassy. Candied ginger is spicy and sweet, with a chewy texture and a sugary crust. One complements the next, and together they pair with pecans for a spectacular cake that can be dressed up with ice cream for dessert or toasted plain for breakfast.

PREPARATION TIME: *45 minutes*
BAKING TIME: *1 hour to 1 hour 20 minutes*
MAKES: *1 loaf cake, 8 servings*
EQUIPMENT: *One 9-by-5-by-3-inch loaf pan, buttered and floured*

2¼ cups all-purpose flour

1½ teaspoons ground ginger

¼ teaspoon baking soda

¼ teaspoon salt

1½ sticks (12 tablespoons) unsalted butter, softened

1¾ cups sugar

3 tablespoons (2 ounces) freshly grated ginger

4 large eggs, separated

⅔ cup sour cream

¾ cup (3 ounces) finely chopped pecans

½ cup diced (¼-inch) candied ginger

1. Preheat the oven to 350°F.
2. Mix the flour, ground ginger, baking soda, and salt together in a bowl. Set aside. In the bowl of a standing mixer fitted with the paddle attachment, cream the butter with 1¼ cups sugar on medium speed until soft, about 2 minutes. Add the fresh ginger and beat for another minute. Beat in the egg yolks one at a time, scraping down the sides of the bowl and mixing well after each addition. Reduce the speed to low and add half the dry ingredients, then all the sour cream, then the remaining dry ingredients, mixing each just until incorporated and scraping down the sides of the bowl after each addition. Transfer the batter into a large bowl. Stir in the pecans and candied ginger. Wash and dry the mixer bowl thoroughly.

3. In the clean bowl of the standing mixer fitted with the whip attachment, whisk the egg whites on medium speed until opaque and frothy, about 3 minutes. With the motor running, gradually add the remaining ½ cup sugar in a slow, steady stream. Whisk until the whites hold a soft peak, about 3 minutes.

4. Gently stir one-third of the whites into the batter to lighten it, scraping the sides and bottom of the bowl as you fold. Fold in the remaining whites. Scrape the batter into the prepared pan. Bake until a toothpick inserted into the center of the loaf comes out clean, 80 to 90 minutes.

5. Cool the cake in the pan on a rack for 5 to 10 minutes. Invert the pan to release the cake onto the rack. Turn the cake top side up and cool completely before serving. Wrap and store any extra cake at room temperature for up to 3 days.

# Banana-Walnut Cake

Barbara Gottstein, Andrea's college roommate, is a banana cake fan, and this a slightly modified version of her recipe. No one loves it more than Sean, Andrea's son. At home he hopes his lack of interest in ripe bananas will ultimately lead to his mom baking a cake with them in their overripe state. Tender and rich, this is a no-fail, easy-to-prepare family favorite.

PREPARATION TIME: *30 minutes*
BAKING TIME: *55 minutes to 1 hour*
MAKES: *1 loaf cake, 8 servings*
EQUIPMENT: *One 9-by-5-by-3-inch loaf pan, buttered and lined with parchment paper*

2 cups all-purpose flour

1 teaspoon ground cinnamon

¼ teaspoon freshly grated nutmeg

1 teaspoon baking soda

½ teaspoon salt

1 stick (8 tablespoons) unsalted butter, softened

½ cup granulated sugar

¼ cup packed light brown sugar

2 eggs

1 tablespoon vanilla extract or dark rum

3 very ripe bananas

1 cup (3½ ounces) chopped walnuts, toasted

1. Preheat the oven to 350°F.
2. In a medium bowl, sift together the flour, cinnamon, nutmeg, baking soda, and salt and set aside. In the bowl of a standing mixer fitted with the paddle attachment, cream the butter, granulated sugar, and brown sugar on medium speed for 2 minutes. Add the eggs one at a time, making sure each is fully incorporated before adding the next. Mix in the vanilla or rum. Turn the speed to low and add the bananas, one at a time, mixing until they are fully mashed. Add the dry ingredients to the banana mixture, mixing only until incorporated. Remove the bowl from the machine and stir in the walnuts.
3. Transfer the batter to the prepared pan and bake for 55 minutes to 1 hour, or until the cake is well risen and a thin knife or toothpick inserted in the center comes out clean. Cool the cake in the pan on a rack for 15 minutes and then unmold. Allow it to cool fully before serving.

# Cupavci
## CHOCOLATE COCONUT TORTE

Cara's friend Nancy Ladisic gave her this recipe with a large pile of the perfectly shaped cubes one year for Christmas, and we thought they were delicious. Nancy is from Croatia where cupavci is a commonly prepared festive sweet. It has been served for generations by Nancy, her mother, and her mother's mother on birthdays, Easter, and Christmas. Piled high in a pyramid, it is also presented at Croatian weddings instead of a conventional cake. The baked cake is as light as can be. It is cooled, cut into cubes, and individually cloaked in a deep chocolate-coconut crust.

PREPARATION TIME: *1 hour 10 minutes*
BAKING TIME: *20 to 25 minutes*
MAKES: *Twenty-four 2-inch squares*
EQUIPMENT: *One 9-by-13-inch baking pan at least 2 inches deep, buttered and lined with parchment paper*

### FOR THE CAKE

5 large eggs, separated

1¼ cups sugar

¾ cup canola oil

1 tablespoon baking powder

1¼ cups all-purpose flour

### FOR THE GLAZE

1 cup whole milk

1½ teaspoons sugar

1½ teaspoons unsalted butter

3½ ounces coarsely chopped bittersweet chocolate

2 cups (6 ounces) unsweetened coconut flakes

1. Preheat the oven to 375°F.
2. In the bowl of a standing mixer fitted with the whip attachment, whisk the egg yolks and ⅝ cup sugar together on medium speed until the yolks are a little lighter and thicker, about 3 minutes. With the mixer running slowly, add the oil, baking powder, flour, and ¼ cup boiling water. Set aside.
3. Clean the mixing bowl and the attachment and whip the egg whites on high speed until they are frothy, about 3 minutes. Gradually add the remaining ¾ cup sugar. Whip until the whites are stiff and shiny. Fold them into the egg yolk–flour mixture in three additions and pour the batter into the prepared pan. Bake for 20 to 25 minutes, or until the cake is golden and set. Remove from the oven and cool in the pan on a rack. When it is completely cool, cut it into 2-inch cubes.

*continued*

4. While the cake is cooling, prepare the glaze: Bring the milk, sugar, and butter to a boil over medium-high heat in a medium saucepan. Add the chopped chocolate and remove the pan from the heat. Allow the mixture to stand for 5 minutes, then whisk it smooth. Place the coconut on a flat plate. While the glaze is still warm but not hot, dip the cooled cake cubes into the glaze, working with a few at a time. Remove them with a slotted spoon, allowing the excess glaze to drip back into the pan. Drop the cubes onto the coconut and gently rotate them so all sides are covered. Place them on a serving platter as you go, until all the cubes are covered. They can be stored in an airtight container for up to 3 days.

# Hazelnut–Olive Oil Ring

The unique flavor of this cake shines through when you use mild olive oil. Extra-virgin oil, with its bold flavor, would overpower the hazelnuts, knocking them out of their starring role. Without butter and cream, we view this cake as a healthy one. Every bit of anticipated moistness is provided by the oil and nuts, and no one misses the rich dairy ingredients. We serve it as we would a simple angel food cake, topped with fresh berries in the spring and summer, or poached fall fruit in the autumn and winter.

PREPARATION TIME: *20 minutes*
BAKING TIME: *35 minutes*
MAKES: *One 10-inch cake, 10 to 12 servings*
EQUIPMENT: *One 10-inch tube pan, lightly buttered and floured*

1¼ cups (4½ ounces) hazelnut flour or finely ground hazelnuts

1¼ cups all-purpose flour

¼ cup confectioners' sugar, plus more for finishing

2½ teaspoons baking powder

¼ teaspoon salt

3 large eggs

¾ cup granulated sugar

½ cup olive oil

½ cup Frangelico or other hazelnut liqueur

1. Preheat the oven to 350°F.
2. Place the hazelnut flour or ground hazelnuts in a bowl. Sift the all-purpose flour, ¼ cup confectioners' sugar, baking powder, and salt over the hazelnut flour and stir to mix well.
3. In the bowl of a standing mixer fitted with the whip attachment, whisk the eggs on medium speed until they are frothy, about 3 minutes. With the mixer running, add the granulated sugar a little at a time and whip for another 3 to 4 minutes, or until the eggs have lightened and thickened.
4. Fold the flour-hazelnut mixture into the egg mixture in 2 or 3 additions, using a rubber spatula and scraping the sides of the bowl as you fold. Stir the olive oil and Frangelico into the batter. Scrape the batter into the prepared pan and bake until the cake pulls away from the sides of the pan and springs back when pressed lightly, about 35 minutes.
5. Unmold the cake immediately: Carefully slide a sharp knife or spatula around the sides of the cake and then invert the pan onto a cooling rack. Dust it lightly with confectioners' sugar and serve at room temperature.

*Dione Lucas's Flourless Hazelnut Roulade (page 319)*

# Dione Lucas's Flourless Hazelnut Roulade

This is a classic. Codified many years ago by the English chef Dione Lucas, this flourless cake, rolled and filled with sweetened whipped cream, may have slipped out of prominence, but we believe it deserves a second look. Dione Lucas was the first woman to graduate from the Cordon Bleu in Paris and the first to host a TV cooking show. Many a midcentury housewife tried to perfect this roulade, and we believe it can be easily done. First, understand that the "cake" portion of this recipe is like a fallen soufflé, made from a base of egg yolks and hazelnuts and leavened with airy beaten egg whites. Next, you need to cover the baked and fallen cake with a damp towel as it cools, so you can roll it without cracking it. Make it the day you plan to serve it—it is not known for its longevity. Thanks to Bonnie Slotnick for passing on the original recipe. We have adapted it slightly, using hazelnuts instead of walnuts.

PREPARATION TIME: *55 minutes*
BAKING TIME: *15 to 18 minutes, plus 1 hour 15 minutes to chill*
MAKES: *One 16-inch roulade, 10 servings*
EQUIPMENT: *1 rimmed baking sheet, buttered and lined with buttered parchment paper*

6 large eggs, separated

¾ cup granulated sugar

1½ cups (5¼ ounces) hazelnut flour or ground hazelnuts

½ teaspoon ground cinnamon

2 tablespoons confectioners' sugar

**FOR THE FILLING**

1½ cups heavy cream, chilled

¾ cup confectioners' sugar

½ teaspoon vanilla extract

1 tablespoon sour cream

Confectioners' sugar for finishing

1. Preheat the oven to 350°F.
2. In the bowl of a standing mixer fitted with the whip attachment, whisk the egg yolks on medium speed. Gradually sprinkle in ½ cup granulated sugar and whisk until the eggs are thick and a pale buttercup yellow, about 10 minutes. Stir together the hazelnut flour and cinnamon. Fold this mixture into the lightened egg yolk, place in a clean bowl, and set aside.
3. Clean the mixing bowl and the attachment and whip the egg whites on high speed until they are frothy and bubbly, about 3 minutes. Gradually sprinkle in the remaining ¼ cup granulated sugar and whisk until the egg whites are stiff but not dry, about 3 more minutes. Scoop a heaping spoonful of the whites into the egg yolk mixture and stir them together. This will lighten the egg yolk mixture and make it easier to fold the remaining whites into the yolks while maintaining the most airiness.

*continued*

4. In 2 batches, fold the whites into the yolks. Pour the mixture into the prepared pan. Using a spatula, level the top of the batter. Bake for 15 to 18 minutes, until the puffy top feels firm and the cake is a light golden brown. Dampen a kitchen towel and wring out all the extra moisture. Place the cloth over the cake and cool it in the refrigerator for 15 minutes. When it is completely cool, remove it from the fridge, take off the towel, and sprinkle 2 tablespoons confectioners' sugar on top.

5. Make the Filling: In the bowl of a standing mixer fitted with the whip attachment, whisk the chilled cream with the confectioners' sugar, vanilla, and sour cream until soft peaks form. Set aside.

6. Stretch a piece of aluminum foil 20 inches long on the counter. Turn the sugared side of the cake onto the foil and remove the parchment paper. Spread the whipped cream over the cake, leaving a ½-inch border all around. Working with an 18-inch edge farthest from you, lift the long edge of the foil up with the edge of the cake. Begin rolling the cake into a log, using the foil as your guide. Roll it toward you as tightly as you can. Twist the ends of the foil shut and refrigerate the roulade for 1 hour or overnight. When you are ready to serve, unwrap the foil, trim the ends, and dust the top of the roulade with confectioners' sugar. Slice it into 1½-inch pieces and serve. Refrigerate any left-overs, wrapped airtight, for up to 1 day.

# Peanut Butter and Jelly Cupcakes

Baking should be fun, and we think these cupcakes are loads of fun: a cross between the elegant and the commonplace. We have created a peanutty butter cake that is tender enough to be eaten alone but is filled with jelly like a doughnut, offering the most comfortable of childhood favorites in a form for adults. Our families always chuckle with delight when we make these cupcakes; they love the contrast of the familiar flavors and the unusual presentation.

PREPARATION TIME: *1 hour*
BAKING TIME: *25 to 30 minutes*
MAKES: *21 cupcakes*
EQUIPMENT: *Two 12-cup muffin tins lined with paper liners*

### FOR THE CUPCAKES

1½ cups all-purpose flour

2 teaspoons baking powder

¼ teaspoon baking soda

½ teaspoon salt

½ cup (2½ ounces) finely ground roasted peanuts

1½ sticks (12 tablespoons) unsalted butter, softened

⅔ cup granulated sugar

⅔ cup packed light brown sugar

⅔ cup smooth natural peanut butter

3 large eggs

½ cup sour cream

1 teaspoon vanilla extract

1 cup grape jelly or seedless raspberry jam

### FOR THE ICING

¾ stick (6 tablespoons) unsalted butter, softened

3 ounces cream cheese, softened

½ cup confectioners' sugar

½ cup smooth natural peanut butter

½ teaspoon vanilla extract

¼ cup whole milk

1. Preheat the oven to 375°F.
2. Sift the flour, baking powder, baking soda, and salt together into a bowl. Stir in the ground peanuts.
3. In the bowl of a standing mixer fitted with the paddle attachment, beat the butter with the two sugars on medium-high speed until light, about 5 minutes. Stop the mixer and scrape down the sides of the bowl occasionally. Turn the mixer to low and beat in the peanut butter, mixing to incorporate, about 30 seconds.

*continued*

4. In a small bowl, whisk the eggs with the sour cream and vanilla. With the mixer still on low speed, and scraping down the sides of the bowl after each addition, add half the dry ingredients and mix to incorporate, then all the egg–sour cream mixture, and finally the remaining dry ingredients.

5. Scrape the batter into the prepared tins, filling 21 of the cups two-thirds full. Bake for 25 to 30 minutes or until the cupcakes are well risen and spring back slightly when touched. Cool the cupcakes completely in the tins on racks. Wash and dry the mixer bowl.

6. While the cupcakes are baking, prepare the icing: In the clean bowl of the standing mixer fitted with the paddle attachment, beat the butter and cream cheese to combine, about 30 seconds. Add the confectioners' sugar and beat on low speed for 2 minutes. Scrape down the sides of the bowl, add the peanut butter and vanilla, and beat for another 2 minutes. Add the milk and mix for 2 minutes more. Set the icing aside until you are ready to use it.

7. While the cupcakes are cooling, place the jelly or jam in a bowl and whisk until smooth and spreadable. Cut a deep cone shape in the top of each cooled cupcake with a sharp knife and remove the center. Spoon 1 teaspoon jelly into the hole and return the top to close it. Repeat with the remaining cupcakes. Spread the icing on top and serve. The cupcakes are best eaten on the same day. Store any leftovers in an airtight container in the refrigerator for up to 3 days.

# Chocolate-Almond Cupcakes

Nearly everyone loves chocolate, and these are a glowing example of rich, finger-licking chocolate at its best. The almonds stand out against their dark brown background like stars in the nighttime sky. We understand the popularity of cupcakes. With built-in portion control, a hopeful blast of flavor, and a tightrope balance of cake and frosting, cupcakes can be daily snacks or special-occasion desserts. These are casual enough to be snacks and also dressy enough for an elegant finish. Your pick, but don't expect longevity from the batch. Everyone loves them.

PREPARATION TIME: *40 minutes*
BAKING TIME: *20 to 25 minutes*
MAKES: *24 cupcakes*
EQUIPMENT: *Two 12-cup muffin tins lined with paper liners*

### FOR THE WHIPPED CREAM

2 cups heavy cream

2 cinnamon sticks

1 tablespoon vanilla extract

¼ cup confectioners' sugar, sifted

### FOR THE CUPCAKES

⅔ cup Dutch process cocoa powder (see box page 90)

⅓ cup Amaretto or other almond liqueur

2 cups all-purpose flour

½ cup (1¾ ounces) almond flour

1¼ teaspoons baking soda

1 teaspoon ground cinnamon

¼ teaspoon baking powder

¼ teaspoon salt

1¼ sticks (10 tablespoons) unsalted butter, softened

1 cup granulated sugar

⅔ cup packed light brown sugar

2 large eggs

1 large egg yolk

½ cup (2¼ ounces) finely chopped slivered almonds

1. Preheat the oven to 325°F.
2. Make the whipped cream: Bring 1 cup cream and the cinnamon sticks to a boil over medium-high heat in a small saucepan. Turn off the heat and let stand for 15 minutes. Add the remaining 1 cup cream and chill thoroughly. The cream can be prepared to this point a few days in advance and stored in an airtight container in the refrigerator.
3. Make the cupcakes: Stir the cocoa with 1 cup boiling water in a medium bowl until the cocoa is dissolved and melted. Stir in the amaretto and set aside to cool.
4. Sift the flours, baking soda, ground cinnamon, baking powder, and salt together into a separate bowl. Mix well.

*continued*

5. In the bowl of a standing mixer fitted with the paddle attachment, cream the butter, granulated sugar, and brown sugar on medium speed until light, about 5 minutes, stopping the mixer to scrape down the sides of the bowl occasionally. Reduce the speed to low and add eggs and egg yolk. Add one-third of the dry ingredients, then one-half of the cocoa mixture, mixing each addition just until incorporated and scraping down the sides of the bowl after each. Repeat with one-half of the remaining dry ingredients and the remaining cocoa mixture, then finish with the remaining dry ingredients. Stir in the chopped slivered almonds.

6. Scrape the batter into the prepared tins, filling the cups two-thirds full, and bake until the cupcakes are well risen and spring back slightly when touched, 20 to 25 minutes. Cool in the pan on a rack before unmolding. Wash and dry the mixer bowl.

7. Remove the cinnamon sticks from the chilled cream. Place it in the clean bowl of the standing mixer fitted with the whip attachment, and whip the cream on medium speed until it thickens slightly. With the mixer running, gradually add the confectioners' sugar and whip until the cream is firm but not overwhipped, 3 to 4 minutes. Chill until ready to use.

8. When the cupcakes are cool enough to handle, cut a deep cone shape in the top of a cupcake with a knife. Remove the center and fill with 1 teaspoon whipped cream. Return the top and close. Repeat with remaining cupcakes. Chill until ready to serve. Spread a bit of the remaining whipped cream on top of each cupcake. Store any leftovers in an airtight container in the refrigerator for up to 3 days.

# Cranberry-Pistachio Biscotti

These festive red-and-green biscotti are one of the basics of our holiday cookie baking sprees. Rich, sturdy, colorful, and linear, they add a beautiful counterpoint to some of the less vibrant, round treats. These are crumblier than many other biscotti because they are made by cutting butter into the dry ingredients. Different biscotti may have no added fat, or may have some oil mixed in. Instead, this process will make a cakier, crumblier, and ultimately richer cookie. This type of biscotti is always twice-baked, first in large logs, and next when cooled, sliced, and toasted at a lower temperature. The second baking ensures the driest and toastiest of textures. Many like to dunk these in a hot beverage, but we like them just the way they are.

PREPARATION TIME: *30 minutes*
BAKING TIME: *40 to 45 minutes for 2 sheets, plus 45 minutes to cool*
MAKES: *75 cookies*
EQUIPMENT: *2 rimmed baking sheets lined with parchment paper*

3½ cups all-purpose flour

1¾ cups sugar

1 teaspoon baking powder

½ teaspoon salt

1 stick (8 tablespoons) unsalted butter, chilled

1 cup dried cranberries

2 cups (10 ounces) unsalted pistachios

4 large eggs

2 teaspoons vanilla extract

1. Preheat the oven to 350°F.
2. In the bowl of a standing mixer fitted with the paddle attachment, mix the flour, sugar, baking powder, and salt on low speed.
3. Cut the butter into 8 to 12 pieces and add to the flour mixture. Beat on medium-low speed until the flour resembles coarse meal. Stir in the cranberries and pistachios until they are evenly coated with the dry ingredients.
4. In a small bowl, whisk the eggs and vanilla together. Add to the flour mixture and beat on low speed until incorporated. The dough will be sticky.
5. Turn the dough out onto a floured work surface and divide into 3 equal pieces. Working with floured hands, roll 1 piece into a log about 16 inches long. Transfer the log to one of the prepared pans and press gently with your hands to flatten. Repeat with the remaining pieces of dough and pans, placing 2 logs on one of the pans. Bake until the logs have spread and are well risen, golden, and firm to the touch, 25 to 30 minutes. Remove and cool on the pans. Do not turn the oven off.

*continued*

6. Lower the oven to 300°F. When the logs have cooled, carefully transfer them to a cutting board. Using a serrated knife, slice them one by one at a 45-degree angle into ½-inch slices. Return these slices to the pans, arranging them on their sides so they are lying flat, and bake until toasted and crisp, 15 to 20 minutes. Cool on a rack. Repeat as needed with the remaining logs and cooled pans until all the biscotti are baked, or freeze the logs for future use. The cooled biscotti can be stored in an airtight container for up to 1 week.

# Lillian Osband's Mandelbrot

Cara's grandmother Lillian Osband, known to her family as Lilly, was a health-food fanatic before it was fashionable. She eschewed frying, cut back on fat, and looked for ways to use "healthy" ingredients, including soy flour, even though she had to trek to a remote "natural store" in Brooklyn to purchase it. Whether because of her eating habits or because of those long walks to that out-of-the-way store, Lilly lived to be ninety-six and was vital until the end of her life. At Cara's house, sweets were served very rarely, and when Lilly arrived for a weekend visit, she'd often bring home-baked Mandelbrot, the Jewish version of a twice-baked cookie. Lilly's Mandelbrot had little oil and contained soy flour, and Cara loved them. They were doled out as if they were little gold bars and always made for a thrilling weekend.

PREPARATION TIME: *30 minutes*
BAKING TIME: *40 to 45 minutes for 2 sheets, plus 45 minutes to cool*
MAKES: *60 cookies*
EQUIPMENT: *2 rimmed baking sheets lined with parchment paper*

| | |
|---|---|
| 2 cups all-purpose flour | ¾ cup dried currants |
| 1 cup soy flour | 1 cup (3½ ounces) walnut pieces |
| 1½ cups sugar | ½ cup vegetable oil |
| 1 tablespoon baking powder | 3 large eggs |
| 2 teaspoons ground cinnamon | 2 teaspoons vanilla extract |
| Pinch freshly grated nutmeg | 1 tablespoon freshly grated orange zest |

1. Preheat the oven to 350°F.
2. Mix the flours, sugar, baking powder, cinnamon, and nutmeg in a large bowl. Stir in the currants and walnuts and set aside.
3. In a small bowl, whisk the oil, eggs, and vanilla and stir in the zest. Add the oil mixture to the flour mixture and stir to combine until a uniform dough forms. (Knead a little by hand if necessary.)
4. Transfer the dough to a lightly floured surface and divide it into 2 pieces. Working with floured hands, roll 1 piece into a log about 16 inches long. Transfer the log to one of the prepared pans and press gently with your hands to flatten. Repeat with the remaining piece of dough and pan. Bake until the logs are well risen, golden, and firm to the touch, 20 to 25 minutes. Remove and cool on the pans, about 45 minutes. Lower the oven temperature to 300°F.

*continued*

5. When the logs have cooled, carefully transfer them to a cutting board. Using a serrated knife, slice them one by one at a 45-degree angle into ½-inch slices. Return these slices to the pans, arranging them on their cut sides, and bake until toasted and crisp, 15 to 20 minutes. Cool the cookies on the pans for 5 minutes and then transfer to a rack. They can be stored in an airtight container for up to 1 week.

# White Chocolate–Salted Macadamia Nut Cookies

Sweet and salty dessert combinations have zoomed up the charts of desirability, and with recipes like this in the repertoire, we understand why. Roughly chopped macadamias provide the crunch and the salt, and a combination of chocolates provides the sweet. These also fall into the "I can't eat just one" category, so be prepared for the onslaught of happy eaters. Crisp when they are finished; err on the side of underbaking these cookies if you are not precisely sure of doneness. They won't feel firm when they come out of the oven, but they will continue to bake just a bit and will crisp up as they cool on the pans.

PREPARATION TIME: *30 minutes*
BAKING TIME: *15 to 18 minutes for 2 sheets*
MAKES: *65 cookies*
EQUIPMENT: *2 rimmed baking sheets lined with parchment paper*

2½ cups all-purpose flour

1 teaspoon baking soda

2 sticks (16 tablespoons) unsalted butter, softened

1 cup granulated sugar

½ cup packed light brown sugar

2 large eggs

2 teaspoons vanilla extract

¾ cup (6 ounces) semisweet chocolate chips

12 ounces white chocolate, chopped

2 cups (10 ounces) coarsely chopped salted macadamia nuts

1. Preheat the oven to 350°F.
2. Mix flour and baking soda together and set aside.
3. In the bowl of a standing mixer fitted with the paddle attachment, beat the butter and sugars on medium speed until very light, about 5 minutes. Add the eggs and vanilla, stopping once to scrape down the sides of the bowl with a rubber spatula. Remove the bowl from the mixer and stir in the flour and baking soda. Stir in the chocolates and the macadamia nuts.
4. Place heaping teaspoons of dough 2 inches apart on the prepared pans. Bake until golden and set, 12 to 15 minutes.
5. Cool the cookies on the pans on a rack. Repeat as needed with the remaining dough and cooled pans until all the cookies are baked, or freeze the dough for future use. Store the cooled cookies for up to 3 days in an airtight container.

# Chewy Oatmeal Pecan-Raisin Cookies

To us, oatmeal cookies, like their all-American cousin chocolate chip, mean home, hearth, and all things delicious and simply baked. These are packed with dried fruit and pecans and flavored with maple syrup, and the balance between the sweet light golden raisins and the tart dark cranberries is just right. We prefer grade B maple syrup for its deeper color and richer flavor. With pecans from Georgia, maple syrup from Vermont, cranberries from New Jersey, and raisins from California, these cookies are a cross-country representation of American wholesomeness. Sonia Dreryan, Andrea's sister's friend, passed along the original from which this recipe is adapted. If you prefer your cookies crisp, bake these for fifteen minutes.

PREPARATION TIME: *30 minutes*
BAKING TIME: *12 to 15 minutes for 2 sheets*
MAKES: *100 cookies*
EQUIPMENT: *2 rimmed baking sheets lined with parchment paper*

2 cups all-purpose flour

1 teaspoon ground cinnamon

1 teaspoon baking powder

½ teaspoon baking soda

½ teaspoon salt

2 sticks (16 tablespoons) unsalted butter, softened

1½ cups packed light brown sugar

¼ cup maple syrup

2 large eggs

1 tablespoon vanilla extract

2 cups dried cranberries

2 cups golden raisins

2 cups (8 ounces) coarsely chopped pecans

2 cups rolled oats

1. Preheat the oven to 350°F.
2. Stir together the flour, cinnamon, baking powder, baking soda, and salt in a medium bowl and set aside.
3. In the bowl of a standing mixer fitted with the paddle attachment, beat the butter, brown sugar, and maple syrup on medium speed until light and fluffy, about 5 minutes. Add the eggs and beat until incorporated. Beat in the vanilla.
4. Remove the bowl from the mixer and stir in the dried fruits and pecans, using a rubber spatula. Gently fold in the flour mixture. Add the oats and fold with the rubber spatula, making sure they are evenly distributed.
5. Drop tablespoons of the dough 2 inches apart on the prepared pans. Bake until golden and set, 12 to 15 minutes. Cool the cookies on the pans on a rack. Repeat as needed with the remaining dough and cooled pans until all the cookies are baked, or freeze the dough for future use. Store the cooled cookies for up to 3 days in an airtight container.

# Nutty Peanut Butter Bites

These cookies are chunky and crisp, as all good peanut butter cookies should be. They have a sandy texture, and we like them small—just an intense, peanut-packed morsel. Barbara Pugliese, a dear friend, great baker, and former colleague at ICE, has been making these as long as we've known her, and she was happy to share the recipe.

PREPARATION TIME: *45 minutes*
BAKING TIME: *12 to 15 minutes for 2 sheets*
MAKES: *48 cookies*
EQUIPMENT: *2 rimmed baking sheets lined with parchment paper*

1½ cups all-purpose flour

¾ teaspoon baking soda

¼ teaspoon salt

1 stick (8 tablespoons) unsalted butter, softened

½ cup smooth natural peanut butter

½ cup granulated sugar

½ cup packed light brown sugar

1 large egg

½ teaspoon vanilla extract

¾ cup (3¾ ounces) coarsely chopped salted roasted peanuts

1. Preheat the oven to 350°F.
2. Stir together the flour, baking soda, and salt in a medium bowl and set aside.
3. In the bowl of a standing mixer fitted with the paddle attachment, beat the butter, peanut butter, and sugars on medium speed until light and fluffy, about 5 minutes. Add the egg and vanilla and beat until incorporated. Add the flour mixture and beat just until combined.
4. Remove the bowl from the mixer and stir in the peanuts.
5. Using a small ice cream scoop or a tablespoon, drop scoops of dough onto the prepared pans about 2 inches apart. Press each scoop gently with the back of the spoon or the palm of your hand to form it into a disk and flatten it slightly. Bake until golden brown, 12 to 15 minutes. Transfer the cookies to a rack to cool. Repeat as needed with the remaining dough and cooled pans until all the cookies are baked, or freeze the dough for future use. Store the cooled cookies in an airtight container for up to 1 week.

*Benne Wafers (page 333)*

# Benne Wafers

Benne wafers are a southern specialty. Sesame seeds were brought to the American South during the slave trade, when many foodstuffs traveled back and forth across the Atlantic Ocean. The word *benne* translates as "good luck" in Bantu, an African language that was brought to these shores along with the seeds. Maybe they were lucky because they made it through the arduous journey, and maybe part of their association with luck lies with their plentitude. These thin, crisp cookies are packed with the tiny, tasty seeds. Our recipe comes from our mentor, Nick Malgieri, and we love its authentic southern charm.

PREPARATION TIME: *20 minutes*
BAKING TIME: *10 to 12 minutes for 2 sheets*
MAKES: *90 cookies*
EQUIPMENT: *2 rimmed baking sheets lined with parchment paper*

2½ cups (12½ ounces) sesame seeds

1½ cups all-purpose flour

1 teaspoon baking powder

½ teaspoon salt

2 sticks (8 ounces) unsalted butter, softened

1 cup packed light brown sugar

⅓ cup granulated sugar

1 tablespoon vanilla extract

1 tablespoon sesame oil

1 large egg

1 large egg yolk

1. Preheat the oven to 375°F.
2. Stir the sesame seeds, flour, baking powder, and salt together in a bowl and set aside.
3. In the bowl of a standing mixer fitted with the paddle attachment, beat the butter with the sugars until light, about 5 minutes. Beat in the vanilla, sesame oil, egg, and egg yolk and mix thoroughly. Remove from the mixer and stir in the flour-and-seed mixture.
4. Drop heaping teaspoons of the dough 1 to 2 inches apart on the prepared pans and flatten slightly. Bake for 10 to 12 minutes, until the cookies spread, firm slightly, and are lightly colored around the edges. Cool them on a rack. Repeat as needed with the remaining dough and cooled pans until all the cookies are baked, or freeze the dough for future use. Store the cooled cookies between sheets of parchment paper in an airtight container for up to 1 week.

# Chocolate–Pumpkin Seed Crinkles

These dark, slightly spicy treats recall the flavors of Mexico, and pumpkin seeds make the geographical allusion all the more complete. Many cups of steaming Mexican hot chocolate have been frothed in our homes, spiced with cinnamon and scented with a tiny touch of cayenne. We've put those flavors into a cookie.

The technique of making these morsels is easy; they can be mixed by hand, and the dough must rest in the refrigerator to firm up before baking. Well-wrapped and chilled for hours or even a day, these cookies are a star in our pantheon of convenience. Tossing the rounds of dough in confectioners' sugar before baking creates the crinkles—jagged white lines that open to reveal their dark interiors. We underbake these just a tiny bit when we crave a softer cookie.

PREPARATION TIME: *45 minutes, plus 4 hours to chill the dough*
BAKING TIME: *10 to 12 minutes for 2 sheets*
MAKES: *80 cookies*
EQUIPMENT: *2 rimmed baking sheets lined with parchment paper*

¼ cup vegetable oil

½ stick (4 tablespoons) unsalted butter, melted

4 ounces semisweet chocolate, melted

1¾ cups granulated sugar

4 large eggs

1 teaspoon vanilla extract

2 cups all-purpose flour

2 teaspoons baking powder

1 teaspoon ground cinnamon

½ teaspoon cayenne pepper

¼ teaspoon salt

1 cup (6½ ounces) semisweet chocolate chips

1 cup (5½ ounces) coarsely chopped pumpkin seeds, toasted

1 cup confectioners' sugar

1. Combine the oil, butter, chocolate, and granulated sugar in a medium bowl. Add the eggs one at a time, whisking to blend between additions. Whisk in the vanilla.

2. Sift the flour, baking powder, cinnamon, cayenne, and salt into a medium bowl. Whisk briefly to combine, then stir into the chocolate mixture. Stir in the chocolate chips and pumpkin seeds. Cover the bowl with plastic wrap and refrigerate for at least 4 hours, or overnight. The dough can be prepared up to this point and kept in the refrigerator for 3 days, well wrapped.

3. When you are ready to bake the cookies, preheat the oven to 350°F.

4. Sift the confectioners' sugar into a large bowl. Drop 1 teaspoon (½ ounce) of the cold dough into the confectioners' sugar and use your hands to form it into a ball coated with the sugar. Place it on one of the prepared pans and repeat with the remaining dough, leaving at least 2 inches between the cookies on all sides. Bake until the cookies have puffed and spread and their surfaces are crackled, 10 to 12 minutes. Cool on the pans on a rack. Repeat as needed with the remaining dough and cooled pans until all the cookies are baked, or freeze the dough for future use. Store the cooled cookies stacked between layers of parchment paper or wax paper in an airtight container for up to 3 days.

# Butter Pecan Sandies

The New York Philharmonic is filled with avid cookie eaters. Every trip they take to perform outside of Avery Fisher Hall involves hundreds of cookies baked for them by Cara. She has performed this task for 18 years, and during that stretch, certain cookies have risen in popularity. These Butter Pecan Sandies have been a constant favorite. They are slice-and-bake cookies, and remarkably simple to prepare. Storing the dough well wrapped in the freezer and ready for baking makes short work of filling trays and trays of cookies. Allow the dough to defrost slightly, but not entirely, in the refrigerator before you slice them, and use a sharp knife that will easily cut through the pecans.

PREPARATION TIME: *20 minutes, plus 4 hours to chill the dough*
BAKING TIME: *12 to 15 minutes for 2 sheets*
MAKES: *60 cookies*
EQUIPMENT: *2 rimmed baking sheets lined with parchment paper*

2 sticks (16 tablespoons) unsalted butter, softened

1 cup confectioners' sugar

1 tablespoon vanilla extract

¼ teaspoon salt

1½ cups all-purpose flour

2 cups (8 ounces) chopped pecans

1. In the bowl of a standing mixer fitted with the paddle attachment, beat the butter and sugar on medium speed until light and fluffy, about 5 minutes. Add the vanilla and salt and beat until incorporated. Turn the mixer to low speed and add the flour, beating just until incorporated. Gently stir in about half the pecans.

2. Divide the dough into 2 equal pieces and roll each piece into a cylinder about 10 inches long. Place half of the remaining pecans on a piece of parchment paper or wax paper and roll one of the cylinders in the pecans, pressing lightly with your hands so the nuts adhere to the log. Repeat with the second cylinder of dough and remaining pecans. Wrap each log in clean parchment paper or wax paper and twist the ends to seal. Refrigerate until firm, at least 4 hours or overnight. The dough can be frozen at this point for up to 1 month. Thaw overnight in the refrigerator and proceed.

3. When ready to bake, preheat the oven to 350°F.

4. Remove the logs from the refrigerator and rest for 10 minutes. Cut the logs into ⅜-inch slices and place them on the prepared pans about 1 inch apart. Bake until the bottoms and edges of the cookies are just beginning to brown, 12 to 15 minutes.

Cool the cookies on the pans on racks. Repeat as needed with the remaining dough and cooled pans until all the cookies are baked, or freeze the dough for future use. Store the cooled cookies stacked between layers of parchment paper or wax paper in an airtight container for up to 1 week.

*Lemon–Poppy Seed Cookies (page 339)*

# Lemon–Poppy Seed Cookies

We love the look of these cookies, pale golden rounds speckled with dark-blue poppy seeds, surrounded by shards of toasty sliced almonds. The classic combination of lemon and poppy seeds so commonly found in cakes is slightly unusual in a cookie, but it works. A ring of sliced almonds on the outside gives the cookies a tailored, finished look. Also of the slice-and-bake variety, we depend on the convenience of making them. They are a New York Philharmonic favorite, making a long-running appearance on Cara's voluminous cookie trays. Orchestra members vote for their favorites by consuming them first, and these always go in the blink of an eye. *(See additional photo page 290.)*

PREPARATION TIME: *20 minutes, plus 4 hours to chill the dough*
BAKING TIME: *12 to 15 minutes for 2 sheets*
MAKES: *70 cookies*
EQUIPMENT: *2 rimmed baking sheets lined with parchment paper*

**2 sticks (16 tablespoons) unsalted butter, softened**

**⅔ cup granulated sugar**

**2 egg yolks**

**1½ teaspoons vanilla extract**

**1 tablespoon freshly grated lemon zest**

**⅓ cup (1½ ounces) poppy seeds**

**2 cups all-purpose flour**

**1 cup (4 ounces) lightly crushed sliced almonds**

1. In the bowl of a standing mixer fitted with the paddle attachment, cream the butter and sugar on medium speed until light and fluffy, about 5 minutes. Add the egg yolks and vanilla and beat until combined. Turn the mixer to low speed and add the lemon zest and poppy seeds. Carefully add the flour, mixing just until incorporated.

2. Divide the dough in half and roll each half into a 12-inch cylinder. Place half the sliced almonds on a piece of parchment paper or wax paper and roll 1 log in the almonds, pressing lightly so they adhere to the log. Repeat with the second log of dough and the remaining almonds. Wrap each log in parchment paper or wax paper and twist the ends. Refrigerate for at least 4 hours or overnight, until firm.

3. When ready to bake, preheat the oven to 350°F.

4. Remove the logs from the refrigerator and rest for 10 minutes. Cut the logs into ⅜-inch slices and place them on the prepared pans 1 inch apart. Bake until the bottoms and edges of the cookies are just beginning to brown, 12 to 15 minutes. Cool the cookies on the pans on a rack. Repeat as needed with the remaining dough and cooled pans until all the cookies are baked, or freeze the dough for future use. Store the cooled cookies between layers of parchment paper or wax paper in an airtight container for up to 1 week.

# Classic Walnut Rugelach

*Rugelach* means "little twists" in the Yiddish language, and they are pastries of Ashkenazi Jewish origin. The original dough was made in the shtetls of Eastern Europe with sour cream, and the substitution of cream cheese is most likely an American alteration. They are rich and a little sweet, and are from a time when their ingredients were a luxury. When Cara was in college her father learned to bake these rugelach, filled with currants and chopped walnuts. He would layer them in waxed paper, pack them into small coffee cans and ship them to her. They were a great luxury then, too, when college cafeteria food was the norm, and home-baked treats were few and far between.

PREPARATION TIME: *55 minutes, plus 1 hour to chill the dough*
BAKING TIME: *25 to 30 minutes for 2 sheets*
MAKES: *48 cookies*
EQUIPMENT: *2 rimmed baking sheets lined with parchment paper*

**FOR THE DOUGH**

2 sticks (16 tablespoons) unsalted butter, softened

8 ounces cream cheese, softened

2 cups all-purpose flour

**FOR THE FILLING**

½ cup currants

½ cup (1¾ ounces) finely chopped walnuts, toasted

½ cup sugar

½ teaspoon ground cinnamon

½ cup apricot jam, stirred

**FOR THE TOPPING**

¼ cup whole milk

¼ cup sugar

1. Make the dough: In the bowl of a standing mixer fitted with the paddle attachment, beat the butter and cream cheese until combined, about 2 minutes. Stir in the flour and mix only until incorporated. Refrigerate the dough until it is firm, about 1 hour.
2. Make the filling: While the dough is chilling, toss the currants, walnuts, sugar, and cinnamon together in a small bowl. Set aside.
3. Preheat the oven to 350°F.
4. Divide the dough into 4 equal pieces. Work with 1 piece of dough at a time and keep the rest in the refrigerator. On a lightly floured work surface, roll the dough into a very thin circle about 10 inches in diameter. Spread 2 tablespoons of the apricot jam onto the surface of the dough, leaving a ½-inch margin around the perimeter. Sprinkle ¼ of the currant-nut filling evenly over the jam.

5. Using a pizza wheel, cut the dough into 12 triangular wedges (like pizza slices). Starting with the outer edge, roll one wedge into a crescent. Gently curve the ends of the crescent inward and place it on one of the prepared pans. Repeat with the remaining wedges, leaving 1 inch around the cookies on the pan. Repeat this process with the remaining 3 pieces of dough and the remaining filling.

6. For the toping: Brush the tops of the dough with the milk and sprinkle them with the sugar. Bake until the cookies are a very pale golden color, 25 to 30 minutes. Remove them from the pan immediately and cool on a rack. Store the cookies stacked between layers of parchment paper or wax paper in an airtight container for up to 1 week.

# Poppy Seed Hamantaschen

The poppy seed filling in this Purim holiday treat is the classic. First ground slightly, the navy blue seeds are then cooked in milk, where they swell and thicken the filling. The triangular shape of this cookie is said to mimic the hat of Haman, the villain in the Purim story. While good triumphed over evil in the tale, we are glad that this treat was created to celebrate the wrongdoer's hat. We have made hamantaschen with different fruit fillings, and even with chocolate, but the poppy seed centers always prevail. Purim is the most festive of Jewish holidays, with parties and costumes and loads of treats. This one is the best of all.

PREPARATION TIME: *55 minutes, plus 3 hours to chill the dough*
BAKING TIME: *15 to 18 minutes for 2 sheets*
MAKES: *24 pastries*
EQUIPMENT: *3 rimmed baking sheets lined with parchment paper*

### FOR THE DOUGH

2 sticks (16 tablespoons) unsalted butter, softened

8 ounces cream cheese, softened

½ cup sugar

2 large egg yolks

½ teaspoon salt

4 cups all-purpose flour

### FOR THE FILLING

1 cup (5 ounces) poppy seeds

1 cup whole milk

2 tablespoons unsalted butter

2 tablespoons honey

½ cup (2¼ ounces) finely chopped slivered almonds

½ teaspoon freshly grated lemon zest

¼ cup golden raisins

¼ cup sugar

1 tart apple, peeled, cored, and grated

### FOR FINISHING

1 large egg, lightly beaten with a pinch of salt

1. Make the dough: In the bowl of a standing mixer fitted with the paddle attachment, beat the butter, cream cheese, and sugar on medium speed until light and fluffy, about 5 minutes. Beat in the egg yolk and salt. Scrape down the sides of the bowl. Add the flour and mix just until incorporated. Wrap the dough in plastic and refrigerate until it is firm, at least 3 hours, or overnight.

2. Make the filling: Using a small spice grinder or a food processor, grind the poppy seeds to a rough paste. Transfer them to a small saucepan. Add the milk, butter, honey, almonds, lemon zest, and raisins and bring to a boil over medium heat. Add the sugar and grated apple, reduce the heat to low, and continue to cook, stirring occasionally,

until the mixture thickens, 25 to 30 minutes. Allow the filling to cool completely before forming the pastries. The filling can be made up to this point and stored in the refrigerator for up to 3 days.

3. When you are ready to bake, preheat the oven to 350°F.

4. Divide the dough into 2 equal pieces. Work with 1 piece of dough, keeping the other one in the refrigerator. On a lightly floured work surface, roll the dough ¼-inch thick. Using a 4-inch round cookie cutter, cut out circles and line them up on the prepared pans ¼-inch apart. Repeat with the remaining dough. Wrap the scraps and chill to reroll later. Reroll the reserved scraps only once, or the dough will toughen.

5. Brush the surface of the circles with the lightly beaten egg. Drop a heaping tablespoon of filling in the center of each circle. Fold in the sides in three places, leaving a triangle shape in the center with the filling exposed. The sides should not overlap; they should just touch each other. Where the sides meet, pinch them together to seal. Brush the pastry dough with the beaten egg and bake until they are lightly golden, 15 to 18 minutes. Cool on the pans on racks. Store the cooled cookies stacked between layers of parchment paper or wax paper in an airtight container for up to 1 week.

# Linzer Hazelnut Spirals

These lovely Linzers are a dramatic twist on the more traditional Linzer tarts. They are easier to prepare, saving the steps of cutting, matching, and sandwiching the cookies together with raspberry jam. This dough can be prepared ahead and frozen, then sliced and baked when needed, an enormous boon to the avid cookie baker. Linzer cakes have been made for centuries in the Austrian town of Linz, and the handheld cookie with jam peeking through the top evolved from its full-size predecessor. We've taken it a step further, but the ingredients remain the same, a slightly spicy ground nut–filled gluten-free pastry packed with a sweet berry center.

PREPARATION TIME: *45 minutes, plus 5 hours to chill the dough*
BAKING TIME: *15 to 18 minutes for 2 sheets*
MAKES: *50 cookies*
EQUIPMENT: *2 rimmed baking sheets lined with parchment paper*

### FOR THE DOUGH

1½ sticks (12 tablespoons) unsalted butter, softened

6 ounces cream cheese, softened

1½ cups (5¼ ounces) hazelnut flour

1 teaspoon ground cinnamon

¼ teaspoon freshly grated nutmeg

### FOR FILLING AND FINISHING

1 cup seedless raspberry jam

2 large egg whites

Pinch salt

½ cup (2½ ounces) finely chopped hazelnuts

½ cup sugar

1. Make the dough: In the bowl of a standing mixer fitted with the paddle attachment, beat the butter and cream cheese on medium speed until combined, 1 to 2 minutes. Add the hazelnut flour, cinnamon, and nutmeg and mix just until incorporated. Wrap the dough in plastic wrap and refrigerate until firm, about 1 hour.

2. Make the filling and finishing: Place the raspberry jam in a small bowl and whisk vigorously to loosen it. In another small bowl, whisk together the egg whites and salt. In a third bowl, combine the hazelnuts and sugar.

3. Preheat the oven to 350°F.

4. Divide the dough into 2 equal pieces. On a lightly floured work surface, roll 1 piece of dough into a 10-by-15-inch rectangle. Make sure the 10-inch side is facing you. Using a pastry brush, paint the surface of the dough with ½ cup jam. Roll the dough from the 10-inch side. Place the log in the refrigerator and repeat with the second piece of dough. Both logs should be chilled for 4 hours or overnight before slicing.

5. Starting with the first chilled log, use a sharp knife to trim the end and cut the log into ⅜-inch slices. Place the cookies cut side down on the pan, at least 1½ inches apart. Repeat with the second log. Once the cookies are arranged on the pans, brush the tops with the remaining egg white and sprinkle them with the hazelnut-sugar mixture. Bake until slightly browned on top, 15 to 18 minutes. Cool on the pans for about 5 minutes and then transfer the cookies to a rack. Repeat as needed with the remaining dough and cooled pans until all the cookies are baked. Store the cooled cookies between layers of parchment paper or wax paper in an airtight container for up to 1 week.

# Nut-Studded Shortbread

Shortbread is Scotland's great contribution to the cookie universe, and butter is at the heart of shortbread. You should use the purest butter you can find, and make sure your butter is at room temperature before you begin. The crumbly texture of the cookie depends on it. While the butter and sugar may be beaten until light in both color and texture, mixing must come to a halt right after the flour and nuts are added. Overbeating will cause a tough cookie, and the beauty of shortbread lies in that tender, crumbly texture. Feel free to mix and match the nuts. While they all make a contribution, any combination you have on hand will work. Once the dough is mixed we handle it carefully, always rolling it out on a clean, very lightly floured surface, for added flour could stiffen the cookie. We reroll the scraps as briefly as possible, incorporating as little surface flour as we can—another tactic to keep the cookie as crumbly as shortbread should be.

PREPARATION TIME: *55 minutes*
BAKING TIME: *20 to 25 minutes for 2 sheets*
MAKES: *48 cookies*
EQUIPMENT: *2 rimmed baking sheets lined with parchment paper*

**4 sticks (1 pound) unsalted butter, softened**

**1¼ cups superfine sugar**

**3¾ cups all-purpose flour**

**¼ cup (1 ounce) finely chopped pecans**

**¼ cup (1 ounce) finely chopped walnuts**

**¼ cup (1¼ ounces) finely chopped pistachios**

**¼ cup (1¼ ounces) finely chopped Brazil nuts**

**¼ cup (1¼ ounces) finely chopped almonds**

**¼ cup (1¼ ounces) finely chopped hazelnuts**

**¼ cup (1¼ ounces) finely chopped roasted cashews**

**Confectioners' sugar**

1. Preheat the oven to 325°F.
2. In the bowl of a standing mixer fitted with the paddle attachment, cream the butter and sugar on medium speed until they are very light and fluffy, about 10 minutes. Scrape down the sides of the bowl as needed to make sure the butter is being incorporated evenly. Reduce the speed to low and add the flour ½ cup at a time, mixing just until it is incorporated. Remove the bowl from the mixer and stir in the nuts, using a rubber spatula, until they are evenly distributed.

3. Cut the dough into 2 equal pieces. On a lightly floured work surface, press 1 piece of dough into a rough square. Pass lightly over the top of the dough with a rolling pin to flatten it to about 3/8-inch thick. Dust with flour as needed. Using a bench scraper or knife, cut the dough into 1½-inch strips and then cut each strip into 3-inch pieces (that is, 1½-by-3-inch rectangles). Reserve the scraps. Place the cookies on one of the prepared pans. Prick the top of each cookie about 4 times with the tines of a fork down the length of the cookie.

4. Bake the cookies until they are beginning to brown slightly around the edges and on the bottom, 15 to 20 minutes. Cool the cookies on the pans, so they firm up a bit. Repeat as needed with the remaining dough and cooled pans until all the cookies are baked. You can carefully reroll the scraps. Store the cooled cookies stacked between layers of parchment paper or wax paper in an airtight container for up to 1 week.

# Pecan Nut Cups

When the busy Christmas baking season rolls around, Andrea begins her annual cookie baking spree. These gems barely get a chance to cool and be packed with their brethren, because they are pulled off the racks by her family when her back is turned. The recipe came from her grandmother Antoinette Bianco, who made them with walnuts. Andrea changed the featured nut to pecans, and the cookie resembles a mini pecan pie.

PREPARATION TIME: *45 minutes, plus 1 hour to chill the dough*
BAKING TIME: *20 to 25 minutes for 2 sheets*
MAKES: *48 cookies*
EQUIPMENT: *Two 12-cup mini muffin tins lightly coated with nonstick spray*

### FOR THE DOUGH

2 sticks (16 tablespoons) unsalted butter, softened

6 ounces cream cheese, softened

2 cups all-purpose flour

### FOR THE FILLING

1 cup (4 ounces) coarsely chopped pecans

¾ cup packed dark brown sugar

1 large egg

1 teaspoon unsalted butter, softened

1 teaspoon vanilla extract

Confectioners' sugar for finishing

1. Make the dough: In the bowl of a standing mixer fitted with the paddle attachment, beat the butter and cream cheese on medium speed until combined, about 2 minutes. Stir in the flour and beat just until incorporated. Wrap the dough in plastic and chill for 1 hour.

2. Make the filling: Place the nuts and brown sugar in a small bowl and toss with a fork to combine. Add the egg, butter, and vanilla, mixing after each addition with the fork. Set aside.

3. Preheat the oven to 350°F.

4. Pinch off a walnut-sized piece of dough and roll it into a ball between your palms. Place it in one of the cups in a tin. Using your fingers, press the dough into the bottom and sides of the cavity. Make sure to cover the sides and bottom evenly. The result should look like a small pie shell, and the dough should easily stick to the sides. Repeat until all the cups are filled. Fill each dough cup about two-thirds full with filling. Bake until the edges of the dough are a light golden color and the filling has puffed nicely on top, 20 to 25 minutes. Cool in the pans for 5 minutes and then use a butter knife or a small metal spatula to remove the nut cups from the pans and transfer them to a cooling rack.

5. Repeat with the remaining dough and filling, but be sure the pans are cool before you reuse them. A hot pan will cause the dough to melt and not stick to the sides properly.

6. When the nut cups have cooled, dust them lightly with confectioners' sugar. Store in an airtight container for up to 1 week (if they last that long).

# Pistachio-Lemon Squares

Cara's lemon squares are renowned. Years ago, the *New York Daily News* dubbed her the "citrus sage" because of these cookies. Recipes for lemon squares abound, but these are easy to prepare and yield the best balance between sweet and tart, crumbly and custardy. They stand out for their intensity of lemony flavor, and there are enough eggs in the topping so they need no additional starch to set them. Andrea had the great idea of adding pistachios to the crust. Are they wonderful without them? Sure. But they add that unbeatable color and a crunchy something to the crust. Don't make them instead of the classic; just do them in addition. We've intentionally left the pan free of a parchment-paper lining. Years of baking lemon squares have taught us that an unlined pan allows the dough to cling to the sides. This keeps the topping from slipping over the edge and under the crust while baking, yielding a smooth and even surface. The custard edges may brown a little where the topping meets the sides of the pan, and we trim them off with a knife or a bench scraper. Even without parchment the squares lift easily out of the pan with an offset spatula.

PREPARATION TIME: *30 minutes*
BAKING TIME: *55 minutes to 1 hour*
MAKES: *50 squares*
EQUIPMENT: *One 12-by-18-inch baking pan*

## FOR THE DOUGH

4 sticks (1 pound) unsalted butter, softened

1 cup confectioners' sugar

1 teaspoon vanilla extract

4 cups all-purpose flour

2¼ cups (11¼ ounces) ground pistachios

## FOR THE FILLING

8 large eggs

4 cups granulated sugar

¾ cup freshly squeezed lemon juice, strained

3 tablespoons finely grated lemon zest

Confectioners' sugar for finishing

1. Preheat the oven to 350°F.
2. Make the dough: In the bowl of a standing mixer fitted with the paddle attachment, beat the butter on medium speed until completely softened, about 2 minutes. Beat in the confectioners' sugar and vanilla and continue to mix until lightened, an additional 2 minutes. Reduce the speed to low, add the flour and ¼ cup ground pistachios, and mix until incorporated. Transfer the dough to the baking pan and press it evenly over the bottom and slightly up the sides. Use the back of a spoon to smooth the dough. Bake until golden and baked through, 25 to 30 minutes.

*continued*

3. Make the filling: Whisk the eggs in a large bowl just to break them up. Whisk in the granulated sugar, then the lemon juice and zest. Do not overmix, as this will cause coarse-textured foam to form on the top when the squares are baked.

4. As soon as the dough is baked, remove it from the oven. (Do not turn the oven off.) Cover the surface with the remaining 2 cups ground pistachios. Pour the lemon filling on top of the dough and pistachios. Immediately return the pan to the oven and continue baking until the topping is set and firm. This will take an additional 25 to 30 minutes. Cool in the pan on a rack.

5. When completely cool, cut into 2-by-2-inch squares right in the pan. First trim the edges with a large knife, then make marks 2 inches apart around the edges and cut into squares. Lift the squares out of the pan carefully with a small offset spatula. The first square may be a bit difficult to remove, but the rest will come out easily. Dust with confectioners' sugar before serving. Store the squares in a tin or a plastic container with a tight-fitting lid for 3 to 4 days.

# Peanut-Fudge Brownies

Who could resist a brownie nestled in a peanut-packed crust? Not us. The idea for this dynamic dessert duo came from Ellie Ference. Her son Michael is Andrea's brother-in-law, and brownies studded with peanuts instead of walnuts or pecans are a Ference family favorite. We have poured Ellie's brownie mix into a crumbly peanut crust, which is pressed into a pan and cooked through before filling. A bit of reserved crust is dropped on the top before baking, creating peanut crumbs that look like streusel. This brownie is moist, not cakey or dry, and appeals to the rich-and-gooey-brownie lover in us both.

PREPARATION TIME: *50 minutes*
BAKING TIME: *1 hour*
MAKES: *24 squares*
EQUIPMENT: *One 9-by-13-inch baking pan, buttered and lined with parchment paper*

### FOR THE DOUGH

2 sticks (16 tablespoons) unsalted butter, softened

¼ cup smooth natural peanut butter

½ cup confectioners' sugar

½ teaspoon vanilla extract

1½ cups all-purpose flour

½ cup (2½ ounces) finely ground roasted peanuts

### FOR THE FILLING

1¾ sticks (14 tablespoons) unsalted butter, melted

2 cups granulated sugar

4 large eggs

2 tablespoons smooth natural peanut butter

3 ounces unsweetened chocolate, melted

1 teaspoon vanilla extract

1 cup all-purpose flour

¼ teaspoon salt

1 cup (5 ounces) chopped roasted salted peanuts

Confectioners' sugar for finishing

1. Preheat the oven to 325°F.
2. Make the dough: In the bowl of a standing mixer fitted with the paddle attachment, beat the butter with the peanut butter on medium speed for 2 minutes. Beat in the confectioners' sugar and vanilla and continue to mix until lightened, 2 additional minutes. In a small bowl, stir together the flour and ground peanuts. Reduce the speed of the mixer to low and gradually add the flour mixture. Beat until incorporated. Remove and reserve ¾ cup of the dough for the topping. Press the remainder of the dough evenly into the

*continued*

bottom and slightly up the sides of the prepared pan. Use the back of a spoon to smooth it. Bake until golden and baked through, 20 to 25 minutes.

3. Make the filling: Whisk the butter, granulated sugar, eggs, and peanut butter together in a large bowl. Add the melted chocolate and stir to combine. Stir in the vanilla, flour, and salt. Fold in ¾ cup chopped peanuts.

4. As soon as the dough is baked, remove it from the oven. (Do not turn the oven off.) Pour the filling on top of the baked dough. Gently crumble the reserved 1 cup dough on top of the brownie filling, and then sprinkle the remaining ¼ cup peanuts on top. Return the pan to the oven and bake until the brownies feel firm when pressed lightly, 25 to 30 minutes. Cool in the pan on a rack.

5. When ready to serve, cut the squares directly in the pan. Cut the 9-inch side into 4 strips and cut the 13-inch side into 6 strips. Lift the brownies out of the pan carefully with a small metal offset spatula. The first square may be a bit difficult to remove, but the rest will come out easily. Dust lightly with confectioners' sugar before serving. Store the squares stacked between layers of parchment paper or wax paper in an airtight container for 3 days.

# Coconut Macaroons

French or American, macaroons are chewy cookies that consist mostly of egg whites and often include ground almonds or coconut. We bake them at Passover because they never include flour and adhere to the dietary restrictions of that holiday, but it would be silly to restrict them to one time of year. They are tasty and simple to prepare. Perfectly whipped egg whites are the key to macaroon success. Room temperature whites whip best and to maximum volume. If you do not have time to bring your eggs in the shell to room temperature before separating the white and the yolk, place them in a bowl of warm water for several minutes. Always add sugar slowly, in a thin stream, when whipping whites. Too much sugar going in at once will deflate the whites and rob you of some of the volume. Make sure to whip the whites until they are shiny and stiff. That means they stand up and point skyward, well formed and upright, when you pull the beater out of the bowl.

PREPARATION TIME: *20 minutes*
BAKING TIME: *20 to 25 minutes for 2 sheets*
MAKES: *60 macaroons*
EQUIPMENT: *2 rimmed baking sheets lined with parchment paper*

4 large egg whites, at room temperature

¼ teaspoon salt

1 cup sugar

1½ cups (4½ ounces) unsweetened coconut flakes

1 cup (4 ounces) sweetened shredded coconut

1. Preheat the oven to 325°F.
2. In the bowl of a standing mixer fitted with the whip attachment, whisk the egg whites and salt on medium speed until soft peaks form. Add the sugar slowly and continue whipping until all the sugar has been added and the whites are stiff and shiny. Remove the bowl from the mixer and fold in both kinds of coconut. Be careful not to overmix the batter.
3. Drop tablespoons of batter onto the prepared pans, leaving about 1 inch between the macaroons on all sides. Bake until the macaroons are golden brown, puffed, and shiny, 20 to 25 minutes. Cool the cookies on the pans on a rack. When they are cool enough to touch, they should be easy to remove. Transfer them to a rack to cool thoroughly. Repeat as needed with the remaining dough and cooled pans until all the macaroons are baked. Store the cooled macaroons between layers of parchment paper or wax paper in an airtight container for up to 2 days.

# Hazelnut and Vanilla Cream Macarons

French style macarons are all the rage, and we certainly understand their popularity. Light as air, they are crisp when baked. When filled with buttercream, they take on a richness that perfectly balances the light exterior. Pipe the batter to create the domed shape. Then allow the spheres to rest and dry out. When dry, a thin crust is created atop the cookies. They are then baked, and the dry dome will lift, allowing the batter to peek through at the bottom of each cookie. This creates the characteristic "foot" at the edge of each sweet. Sandwiched with buttercream after they are baked and then stored in the refrigerator, they take on a compelling moistness that is addictive. There are many different methods for making French macarons, but this version, adapted from a recipe by Kathryn Gordon in *Les Petits Macarons: Colorful French Confections to Make at Home*, is one of the simplest.

PREPARATION TIME: *55 minutes, plus 24 hours to age the egg whites*
BAKING TIME: *20 to 25 minutes for 2 sheets*
MAKES: *50 macarons*
EQUIPMENT: *2 rimmed baking sheets lined with parchment paper or silicone sheets; a piping bag filled with a ½-inch round tip; a candy thermometer*

### FOR THE BATTER

2 cups (7 ounces) hazelnut flour

1½ cups confectioners' sugar

⅛ teaspoon fine sea salt

1 tablespoon powdered egg white

¾ cup granulated sugar

½ cup (4 ounces) egg whites, from 4 eggs kept at room temperature for 24 hours

½ teaspoon cream of tartar

4 drops gel food coloring (optional)

### FOR THE FILLING

1 vanilla bean

½ cup granulated sugar

4 egg yolks

1½ sticks (12 tablespoons) unsalted butter, cut into cubes and softened

2 teaspoons vanilla extract

1. Place the hazelnut flour, confectioners' sugar, and salt in the bowl of a food processor and process for about 20 seconds. Sift with a strainer and set aside. Sifting helps provide a smooth surface in the finished macarons.

2. In the bowl of a standing mixer fitted with the whip attachment, whisk together the powdered egg white and granulated sugar. Add the egg whites and cream of tartar. Whisk to combine for about 20 seconds. Increase the speed to medium and whip until the meringue is glossy and stiff peaks form, 10 to 11 minutes. The batter is ready when the whisk leaves marks in the bowl and the batter resembles marshmallow fluff. With a

spatula, fold the dry ingredients into the meringue in 3 additions, until they are almost fully incorporated. Add the food coloring, if you like, and finish folding.

3. Place the batter in the piping bag. Only fill the bag halfway; if you overfill the bag, you will not be able to squeeze out the batter. Twist the top of the bag closed. Pipe quarter-sized mounds onto the prepared pans 1½ inches apart. To pipe properly, hold the tip of the bag at a 90-degree angle ¼ inch above the pan. Firmly squeeze without moving the bag until the batter is the right size and about ¼-inch high. As soon as you have reached the desired size, about 1½ inches in diameter, stop squeezing and twist your wrist in a clockwise motion without lifting. Once you are sure no more batter is flowing from the bag, move on to the next cookie. When the pan is filled with unbaked cookies, lift it and drop it on the work surface a few times to deflate the batter.

4. About 30 minutes before baking, preheat the oven to 300°F and bake for an additional 9 to 10 minutes. A foot will form around the bottom of each cookie. Remove them from the oven and cool on the pans on racks. Wash and dry the mixer bowl.

5. While the cookies are baking and cooling, prepare the filling: Split the vanilla bean in half lengthwise and use the back of a paring knife to scrape out the seeds. Place the seeds, pod, sugar, and egg yolks in the clean  bowl of the standing mixer. Place the bowl over a pot of simmering water and whisk continuously until the mixture thickens and reaches 165°F on the candy thermometer, 5 to 7 minutes. Remove the bowl from the heat and remove and discard the vanilla bean pod. Place the bowl on the mixer fitted with the whip attachment, and whisk the mixture on medium-high speed to cool, about 5 minutes. When the bottom of the bowl cools to below body temperature, add the cubed butter. Continue whipping on medium-high speed for about 10 minutes, until the mixture is fluffy. Add the vanilla extract and mix to combine, about 30 seconds.

6. Lift the cooled macarons from the pans using an offset spatula. Flip half of them over. Pipe ½ teaspoon filling on one macaron and top with a second macaron to form a sandwich. Repeat with the remaining macarons. Serve immediately, or store in the refrigerator in an airtight container for up to 4 days. Filled macarons can be frozen for up to 1 month.

NOTE: If your macarons crack during baking, try doubling the pans to insulate from the heat.

*White Chocolate–Orange–Almond Bark (page 357)*

# White Chocolate–Orange–Almond Bark

Bark is the easiest of all candy to make. After you temper the chocolate, the task is quickly accomplished with a little stirring, spreading, and scattering. Start with the highest quality white chocolate. Less expensive white chocolates have little cocoa butter, too much sugar to compensate for this, and lackluster flavor. Stir in the puffed-rice cereal to add an airy crunch. Spread the chocolate mixture on the prepared pan, toss the almonds and orange peel on top, and allow the confection to set. An elegant, flavorful dessert is created without ever turning on the oven. *(See additional photo page 290.)*

PREPARATION TIME: *15 minutes*
MAKES: *1½ pounds*
EQUIPMENT: *1 rimmed baking sheet lined with parchment paper or wax paper*

**1½ pounds good white chocolate, tempered (see box page 358)**

**1 cup (1 ounce) unsweetened puffed-rice cereal, such as Rice Krispies**

**1 cup (4½ ounces) roughly chopped slivered almonds, toasted**

**1 cup (7 ounces) candied orange peel, chopped into ¼-inch pieces**

1. Place the tempered chocolate in a large mixing bowl. Stir in the cereal and mix.

2. Working quickly, using an offset spatula, spread the mixture on the prepared pan and scatter the almonds and candied orange peel on top, pressing lightly. Allow the bark to harden, which takes about 10 minutes at a cool room temperature. Break the candy into irregular bite-sized pieces and serve. Store in an airtight container for up to 1 week.

## *Tempering Chocolate*

Tempering chocolate is not as daunting as it sounds. Basically, all you are doing is melting the chocolate and reconnecting the sugar crystals to each other in a uniform way so the resulting chocolate looks attractive. Tempered chocolate will stay shiny when used as a coating, and it will produce the requisite snap when bitten.

A few home tempering machines are on the market, but there's no need to invest in expensive equipment when you likely already own what we consider the best tool for tempering chocolate: the microwave oven. That may surprise you, but we've tested all kinds of methods, from classic techniques to some modern ones, and using a microwave oven is by far the easiest, quickest, and cleanest way to temper chocolate.

A few simple rules: First, always work with top-quality chocolate. So much good chocolate is available in supermarkets and specialty stores today that there's no excuse not to purchase the best, and even tempering won't save mediocre chocolate. Second, do not work with less than 1 pound of chocolate at a time. Even if your recipe calls for less, tempering at least 1 pound when using the microwave protects the chocolate from scorching.

Start with small pieces of chocolate, chopped into ½-inch pieces or purchased in small disks called *pistoles*. Place three-quarters of the chocolate into a microwave safe bowl. Melt it on medium power in 30 second intervals, stirring after each, until the entire bowl is melted. When it is ready, a chocolate thermometer will read between 100 and 110°F. Gradually stir in the reserved quarter of unmelted chocolate bit by bit, ensuring that the chocolate is entirely melted before you stir in the next bit. This process will bring the temperature of the chocolate down, and this is your goal. Bring the temperature down to 90°F if you are tempering bittersweet chocolate, 88°F if you are tempering milk or white chocolate. Use your thermometer to maintain this temperature, and you are ready to enrobe your treats. If your chocolate starts to solidify, stir in the edges and pop the bowl back into the microwave for a few seconds. Your vigilance with the temperature will be rewarded with a streak-free, snappy coating.

# Crackling Peanut Brittle

Two things make this peanut brittle unique. First, the addition of honey-roasted peanuts instead of the unsalted kind adds an unexpected twist to a ubiquitous sweet. Next, the little bit of baking soda added at the end aerates the brittle, yielding a candy with a lighter texture than usual. Start this recipe with all of your ingredients at hand and be ready to work quickly once your cooked syrup reaches 300°F. Prepare your baking sheet before you start, and lightly butter an offset spatula. Once the brittle is poured onto the pan it will cool rapidly, and spreading it may be difficult. Proper preparations will get the job done easily.

PREPARATION TIME: *15 minutes*
COOKING TIME: *45 minutes, plus 30 minutes to cool and set*
MAKES: *1½ pounds*
EQUIPMENT: *1 rimmed baking sheet, heavily buttered; a candy thermometer*

1½ cups sugar

¾ cup dark corn syrup

2 tablespoons unsalted butter

¼ teaspoon salt

½ teaspoon vanilla extract

2 cups (10 ounces) chopped honey-roasted peanuts

1 teaspoon baking soda

1. Place the sugar, corn syrup, ½ cup water, butter, and salt in a medium heavy-bottomed saucepan and stir to combine. Place the saucepan over medium heat and bring the mixture to a boil, stirring occasionally so the sugar melts evenly. Reduce the heat to low, cover the pan, and boil the syrup for 5 minutes. Insert a candy thermometer and continue to cook the syrup without stirring until it reaches 300°F, about 40 minutes. It will be a deep golden color.

2. Remove the syrup from the heat and stir in the vanilla and peanuts, then stir in the baking soda. The mixture will foam when the baking soda is added. Pour the mixture onto the prepared pan and, using a buttered metal spatula, spread it as thin as possible. Set the pan aside and allow the brittle to cool and harden, about 30 minutes. After the brittle has cooled completely, break it into approximately 2-inch pieces and serve. Store in an airtight container for up to 1 week.

# Macadamia Crunch

Macadamia crunch is a bit of an indulgence, a fine balance of sweet caramel and rich nuts. As for the peanut brittle, a clean saucepan, a candy thermometer, and a watchful eye are essential to success. Be prepared with all of your ingredients at the ready before you begin, and when the crunch is mixed and you pour it onto your prepared pan, use an offset spatula that is brushed with a bit of melted butter to spread the crunch as thinly as possible, nearly reaching the corners of the pan. Thin crunch makes for the most elegant version of this sweet. We have pushed this treat from extraordinary to extravagant when we break it into large shards and dip the pointed ends in tempered chocolate. *(See photo page 290.)*

PREPARATION TIME: *15 minutes*
COOKING TIME: *45 minutes, plus 30 minutes to cool and set*
MAKES: *1¾ pounds*
EQUIPMENT: *1 rimmed baking sheet, heavily buttered; a candy thermometer*

2 cups sugar

¼ cup light corn syrup

2 tablespoons unsalted butter

¼ teaspoon fine sea salt

2½ cups (12 ounces) finely chopped salted macadamia nuts

1. Pour the sugar, corn syrup, ½ cup water, butter, and salt into a medium heavy-bottomed saucepan and stir to combine. Place the saucepan over medium heat and bring the syrup to a boil, stirring occasionally so the sugar melts evenly. Reduce the heat to low and allow the syrup to boil for 5 minutes. Insert a candy thermometer and continue to cook the syrup without stirring until it reaches 300°F. It will be a deep golden color, about 40 minutes.

2. Remove the syrup from the heat and stir in the macadamia nuts. Pour the mixture onto the prepared pan and, using a buttered metal spatula, spread it as thin as possible. Set the pan aside and allow the candy to cool and harden, about 30 minutes. After the candy has cooled completely, break it into approximately 2-inch pieces. Store the brittle between sheets of wax paper in a tin or plastic container that has a tight-fitting cover for up to 1 week.

# Chocolate-Covered Almonds

Just as savory seasoned nuts make perfect before-meal nibbles, sweetened nuts make perfect after-dinner treats. These almonds get a slim caramel coat before they get a chocolate bath. A final dusting of unsweetened cocoa clings to their dark chocolate exteriors. After dessert is served, a small bowl of these dusky brown bites can keep conversations flowing. They are not too sweet, not too rich, and perfectly satisfying. *(See photo page 290.)*

PREPARATION TIME: *20 minutes*
COOKING TIME: *40 minutes, plus 20 minutes to cool and set*
MAKES: *1½ pounds*
EQUIPMENT: *1 rimmed baking sheet lined with parchment paper or a silicone sheet; a candy thermometer*

¾ cup sugar

3¼ cups (1 pound) whole natural almonds

2 cups Dutch process cocoa powder (see box page 90)

8 ounces tempered bittersweet chocolate (see box page 358)

1. Preheat the oven to 300°F.
2. Combine the sugar and 3 tablespoons water in a medium heavy saucepan over medium heat and bring to 240°F. Add the almonds to the sugar mixture and continue to cook, stirring constantly. The sugar will begin to crystallize. Continue cooking the almonds until the sugar browns, 35 to 40 minutes.
3. Pour the almonds onto the prepared baking sheet and cool for about 20 minutes. As they are cooling, separate them from each other with a fork.
4. Sift the cocoa powder into a large bowl and set aside.
5. Once the nuts have fully cooled, place half of them in a large bowl. Add half the tempered chocolate and stir to combine. Working quickly, separate the nuts with your hands and drop them into the sifted cocoa powder. Shake the bowl to coat the nuts. Transfer them to a sieve and lightly shake them to remove any excess cocoa powder. Repeat with the rest of the nuts, tempered chocolate, and cocoa powder. Store any leftover almonds in an airtight container for up to 1 week.

# APPENDIX

# Nuts and Bolts of Nut Nutrition

| NUT/SEED | Almonds (23 Whole or 1 ounce) | Brazil Nuts (6 pieces or 1 ounce) | Cashews (16 pieces or 1 ounce) | Chestnuts (5 pieces or 1 ounce) | Unsweetened Coconut (1 ounce) | Hazelnuts (21 pieces or 1 ounce) | Macada (11 pie 1 ounce |
|---|---|---|---|---|---|---|---|
| Calories | 163 | 186 | 157 | 103 | 187 | 178 | 20 |
| Total Fat (g) | 14 | 19 | 12 | < 1 | 18.3 | 17 | 22 |
| Protein (g) | 6 | 4.1 | 5.17 | 1.93 | 1.95 | 4.24 | 2.2 |
| Fiber (g) | 3.5 | 2.1 | 0.94 | 2.15 | 4.6 | 2.7 | 2.4 |
| Potassium (mg) | 200 | 187 | 187 | 248.5 | 154 | 193 | 10 |
| Calcium (mg) | 75 | 45 | 10 | 8 | 7 | 32 | 24 |
| Phosphorus (mg) | 137 | 206 | 168 | 45 | 58 | 82 | 53 |
| Magnesium (mg) | 76 | 107 | 83 | 14 | 26 | 46 | 37 |
| Iron (mg) | 1.1 | 0.69 | 1.89 | 0.38 | 0.94 | 1.33 | 0.7 |
| Zinc (mg) | 0.9 | 1.2 | 1.64 | 0.24 | 0.57 | 0.69 | 0.3 |
| Copper (mg) | 0.3 | 0.5 | 0.62 | 0.22 | - | 0.49 | 0.2 |
| Selenium (mcg) | 0.7 | 543.5 | 5.6 | 0.5 | - | 0.7 | 1 |
| Sodium (mg) | - | 1 | 3 | 1 | 10 | - | 1 |
| Vitamin A (IU) | 1 | - | - | 10 | - | 6 | - |
| Vitamin B1 (mg) (Thiamin) | 0.06 | 0.18 | 0.12 | 0.1 | 0.02 | 0.18 | 0.2 |
| Vitamin B2 (mg) (Riboflavin) | 0.32 | 0.01 | 0.02 | 0.08 | 0.03 | 0.03 | 0.0 |
| Vitam B6 (mg) | 0.04 | 0.03 | 0.12 | 0.21 | 0.09 | 0.16 | 0. |
| Vitamin C (mg) | - | 0.2 | 0.1 | 10.9 | 0.4 | 1.8 | 0. |
| Vitamin E (mg) | 7.27 | 1.62 | 0.26 | 0.21 | 0.12 | 4.26 | 0.1 |
| Vitamin K (mcg) | - | - | 9.7 | 3.3 | 0.1 | 4 | - |
| Folate (mcg) | 12 | 6 | 7 | 29.5 | 3 | 32 | 3 |
| Niacin (mg) | 1.03 | 0.08 | 0.3 | 0.56 | 0.17 | 0.51 | 0.7 |

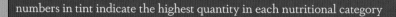 numbers in tint indicate the highest quantity in each nutritional category

| ...uts (...pieces ...ounce) | Pecans (19 halves or 1 ounce) | Pine Nuts (1 ounce) | Pistachios (50 pieces or 1 ounce) | Poppy Seeds (1 table-spoon or 1/4 ounce) | Pumpkin Seeds (1 ounce) | Sesame Seeds (1 table-spoon or 1/4 ounce) | Sunflower Seeds (1 ounce) | Walnuts (14 halves or 1 ounce) |
|---|---|---|---|---|---|---|---|---|
| ...66 | 196 | 191 | 162 | 47 | 163 | 52 | 175 | 185 |
| ...4 | 20 | 19 | 13 | 4 | 14 | 4 | 16 | 18 |
| ...71 | 2.6 | 3.88 | 6.05 | 1.59 | 8.46 | 1.6 | 5.48 | 4.32 |
| ...3 | 2.7 | 1 | 2.9 | 1.7 | 1.8 | 1.1 | 3.1 | 1.9 |
| ...87 | 116 | 169 | 295 | 62 | 223 | 42 | 139 | 125 |
| ...5 | 20 | 5 | 31 | 127 | 15 | 88 | 16 | 28 |
| ...01 | 79 | 163 | 133 | 75 | 333 | 57 | 327 | 98 |
| ...0 | 34 | 71 | 34 | 29 | 156 | 32 | 37 | 45 |
| ...64 | 0.72 | 1.57 | 1.19 | 0.83 | 2.29 | 1.31 | 1.93 | 0.82 |
| ...94 | 1.28 | 1.83 | 0.65 | 0.7 | 2.17 | 0.7 | 1.5 | 0.88 |
| ...19 | 0.34 | 0.38 | 0.38 | 0.14 | 0.36 | 0.37 | 0.52 | 0.45 |
| ...1 | 1.1 | 0.2 | 2.6 | 0.1 | 2.7 | 3.1 | 22.5 | 1.4 |
| ...2 | - | 1 | - | 2 | 5 | 1 | - | 1 |
| ...- | 16 | 8 | 74 | - | 2 | 1 | - | 6 |
| ...12 | 0.19 | 0.1 | 0.24 | 0.08 | 0.02 | 0.07 | 0.09 | 0.1 |
| ...03 | 0.04 | 0.06 | 0.05 | 0.01 | 0.04 | 0.02 | 0.07 | 0.04 |
| ...07 | 0.06 | 0.03 | 0.36 | 0.02 | 0.03 | 0.07 | 0.23 | 0.15 |
| ...- | 0.3 | 0.2 | 0.7 | 0.10 | 0.5 | - | 0.4 | 0.4 |
| ...96 | 0.4 | 2.65 | 0.55 | 0.10 | 0.16 | 0.02 | 7.4 | 0.2 |
| ...- | 1 | 15.3 | 3.7 | - | 1.3 | - | 0.8 | 0.8 |
| ...41 | 6 | 10 | 14 | 7 | 16 | 9 | 67 | 28 |
| ...84 | 0.33 | 1.24 | 0.4 | 0.09 | 1.26 | 0.41 | 1.19 | 0.32 |

# Bibliography

**Books and Television**

American Heart Association. *Enjoy.* New York: Clarkson Potter, 2001.

Bayless, Rick. *Mexican Kitchen: Capturing the Vibrant Flavors of a World-Class Cuisine.* New York: Scribner, 1996.

Bhagwandin, Annie. *The Chestnut Cookbook.* Tucson: Hats Off, 2003.

The Culinary Institute of America. *The Professional Chef.* 8th edition. New Jersey: John Wiley and Sons, 2006.

Fife, Bruce. *Coconut Lover's Cookbook.* Colorado Springs: Piccadilly, 2005.

Gordon, Kathryn, and Anne E. McBride. *Les Petits Macarons.* Philadelphia: Running Press, 2011.

Griffith, Linda, and Fred Griffith. *Nuts: Recipes from Around the World That Feature Nature's Perfect Ingredient.* New York: St. Martin's, 2003.

Grimes, Gwin G. *Nuts: Pistachio, Pecan, & Piñon.* Tucson: Rio Nuevo, 2006.

Hess, Elam S. *800 Proven Pecan Recipes.* Philadelphia: Innes and Sons, 1925.

Kaufman, William I. *The Nut Cookbook.* New York: Doubleday, 1964.

Kennedy, Diana. *The Cuisines of Mexico.* New York: William Morrow, 1972.

Lanier, Pamela. *Sweets and Treats from America's Inns.* Petaluma, CA: Lanier, 1999.

Malgieri, Nick, and Tom Eckerle. *Cookies Unlimited.* New York: HarperCollins, 2000.

*Modern Marvels.* "Nuts." The History Channel Digital Library DVD Documentary, A&E Television Networks, 2006.

Rosengarten, Fredric Jr. *The Book of Edible Nuts.* New York: Dover, 2004.

Sahni, Julie. *Classic Indian Cooking.* New York: William Morrow, 1980.

Salter, Tina, and Holly Stewart. *Nuts: Sweet and Savory Recipes from Diamond of California.* Berkeley, CA: Ten Speed, 2001.

Santibanez, Roberto. *Truly Mexican: Essential Recipes and Techniques for Authentic Mexican Cooking.* New York: Houghton Mifflin Harcourt, 2011.

Siegel, Helene. *Totally Nuts Cookbook.* Berkeley, CA: Celestial Arts, 1997.

Toussaint, Jean-Luc. *The Walnut Cookbook.* Berkeley, CA: Ten Speed, 1998.

Trilling, Susana. *Seasons of My Heart: A Culinary Journey Through Oaxaca Mexico.* New York: Ballantine Books, 1999.

Wolfert, Paula. *The Cooking of the Eastern Mediterranean.* New York: HarperCollins, 1991.

**Web Sites**

www.almondboard.com

www.americanpistachios.org

www.nationalpeanutboard.org

www.nuthealth.org

www.oregonhazelnuts.org

www.uspecans.org

www.walnuts.org

# Sources

**Bonnie Slotnick Cookbooks**
163 West 10th Street
New York, NY 10014
212-989-8962
bonnieslotnickcookbooks.com

**Bazzini**
1035 Mill Road
Allentown, PA 18106
610-366-1606 or 800-228-0172
www.bazzininuts.com

**Kalustyan's**
123 Lexington Avenue
New York, NY 10016
212-685-3451 or 800-352-3451
www.kalustyans.com

**Penzeys Spices**
www.penzeys.com
800-741-7787

**Nuts.com**
www.nuts.com
800-558-6887

**N.Y. Cake**
56 West 22nd Street
New York, NY 10010
212-675-2253 or 800-942-2539
www.nycake.com

**JB Prince**
36 East 31st Street
New York, NY 10016
212-683-3553 or 800-473-0577
www.jbprince.com

**EH Nutrition**
500 Mamaroneck Avenue
Suite 320
Harrison, NY 10528
914-701-0012
www.ehnutrition.com

# Acknowledgments

This book was a collaborative effort, and many people helped guide us through it. We want to thank them all. First and foremost, thank you Maria Guarnaschelli. Our brilliant editor led us to our best, forming and shaping our efforts, creating a beautiful book. The staff at W. W. Norton, including Mitchell Kohles, Melanie Tortoroli, Susan Sanfrey, Nancy Palmquist, and Anna Oler, worked tirelessly to support us and helped us from beginning to end. Also thanks to our copy editor, Liz Duvall; proofreader, Kathleen Sanfrey; indexer, Elizabeth Parson; and publicist Alice Rha.

A very special thanks goes to Nick Malgieri, our dear friend and mentor, who taught us both to bake, launched our careers as chefs and teachers, and introduced us to cookbook writing, as we began testing recipes and working on his books. We are forever grateful. Our efforts were rewarded with an introduction to David Black, our literary agent, who has been a voice of reason and has supported us and this project from the start.

Colleagues at the Institute of Culinary Education were always willing to share recipes and pass along any nut news that came their way. Our good friends Michelle Tampakis and Faith Drobbin taught, baked, listened to us, and most importantly laughed with us as we created and wrote this book. Michael Schwartz, Kathryn Gordon, Gerri Sarnataro, and Ron Ciovolino, all ICE chefs, contributed recipes. Barbara Bria Pugliese left the Institute, but not before she introduced us to dukka, and lots of yummy cookies. Rick Smilow, president of the Institute of Culinary Education, deserves thanks for providing the platform that made this book possible. Michael Handal, Jeff Yoskowitz, Sabrina Sexton, Toba Garrett, Andy Gold, Ted Seigel, James Briscione, Chad Pagano, Scott McMillan, Chris Gesualdi, Michael Laiskonis, and Jenny McCoy always had kind words of encouragement and plates of perfect food to sustain us as we worked. School administrators, including Richard Simpson, Brian Aronowitz, Steve Zagor, Kate McCue, and Susan Streit, were understanding and supportive. Hossannah Asuncion, who is a poet, literally helped supply lost words.

Andrea Gentl and Martin Hyers captured our vision in their photographs in an indescribable way. Michael Pederson created the beautiful plates of food in the studio for Gentl and Hyers to photograph. A.L. Bazzini Company generously supplied beautiful nuts and seeds. Karen Schley cooked her way through the savory chapters and offered sage advice. Susan Ryan baked her heart out, and tested countless recipes to perfection. Natalie Danford, Chris Styler, and Rose Kaplan helped form the book in its very early stages.

Our friends and family helped this project come to life, and our gratitude knows no bounds. The Tutunjians, Lisa, John, Noelle, Barbara, John, and Florence, took the time to review family recipes and taste absolutely everything. Aunt Rosemary Skaff and friend Janine Aractingi were our go-to experts on Syrian cuisine. Cara's friends Emily Cohen, Jane Eger, Janet Freedman, Lesley Heller, Leslie Manisero, Martha McCarty, Gloria Okin, Weslie Rosen, Tracey Zabar, and Melanie Zimmerman lent an ear throughout the process. Sonia Dreryan, Barbara Gottstein, Ellie Ference, and Nancy Ladisic all provided recipes.

Our final thanks go to our husbands, Bruce and Bill, and children, Leah, Sophie, Danielle, and Sean. They tolerated our obsessions and absences, learned to love nuts and seeds almost as much as we do, tested recipes, tasted treats, and blossomed along with this project. Their devotion and support provided the fertile ground in which these nuts and seeds could grow.

# Nut and Seed Index

Note: Page references in *italics* refer to photographs.

# General Index

Note: Page references in *italics* refer to photographs.